HARD DRIVING

HARD DRIVING

THE 1908 AUTO RACE FROM NEW YORK TO PARIS

Dermot Cole

UA **PRESS** CLASSIC REPRINT SERIES

Second Edition, 2020

Published by the University of Alaska Press
Elmer E. Rasmuson Library, 1732 Tanana Loop. Suite 404, Fairbanks 99775

First Edition, 1991
Published by Paragon House
90 Fifth Ave, New York, NY 10011

Library of Congress Cataloging in Publication Data
LCCN 2019949481

*This book is dedicated to my father, William Patrick Cole,
and to the memory of my mother, Anne Elizabeth Cole.*

PREFACE

As CLIMATE CHANGE transforms the northern regions of the globe, the Bering Strait has taken on a new role in worldwide commerce, a thoroughfare for access to the Pacific and Arctic Oceans.

In this age when cruise ships, international freighters and military vessels have started to treat the narrow passage as navigable in summer and beyond, the notion of an ice-locked ocean beyond reach is disappearing.

The ancient route between the continents is still a formidable challenge, however, especially since there is considerably more open water and less ice than in the past.

In some minds, the dream of the Bering Strait tunnel connecting the United States and Russia remains alive, though the prospect of raising tens of billions of dollars is more daunting than the howling winds of the coldest winter night.

That only begins to suggest what Bering Strait symbolizes to those who forever are inspired by the narrow gap on every world map and the possibility of crossing between hemispheres.

Travelers on skis and snowmachines, or with dog teams and bicycles and kayaks have had a mixed record over the years on Bering Strait adventures that often proved impossible.

But the gasoline was stockpiled along the way and newspaper editors assured everyone that it was not impossible, just difficult.

In the four years I worked on this book, rising every morning at 5:00 a.m. to write for two hours before heading to the newspaper office in Fairbanks, I felt that I got to know the characters by tracing their steps from New York to Paris through archival collections and museums.

One of the most distinctive was Norwegian Capt. Hans Hansen, an explorer who wore a military uniform of uncertain origin and promised, "We will either reach Paris or our bodies will be found beside the car."

It was an entirely impractical undertaking, one befitting a young man such as Italian Antonio Scarfoglio, 21, who found fault with just about everyone he met. He had demanded that his father allow him to enter the race after threatening that a denial would force him to drive a motorboat across the Atlantic.

Or the aristocrat Bourcier de St. Chaffray, who called himself "Commissionaire General" of the race, though others called him a windbag and a prig.

The competitors planned to leave Times Square in early February and make the first winter crossing of the United States by automobile. They had tentative plans to dismantle the cars and take them across Bering Strait by skin boats and dog teams or even by ship, depending upon what they found in Alaska.

When I think again of the adventure in 1908, three things stand out.

First, the level of ignorance about conditions in Alaska and northern Russia displayed by the race planners led to many of the troubles the racers encountered during the months they spent outdoors.

"Alaska shelters some pessimists, as do other sections of the country," a *New York Times* reporter wrote after a scouting trip to Alaska on the race route. "These are principally men who know nothing of automobiles and could not understand them."

Second, there was this naïve belief that technology plus determination and publicity could conquer any problem. That combination helped keep the men going when common sense might have told them to quit.

Third, the race was an entertaining distraction and a lighthearted adventure in which an international assortment of mechanics, Army officers, aristocrats, soldiers of fortune, and writers engaged in what was usually a friendly competition, with each group complaining that everyone else was cheating.

It was also an innocent exercise in unofficial diplomacy that played out in an entertaining manner, an episode made all the more poignant by the tragedy of what was soon to follow—World War I.

—DERMOT COLE

March 2019

museums. I would like to thank the staff of the museum and the foundation's automotive library for answering questions and supplying access to research materials.

The German car that participated in the race to Paris, the Protos, has been restored and placed on display in the Deutsches Museum in Munich. Thanks to the Siemens Corporation, which once owned the Protos company, for information and photos about the German car.

In Michigan, the staff at the automotive collection of the Detroit Public Library and the University of Michigan's transportation library in Ann Arbor deserve thanks. While in Michigan during 1986–1987, I participated in the Michigan Journalism Fellows program, an invigorating opportunity for any journalist. Program director Charles Eisendrath and his assistant, Margaret DeMuth, made us feel at home during our stay in Ann Arbor. The other Michigan Fellows gave me encouragement early on. In particular, I would like to thank Joseph Gambardella of *Newsday*, Ellen Soeteber of the *Chicago Tribune*, and Lance Williams of the *San Francisco Examiner*.

Several people read the manuscript or helped with suggestions: Duncan Carter, Sherry Simpson, Patrick Cole, William P. Cole, Terrence Cole, Marjorie Cole, Kent Sturgis, Claus Naske, Martha Eliassen, Dan Joling, and Lael Morgan. Thanks also to P. J. Dempsey, my editor at Paragon House, for her assistance.

Throughout this effort I have been aided immensely by my wife, Debbie, an accomplished editor and critic who has helped me steer clear of the potholes and stay on the right track.

"Alaska shelters some pessimists, as do other sections of the country," a *New York Times* reporter wrote after a scouting trip to Alaska on the race route. "These are principally men who know nothing of automobiles and could not understand them."

Second, there was this naïve belief that technology plus determination and publicity could conquer any problem. That combination helped keep the men going when common sense might have told them to quit.

Third, the race was an entertaining distraction and a lighthearted adventure in which an international assortment of mechanics, Army officers, aristocrats, soldiers of fortune, and writers engaged in what was usually a friendly competition, with each group complaining that everyone else was cheating.

It was also an innocent exercise in unofficial diplomacy that played out in an entertaining manner, an episode made all the more poignant by the tragedy of what was soon to follow—World War I.

—Dermot Cole
March 2019

ACKNOWLEDGMENTS

I HAVE RECEIVED assistance from many individuals and organizations in writing this book. I would particularly like to thank George T. MacAdam and Henry Austin Clark Jr. for their assistance. Mr. MacAdam's father was a *New York Times* correspondent who rode much of the way to Paris in the American car. In my visit with Mr. MacAdam in New Jersey, he graciously shared his memories of his father as well as photographs, journals, and notebooks that provide insight into the race and the contestants. I am grateful for his kindness and encouragement.

Mr. Clark, who for many years ran an automobile museum outside of New York City on Long Island, welcomed me to his home and assisted with photographs and information about the race. An authority on antique automobiles, Mr. Clark once owned the Thomas Flyer, the American car that participated in the race in Paris. He saw to it that the Thomas Flyer was preserved and displayed the car in his museum for fifteen years.

The car has now been restored and is on display at the William F. Harrah Foundation National Automobile Museum in Reno, Nevada. Under its chairman, Ben Dasher, the foundation opened a new home for the museum in 1989. With a diverse collection of more than two hundred cars on display, it is one of the world's finest automotive museums. I would like to thank the staff of the museum and the foundation's automotive library for answering questions and supplying access to research materials.

The German car that participated in the race to Paris, the Protos, has been restored and placed on display in the Deutsches Museum in Munich. Thanks to the Siemens Corporation, which once owned the Protos company, for information and photos about the German car.

In Michigan, the staff at the automotive collection of the Detroit Public Library and the University of Michigan's transportation library in Ann Arbor deserve thanks. While in Michigan during 1986–1987, I participated in the Michigan Journalism Fellows program, an invigorating opportunity for any journalist. Program director Charles Eisendrath and his assistant, Margaret DeMuth, made us feel at home during our stay in Ann Arbor. The other Michigan Fellows gave me encouragement early on. In particular, I would like to thank Joseph Gambardella of *Newsday*, Ellen Soeteber of the *Chicago Tribune*, and Lance Williams of the *San Francisco Examiner*.

Several people read the manuscript or helped with suggestions: Duncan Carter, Sherry Simpson, Patrick Cole, William P. Cole, Terrence Cole, Marjorie Cole, Kent Sturgis, Claus Naske, Martha Eliassen, Dan Joling, and Lael Morgan. Thanks also to P. J. Dempsey, my editor at Paragon House, for her assistance.

Throughout this effort I have been aided immensely by my wife, Debbie, an accomplished editor and critic who has helped me steer clear of the potholes and stay on the right track.

INTRODUCTION

AS A NEWSPAPER editor in Fairbanks, Alaska, I hear about unusual road trips as part of my job.

No one makes it to the northern edge of the American road system without passing on a tale about round-the-clock daylight, close encounters with bears, or other hazards of the Alaska Highway. Some wanderers ride horses from Texas or pedal bicycles five thousand miles from New York City. Others walk or drive anything from Model Ts to Land Rovers. Even those who cover the continent in thirty-foot motor homes equipped with fine china and satellite dishes consider it an accomplishment worth bragging about. "I Drove the Alaska Highway" bumper stickers are always in demand.

The Army built the 1,520-mile road to Alaska during World War II because of the threat of a Japanese invasion. The highway has been steadily improved over the years to the point where anyone can now make the trip. You do need a good set of tires and a stockpile of patience, however. The narrow, bumpy road seems to go on forever through the forests and tundra of British Columbia and the Yukon Territory. It crosses "miles and miles of nothing but miles and miles," as a soldier once said.

Modern travelers are usually surprised to find that the road still ends more than five hundred miles short of the western tip of mainland Alaska. Few of them realize that the first attempt to drive through Alaska occurred before there were any roads at all.

This book tells the story of the most difficult car trip ever attempted: the 1908 auto race from New York to Paris through Alaska and Siberia. Two decades before Charles Lindbergh touched down in Paris, the most daring means of getting to France was by automobile along a land route broken only by the waters of the Bering Strait between Alaska and Siberia.

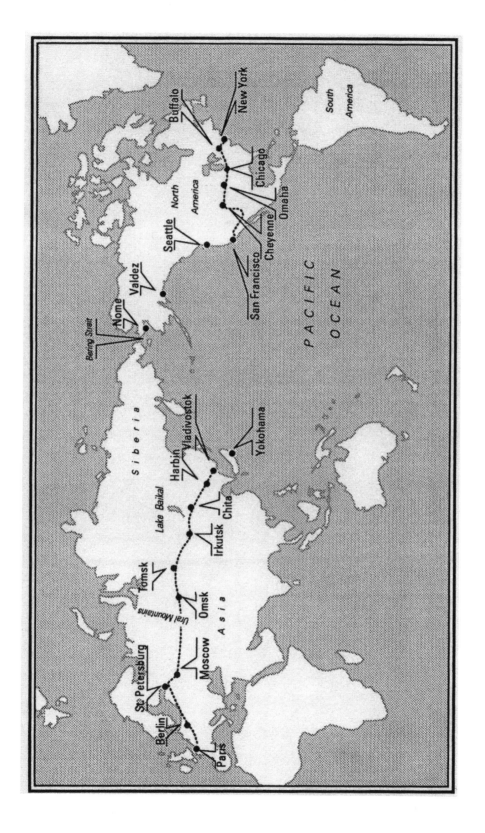

ONE

THE LONG WAY AROUND THE WORLD

IT BEGAN IN Times Square. On February 12, 1908, more than fifty thousand people watched as six automobiles left New York to go around the world to Paris, by way of Alaska and Siberia. Sponsored by *Le Matin* of Paris and the *New York Times*, the race—though little remembered today—rivals Henry Stanley's search for Dr. Livingstone as one of the greatest newspaper stunts of all time.

In Hollywood's version of the contest, the good guys wore white, the bad guys wore black, and the cars crossed the Bering Strait on an iceberg. One reviewer described *The Great Race*, a 1965 film starring Tony Curtis and Jack Lemmon, as a "mammoth comic strip on the screen."[1] The villain's black car had a cone-shaped pole sticking out the front. The pole glowed red-hot and melted the snow, allowing the car to cut through any snowdrift.

The film and the truth parted company in every respect except one: in 1908, six cars did leave New York to go the long way around the world to Paris. None of the drivers ever found a polar bear in the back seat or got into a pie fight, but the true story of what happened is almost as bizarre as the fiction from Hollywood.

On that mild winter day in Manhattan, a total of eighteen drivers, mechanics, and journalists hit Broadway in automobiles that looked

1

like rolling hardware stores. Three cars from France and one each from Germany, Italy, and the United States entered the competition. Members of each crew boasted that they had struck upon the ideal combination of personnel and equipment that would allow them to succeed, while the others would surely fail.

Ropes, lanterns, shovels, extra tires, and spare parts clung to the sides of the cars. The crews had prepared for anything. The men on one auto planned to hoist a sail in Siberia and coast through the snow with the motor shut off.

Hans Hendrik Hansen, a Norwegian who called himself Captain Hansen, had suggested this naval option. "When we come to the long frozen stretches we shall hoist sail and run under auxiliary power," the captain said between puffs on his pipe. "I have done this for hundreds of miles in Siberia and know what to expect." Hansen signed on as a navigator on the de Dion, one of the French cars.[2]

The European teams each carried enough extra gear to "build another car or start an iron foundry," joked a *Times* reporter who looked over the vehicles in Times Square.[3] The car with the sail weighed more than three tons and could run more than fifteen hundred miles between gas stops. It carried 154 gallons of gas in seven tanks, a month's supply of food and an electric hand-cranked generator to power a searchlight. The car also was equipped with front wheels that could be replaced by skis. A compass was mounted in front of the steering wheel.[4] The words *New York to Paris* were painted in large letters on the sides or hoods of the open cars. The smallest car was a twelve-horsepower, one-cylinder Sizaire-Naudin from France.

The American entry was a sixty-horsepower touring car manufactured by the E. R. Thomas Motor Company—the Thomas Flyer. Like the rest of the cars, its steering wheel was on the right-hand side.

The cars gather at the starting line in Times Square on February 12, 1908. From left to right the cars are: the American Thomas Flyer, the Italian Zust, the German Protos, the French de Dion and the French Sizaire-Naudin. (COURTESY OF HENRY AUSTIN CLARK JR.)

It was not until the left-hand drive on the Model T proved a success that the American industry abandoned the European pattern. The Thomas Flyer had large wire hoops mounted over the body, so that a canvas cover could be unfurled, turning the car into a motorized covered wagon. The Thomas Flyer had a pair of fourteen-foot planks strapped to the sides for use in crossing mudholes or gullies.

Charles Godard, driver of the Motobloc, one of the three French cars, boasted that he had placed all the instructions for the race in a sealed bag and would never open it, because he had learned everything he needed to know the year before while driving from Peking to Paris in an event also sponsored by *Le Matin*. In addition to the sealed bag of instructions, he carried a supply of champagne in his well-provisioned car.

Had he cared to look at the documents, Godard would have learned that race officials had suggested that the men bring along bear oil for the arctic portion of the trip. The racers were to smear it over themselves for warmth as they crossed Alaska and Siberia in the open cars. Wide wooden rims that looked like water wheels also found a place on the recommended list of supplies. These were to be attached to the tires, to make it easier to get through the deep snow of the far north.[5]

The first car to reach Paris would receive the "Coupe du Monde," a trophy to be donated by the *New York Times* and *Le Matin*. The most important prize, however, would be worldwide fame and glory. At the time no one had ever crossed the American continent by automobile in the winter, but the newspapers ignored those who said there was no chance of reaching Chicago or San Francisco, let alone Paris.

The *New York Times* claimed that driving in Alaska would not be as hard as many skeptics thought. "Investigation shows that the roads and trails of Alaska are passable and that the obstacles on the hardest parts of the journey on this continent can be overcome," the *Times* said just before the start. "The undertaking is difficult, but we have no doubt that it will be successful."[6]

It was, of course, easy enough to draw lines on a map. Many critics said that was the only geographical research conducted by *Le Matin*'s race planner, an aristocratic thirty-six-year-old Frenchman named G. Bourcier de St. Chaffray. He was a thin man with delicate features who called himself the Commissionaire General of the race. He had closely cropped dark hair and intense blue eyes. *Horseless Age*, a leading American

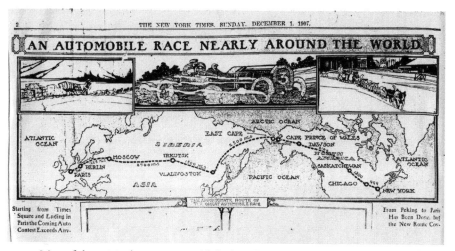

AN AUTOMOBILE RACE NEARLY AROUND THE WORLD.

Map of the original race route published in the *New York Times*, December 1, 1907.

auto magazine, later described St. Chaffray as a "prig and a windbag" who specialized in organizing impossible events. One of his past ventures was a motorboat race from Marseille to Algiers, the magazine said, in which all the boats were lost in the Mediterranean Sea. "He manages to get as much notoriety as possible out of these events before the collapse, and does not seem to take his failure seriously."[7]

St. Chaffray's harshest critic did not refer to him as a prig and a windbag. Eugene Lelouvier chose instead to call the Commissionaire General a liar. Lelouvier was a French adventurer who claimed that he, not St. Chaffray, deserved credit for proposing the race to Paris. To complicate matters and aggravate the Commissionaire General, Lelouvier was driving a car to Paris, even though he had officially withdrawn from the contest. Lelouvier, who started calling himself the Sporting Anarchist, left New York one day before the other racers. He said he would gain his revenge on the Commissionaire General by beating the six official entrants to Paris.

The windbag and the anarchist may have both claimed credit for suggesting the race to Paris, but the real inspiration belonged to another Frenchman, Jules Verne, who invented the sport of racing around the world.

The challenge of circling the globe has proven irresistible to dreamers, adventurers, and sportsmen ever since one of Ferdinand Magellan's little ships took three years to circumnavigate the earth in the early 1520s. But globe trotting did not become an international obsession until the publication of Verne's *Around the World in 80 Days*. In what Verne called a "novel of perpetual motion," he told the story of Phileas Fogg, an Englishman who sipped his morning tea at 8:23 a.m., called for his shaving water at 9:37 a.m., and left for his club every day at 11:30 a.m.

Fogg wagered twenty thousand pounds that he could circle the globe in eighty days—or 115,200 minutes to be exact. When his friends laughed, he solemnly replied: "A true Englishman doesn't joke when he is talking about so serious a thing as a wager." Fogg kept his mind on the clock, whether he was aboard an elephant in India, a steamship on the Pacific, or a passenger train in the American West. After numerous close calls and missed connections, he returned to the club in exactly eighty days, without a second to spare. "Here I am gentlemen," Fogg said as he walked in the door.

Verne's 1873 novel created a sensation in Europe and the United States, and a parade of imitators tried to beat the imaginary record. In 1889, Joseph Pulitzer, publisher of the *New York World*, assigned one of his reporters to the task. Elizabeth Cochrane, known as Nellie Bly to readers of New York's fastest-growing newspaper, made the most of the opportunity.

On the pages of Pulitzer's *World*, her trip around the planet grew into the biggest story since the Civil War. A contest to guess the date of her return to New York generated nearly one million entries. She stopped in France to see Verne, who predicted that she would fail to beat the eighty-day mark. He was wrong. She returned home to a wild celebration with cannon fire after seventy-two days, six hours, eleven minutes, and fourteen seconds. "Father Time Outdone!" proclaimed the headline in the *World*.[8]

Nellie Bly's accomplishment did not appear newsworthy to most other New York newspapers, including the *Sun, Herald, Tribune*, and *Times*. Following the time-honored tradition of ignoring the stunts of competing newspapers if at all possible, they avoided mentioning her trip. Similarly unimpressed was George Francis Train, a sixty-one-year-old American businessman who longed to be the world's fastest human.

Train, who staged an unsuccessful campaign for president in 1872, once boasted that he had been declared a lunatic by no fewer than six judges. Train also claimed that an eighty-day trip he had taken around the world in 1870 was the inspiration for Jules Vernes's novel; at least, as he pointed out, his trip would have been accomplished in eighty days, if he had not been detained for some time in a French jail for siding with rebels in a squabble with the government. He had wrapped himself in a French flag and dared soldiers to fire on the tricolor. Verne filled his books with strange characters, but he denied all knowledge of Train or his travels.

None of New York's newspapers would sponsor Train's attempt to beat Nellie Bly's seventy-two-day record, but he managed to win backing from a paper in Tacoma, Washington, by promising to "put Tacoma on the map." Train had endeared himself to Tacoma, a town with an inferiority complex, by coining such phrases as: "Seattle, Seattle, Death Rattle, Death Rattle; Tacoma, Tacoma, Aroma, Aroma."[9]

For the glory of Tacoma, Train circled the world in sixty-seven days in 1890 and repeated the feat in sixty days in 1892. "I have beaten Phileas Fogg out of sight," Train boasted in his autobiography, which he said he dictated in thirty-five hours. "I have lived fast. I have ever been an advocate of speed."[10]

In the decade after Train's last world ride, advocates of speed turned to the internal combustion engine. Dr. E. C. Lehwess of London made the first attempt to go around the world in a car in 1902, when he rolled away in a bright yellow three-ton truck made in France, the nation that led the world in the early development of the motor vehicle.

One of the world's first motorhomes, the ten-foot-high Panhard-Levassor featured an enclosed living space with hanging bunks and seats, folding tables, and cupboards. The doctor called the box on wheels Passepartout, after the faithful servant of Phileas Fogg. Lehwess had the name painted on the side of the vehicle in an elaborate emblem.

With a crew of nine men and an Irish setter, the expedition filled Passepartout and a second vehicle. The doctor and crew planned to visit France, Belgium, Germany, and Poland before crossing Siberia along the route of the new Trans-Siberian Railroad. The tourists planned to sail to San Francisco and become the first to drive across the United States.

Given the quality of cars in 1902 and the lack of roads, spare parts, and fuel, Lehwess might just as well have planned a trip to the moon. Like Phileas Fogg, however, he kept on in the face of all obstacles. With excess baggage strapped to the roof, the overloaded vehicle carved foot-deep ruts in the European countryside. The truck suffered ignition troubles and blowouts. It was pelted with heavy rain and stones, the latter hurled by villagers who didn't like the noisy contraption that spooked their farm animals.

Lehwess and his companions adhered to a leisurely pace. They stayed two weeks in Paris, attending dinners and races. They stayed nine weeks and three days in Berlin, hitting the dinner circuit and trying to get clearance to enter Russia. Critics joked that a major goal of the expedition was to prove the great "staying power" of Passepartout.

Lehwess displayed more "staying power" in both Warsaw and St. Petersburg, but after nine months on the road, the doctor gave up and returned to London by train. In the end, his dream fell victim to the Russian winter after the engine block cracked about 250 miles east of Moscow.[11]

Over the next few years races and endurance trips emerged as ideal events for advertising and adventure. Charles Glidden of Boston became the champion of long-distance driving. Glidden, a millionaire businessman, believed that riding in a car would help him lose weight and stay healthy. Between 1901 and 1908 he covered forty-six thousand miles and never lost an ounce, but he saw more of the earth than anyone else on wheels.

Wearing a suit and tie, he roamed the world with his wife and a chauffeur. Glidden once calculated that he had written two hundred thousand words, taken two thousand photographs, made one thousand friends, and visited thirty-nine countries on his travels.[12] He also sponsored a series of auto tours in the United States designed to prove that the car was more than a diversion for the rich. The annual Glidden Tours between major cities called the nation's attention to the improvements in the automobile and the need for better highways.

The Glidden Tours and other exhibitions and races played a major role in the promotion of the automobile. Sometimes, it didn't even matter if there were roads between the start and finish lines. In early 1907 *Le Matin* proposed the most ambitious trip yet when it asked: "Will anyone agree to go this summer from Peking to Paris by motorcar?"[13]

Five crews accepted the challenge, including three from France and one each from Holland and Italy. Italian journalist Luigi Barzini, a passenger in Prince Scipione Borghese's car, wrote a book on the journey that remained a best seller in his homeland for twenty years. Barzini acknowledged the many reasons why the nine-thousand-mile trip seemed to be impossible, but said it was best to ignore such arguments: "In great or original undertakings, many points must be left to chance; there must always be some facing of the unknown; the adventure must always be entered upon with a certain amount of unreason."[14]

The drivers shipped their autos to Peking, from where they followed ancient trails of tea caravans northwest to Siberia. For most of the first 150 miles out of Peking, Borghese's car had to be pulled by a horse, a mule, and a donkey, assisted by Chinese workmen. The old man who supervised wore a whistle and held a banner that said "Obey your father's voice."

In many narrow passes the motorists found barely enough room to push the cars over the rocky trails. The racers passed the Great Wall of China and ventured into the Gobi Desert and the Mongolian Plateau, counting only seven trees in one eight-hundred-mile stretch. The cars ran low on gas and water. At times the men sipped oily water from their radiators to relieve their thirst. The Mongolian population of Urga had been warned of the approach of vehicles that could travel without horses. Barzini said the most widespread explanation among the people was that the cars were pulled by invisible horses. "But how can the strangers guide the invisible horse?" a bystander asked.[15]

The prairies and deserts of Mongolia finally gave way to the soggy forests of birch and fir in Siberia. The only thing worse than a Siberian road in the rain was a Siberian road after the rain, Barzini said. At one point Borghese's car flipped over on its top when it fell through a decrepit wooden bridge. The motorists found temporary relief from the decayed bridges and mud-clogged trails by driving along the tracks of the Trans-Siberian Railroad, but the cars took a terrific beating from the railroad ties.

After two months of fighting tough terrain, Borghese arrived in Paris at the offices of *Le Matin*. Twenty days later, the Dutch car and two French entrants finished as well. "We started to show that these little vehicles could go round the world, and the proof of this has now been demonstrated," said Victor Collignon, who drove one of the French cars. Mindful of the hundreds of hours spent pulling the cars out of the mud with the help of Chinese coolies and Mongolian horsemen who wouldn't see another car for years, Prince Borghese would only say: "In the present year of grace it is impossible to go by motor-car alone, comfortably seated upon the cushions of the same, from Peking to Paris."[16]

Not long after the last cars from Peking reached Paris, *Le Matin* carried the idea of hard driving to its logical conclusion; the paper proposed a twenty-thousand-mile journey from New York to Paris. Skeptics on both sides of the Atlantic quickly predicted that the round-the-world race was doomed to fail, but they admitted that the same fate had been forecast for the Peking-to-Paris trip.

The route for the world race led west from New York to Chicago, across the Great Plains and Rocky Mountains, north to Alaska, and west to Siberia. The entire plan rested on the assumption that the cars could enter Siberia at the Bering Strait, the narrow body of water that separates the eastern and western hemispheres. There were no roads on either side of the strait for thousands of miles and much of that territory had yet to be mapped. About twenty-five hundred miles southwest of the landing point in Siberia, the motorists would pick up the Trans-Siberian Railroad and follow it to Europe.

Although some of the worst winter weather on earth strikes the Bering Strait region, at least there was historical precedent for picturing it as the natural place to jump from one continent to another. The first people to come to North America had crossed here ages earlier when lower water levels created a huge land bridge between Alaska and Siberia. As centuries passed, rising water covered the land link, but the Bering Strait remained familiar territory to generations of Eskimos. They ventured out on the ice to hunt bowhead whales and traveled the turbulent waters by skin boat in summer.

By the latter part of the nineteenth century this narrow stretch of icy water began to attract attention from businessmen who saw money to be made by bridging the gap at the Bering Strait. In 1865, Western Union began building a round-the-world telegraph system that would link America with the capitals of Europe by stringing two wires across the Bering Strait. The company cut fifteen thousand telegraph poles and explored six thousand miles of wilderness on both sides of the strait from British Columbia to the Chinese frontier. But Western Union abandoned the proposed telegraph line and left the poles to rot when Cyrus Field succeeded in laying a telegraph cable beneath the Atlantic Ocean in 1867.

Efforts to connect the continents continued even after the telegraph project failed. A telegraph line could be extended across the Atlantic; a railroad could not. Several promoters gave serious thought to a round-the-world railroad with a bridge or tunnel at the Bering Strait.

William Gilpin, the first territorial governor of Colorado, wrote a book in 1890, *The Cosmopolitan Railway: Compacting and Fusing Together All the World's Continents*. He proposed a railroad connecting all the great cities on five continents.

Newspaper stories about the railroad of the future appeared frequently in New York, Paris, and London in the early 1900s. The New York–Paris express was going to whisk a traveler from Manhattan to the Champs-Elysées in twelve days. "We will be running through trains in five or six years," French engineer Loicq de Lobel predicted in 1902. "No more seasickness, no more dangers of wrecked liners, a fast trip in palace cars with every convenience."[17]

While the railroad backers dickered with the Russians, a forty-five-year-old English travel writer became the first man to go from Paris to New York through Siberia and Alaska. He was Harry de Windt, an adventurer in the pattern of Phileas Fogg who always traveled with a servant and stayed in the finest hotels. An admirer said de Windt's long thin face and oversized mustache gave him the look of a "Russian prince, a Wall Street broker, a Paris worldling or the attaché of a British embassy."[18]

De Windt had written about several previous expeditions in books such as *From Pekin to Calais by Land, A Ride to India across Persia and Baluchistan, The New Siberia*, and *On the Equator*. He claimed to have covered one million miles in his lifetime, nearly all of it before the era of air travel. De Windt first attempted to go from New York to Paris in 1896. Before departing Manhattan, he took note of the sorry state of American cuisine, the high prices at the Waldorf, and the gullibility of American newspapers. According to de Windt, a cursory examination of New York journalism left him believing that any fool could walk into a newspaper office, announce plans for a trip to Mars, and be taken as seriously as a professional traveler like himself, a proud member of London's Royal Geographic Society and a nephew of the rajah of Sarawak, Borneo. He complained that a hotel clerk read of his proposed journey to Paris and came up with the idea of riding a white horse to France from New York. "For two days," de Windt said, "the papers were full of this 'explorer,' his portrait was widely published, and leading articles were written on the chimerical enterprise and its chances of success. Moreover, the man actually started, accompanied by a brass band, and cheered by an immense crowd, influenced, as usual, by the hysterical tomfoolery they had read anent this impostor, who, as might have been foreseen, rode quietly back into New York by a different route and was never seen or heard of again! Yet even the best journals were fooled by this buffoon."[19]

De Windt left New York for Paris on May 26, 1896. He and his servant, George Harding, took a train to the West Coast, sailed to Alaska, and hiked over Chilkoot Pass, which became the gateway to the Klondike gold fields a year later. De Windt and his companion passed the undiscovered gold bonanza and floated part of the way down the Yukon in a homemade boat. A ship took them across the Bering Strait to an Eskimo village where de Windt had counted on getting dog teams and sleds. But the village chief, described by de Windt as a "rapacious old scoundrel," refused to cooperate. De Windt complained that the natives of the village of Oumwaidjik showed more interest in his tobacco than in his trip to Paris, and he had to call it off. De Windt's servant hung a Union Jack on a whale rib on the shore, and the whaler *Belvedere* saw it and picked up the two adventurers.

In late 1901 de Windt attempted the trip again, trying to determine the feasibility of the round-the-world railroad. This time he started from his home in Paris with a servant and a photographer. The

London Daily Express, the *Paris Journal,* and the *New York World* helped with expenses. De Windt and his two companions rode four thousand miles in first-class comfort on the Trans-Siberian Railroad to Irkutsk. They proceeded to the Bering Strait by sleighs and sleds pulled by horses, reindeer, and dogs. He said the temperature dropped to seventy-five below zero at one point, freezing a prized bottle of Crimean claret. De Windt said he was no more prepared for the hardships he endured on that trip than an Englishman who "would go out duck-shooting at Christmas time in silk pajamas."[20]

De Windt finally made it to the Bering Strait and across to Alaska, retracing his path of six years earlier. It took him eight months to travel 18,494 miles from Paris to New York. The feat earned de Windt an invitation to the White House for lunch with President Theodore Roosevelt. The president made light of the proposed railroad, contending it was the idea of crooks or cranks. Then Roosevelt "gravely instructed me to reserve for him a first-class compartment (and, if possible, a seat in the dining car) on the first train out from New York for France," de Windt said.[21]

No one ever took the train ride from New York to Paris. The tsar's government, facing growing internal strife in Siberia and elsewhere, feared that the railroad would bring a flood of gold-seeking American colonists to Siberia. A year after rejecting the railroad concession, however, the Russians agreed to open their boundaries to the world auto race, apparently seeing little threat in a small group of men on wheels. "This will cost stupendous sums, but if the money is forthcoming the thing can, of course, be done," said General Rikatcheff, vice-president of the Imperial Geographical Society. "It will not be much of a race, however, for I daresay the cars will have to be dragged over the snow by dogs for a good part of the way."[22]

Several high-ranking tsarist officials, including the ambassador to the United States and Prime Minister Peter Stolypin, received appointments to honorary race committees. So did the chief French proponent of the round-the-world railroad, Loicq de Lobel, who happened to be an old enemy of de Windt's.

Perhaps de Lobel's involvement explains why de Windt wanted nothing to do with the auto race, which he condemned as foolhardy. The two men had argued bitterly years earlier over which one deserved the most credit for researching the railroad scheme. De Windt said the drivers would find little more than a dozen tumbledown shacks and a "hundred miserable natives" between the Bering Strait and Yakutsk, more than twice the distance between New York and Chicago. "A preliminary survey would speedily demonstrate the utter absurdity of the New York–Paris expedition," de Windt said.

He didn't see how anyone could reach the Bering Strait and keep a delicate machine operating. Plus, the ice in the strait didn't always freeze solid and even if it did, the motorists would fail to get over the towering ice ridges created by the drifting sea ice.[23]

With few exceptions, leading automotive journals in England, France, and the United States quickly endorsed de Windt's views on why the race was impossible. But some analysts with superior credentials thought differently. Chief among them was Roald Amundsen, who was one of the world's leading authorities on hard traveling even before he drove a dog team to the South Pole in 1911. As a young man Amundsen had given up medical studies to become an explorer. He had earned worldwide fame in 1906 by completing the first trip along the Northwest Passage between the Atlantic and Pacific oceans.[24]

"I think that the plan for an automobile contest from New York to Paris by way of Bering Strait is feasible in spite of the tremendous difficulties that would be encountered," Amundsen said. "The crossing of Bering Strait on the ice will probably be the most difficult stretch of the journey and eventually the loss of a machine at that point should be considered by the contestants. A folding boat and a sledge should be carried on each car. Concentrated food would be necessary in order to economize space and I would especially recommend pemmican for this purpose."[25]

The world's foremost auto tourist also believed the race could be run. Charles Glidden said, however, that the cars would have to be pushed and hauled by "reindeer, donkeys or coolies" for at least ten thousand miles. He added that since the journey would probably take more than a year, it would be better to employ a combination of hot-air balloons and automobiles to reach Paris.[26]

On paper, the route to Paris led from New York to Chicago and on to Utah. In Utah, the drivers were to head north, traveling through northwest Canada to Alaska. Eleven years earlier one group had tried to drive through Canada during the Klondike Gold Rush. They attempted to reach the gold fields with a steam-powered sleigh that had a locomotive and freight cars attached. Named "I Will," the contraption was supposed to take them cross-country over the mountain passes and tundra. The engine turned a steel drum that had spikes for traction. When the gold seekers tried to leave Edmonton, Alberta, in 1897, the spikes clawed into the earth, and I Will dug itself into a deep hole.[27]

If the New York–Paris racers could succeed in the roadless country where I Will failed, the next obstacle would be the Yukon River, which they would follow about one thousand miles through Alaska to the Bering Sea. The trip had to be made in winter so the cars could run on the frozen river. "The ice would support a New York Central

Railroad train let alone an automobile weighing four thousand pounds or more," said Alaska miner John Riordan. He told a New York newsman the trip to the Bering Sea would be as safe as traveling down Broadway.[28] Broadway had its hazards no doubt, but they did not include temperatures of fifty below zero, frequent blizzards, rugged mountains, and unpopulated wilderness where travelers were more likely to run into a grizzly bear than another human being.

Upon reaching the Bering Strait, the motorists planned to ship the cars by steamer or dog team to Siberia, where the racers would have to travel several weeks before reaching a telegraph line. The *New York Times* said the agents of the Northeastern Siberian Company had never seen an automobile and their reaction to the sight of the machines on Siberian beaches "may perhaps be imagined." The first gas supply point in Siberia was nine hundred miles from the Bering Strait.

Few villages existed in northeast Siberia, but the drivers might from time to time meet a group of natives with a herd of reindeer. "I am convinced that northeast Siberia will be no harder to cross than Alaska," said General Linevitch, aide-de-camp to the tsar. He didn't volunteer his thoughts on the difficulty of crossing Alaska.[29]

Shortly after the organizers announced the race route, Canada's Northwest Mounted Police delivered some bad news: The Mounties said flatly that the cars would never make it through western Canada to Alaska because there was no adequate trail.[30] The race sponsors quickly shifted gears and issued new orders. The racers would skip Canada entirely, go to San Francisco first, and sail to Valdez, Alaska.

At Valdez, known today as the southern terminus of the trans-Alaska pipeline, the drivers were to hook into a one-thousand-mile system of winter trails that would lead them to the gold rush town of Nome and the Bering Sea.

The *New York Times*, which had agreed to be a cosponsor immediately after *Le Matin* proposed the contest, sent a representative to Alaska who reported back that automobiles could travel through Alaska. "The fact is the journey from Valdez is not only feasible, but in a way more easy of accomplishment than many enthusiasts believed," John Klein of the *Times* said. "Alaska shelters some pessimists, as do other sections of the country. These are principally men who know nothing of automobiles and could not understand them. Opposed to this class are the men of the stamp which pioneered the way in the West and later in Alaska, and who have made the country what it is today by a determination to overcome obstacles."[31]

By cosponsoring the race, the *New York Times* elevated the contest above the typical newspaper stunt. Nothing about the *Times* or its publisher, Adolph Ochs, could be described as typical. A dozen years earlier, Ochs had arrived from Tennessee, where he had started as a printer's devil and risen to become one of the leading publishers in the South. At thirty-eight, he borrowed heavily to buy the money-losing *Times* and brought it back to life. He reduced the price from three cents to one cent, and he offered New Yorkers a serious and straightforward treatment of the news. "His newspaper is not clever and it is not especially illuminating," newspaper critic Will Irwin wrote in 1911. "But it comes nearest of any newspaper in New York to presenting a truthful daily picture of life in New York and the world at large."

Ochs was not a literary man. He was an astute businessman, who recognized that a newspaper could be a financial success by appealing to well-educated people interested in business, government, and industry. The 140,000 people who spent a penny to buy the *Times* each day opened a newspaper that took a conservative, measured approach to the world. The *Times* rejected the sensationalism favored by other New York papers such as Pulitzer's *World* or Hearst's *Journal*. The *Times* offered no photographs on the front page, only one-column headlines, and dispassionate accounts of the day's events. There were no comic strips or other signs of frivolity.

Under Ochs and Managing Editor Carr Van Anda, the *Times* had earned a reputation as the most trustworthy and comprehensive newspaper in New York. It advertised itself as the newspaper that would not "soil the breakfast cloth." The air of formality extended to the office as Ochs and Van Anda addressed their subordinates and each other as "Mister."

Ochs did recognize the value of good publicity for his newspaper, however, and he undertook several noteworthy promotions. To mark the opening of the Times Tower in the center of Times Square, he sponsored a display of lights and fireworks on December 31, 1904. It grew into an annual New Year's Eve tradition marking the closing seconds of the year. Ochs sponsored essay contests and offered one hundred dollars to anyone who could think of a perfect slogan for the newspaper. The prize went to D. M. Redfield of New Haven, Connecticut, who penned the words "All the World News, But Not a School for Scandal." The *New York Sun* joked that the *Times* was so dull its motto should have been: "Why is the *New York Times* published? God only knows." Ochs ignored the advice of the *Sun*, and he passed up Redfield's winning entry, deciding that he liked his own idea better: "All the News That's Fit to Print."

Van Anda took that dictum to heart, especially regarding developments in science and technology, where the *Times* had set out to establish itself as the dominant journal of the age.

Journalist Alexander Woollcott once told of the night that Van Anda rode with him on an express train carrying copies of the *Times*

Carr Van Anda, managing editor of the *New York Times*. The *Times*'s involvement in the race to Paris fit with his early attempts to expand the newspaper's coverage of exploration and science. (COURTESY OF THE *NEW YORK TIMES* ARCHIVES)

Adolph S. Ochs, publisher of the *New York Times*. He wanted a newspaper founded on serious coverage of the news, not sensationalism. By cosponsoring the race to Paris, the *Times* elevated the event above the typical newspaper stunt. (COURTESY OF THE *NEW YORK TIMES* ARCHIVES)

to a political convention. Van Anda stood upon the rear platform all the way from New York to Baltimore, watching the towns whiz by. "His delight at this speed was delightfully naïve, he was so pleased and happy. That is why, I imagine, the *Times* has backed the development of aviation—the managing editor simply loved speed."[32]

Ten days before the race to Paris began, the *Times* printed a half-page article by Henry Farman about his 1,630-yard flight near Paris. Most of the airplane flights up until 1908 had not been witnessed by large crowds, and the public was slow to accept the idea that aviation could be more than a circus trick. The world was just beginning to realize that the Wright Brothers had begun a revolution, but it remained easier to imagine the automobile as the ideal machine to move people across the wide-open spaces. And at a time when motoring magazines still debated the question of whether something in the night air made car engines run better in the dark, no one could be certain about the ultimate power of the automobile.

The potential to travel through unexplored regions appealed to the intellectual curiosity of Van Anda, who was largely responsible for building up the news-gathering resources of the *Times*. In this instance, the *Times* agreed to handle all race arrangements between Times Square and Cape Prince of Wales in western Alaska. *Le Matin* would handle preparations from the Bering Strait to Paris.

"While the experience gained by the contestants will be of great benefit in the development of self-moving cars, it will also have its influence in opening up roads. It will tend to bring the ends of the earth closer together," the *Times* said.[33]

After the race made the front page in New York City, it seemed as if there would be dozens of cars racing around the world. The Moon Motor Company of St. Louis was the first American firm to enter. Manufacturer Harry Fosdick said that Prince Borghese's experience in the Peking-Paris drive had shown that a man would succeed if he could adapt to whatever he found beneath his wheels.

The American agent for the Renault Brothers of Paris said that his firm, the largest in France, would enter a car. A French auto expert predicted that one of that nation's cars would undoubtedly win, providing "another demonstration of French energy and the excellence of French motors."[34] The suggestion that a Renault would be at the starting line drew a quick response from Montague Roberts, a twenty-four-year-old driver employed by the New York City dealer for the E. R. Thomas Motor Company of Buffalo, New York. The Buffalo firm had built two thousand cars in the previous six years, including the Thomas Flyer, a high-priced touring car with a reputation for hill-climbing power and speed. It was capable of reaching sixty miles per hour. The preceding summer Roberts had driven a Thomas Flyer to victory in a twenty-four-hour race at Brighton Beach, a racetrack in what would become one of the more crowded sections of Brooklyn. His track record of 997 miles stood only until the next month when a pair of Renault drivers covered 1,070 miles in twenty-four hours. Roberts had already challenged Renault to a deciding twenty-four-hour race when the New York–Paris contest was proposed. "A trip of this sort would suit me just fine and if it were possible to get through I feel sure that I could do it," Roberts said.[35]

The Renault never materialized at the starting line in February. Likewise, the Moon, White, Maxwell, and all of the dozen or so American entries scratched. At the last minute, when it looked as if no American cars would enter, Roberts prevailed on his superiors, and the Thomas Motor Company shipped a car from its factory in Buffalo. E. R. Thomas, owner of the company, had predicted that the cars would not make it as far as Chicago. He said he put aside his doubts only because he wanted at least one of the competitors to fly the Stars and Stripes.[36]

The reluctance of other American manufacturers stemmed in part from a financial panic of the previous fall. Bank runs in various cities provided reason enough for anxiety among those who dealt in luxuries such as automobiles. The cost to take a car to Paris was expected to exceed twenty thousand dollars; a figure far beyond the reach of most of the 250 companies then building cars in the United States. The top four auto companies, Ford, Buick, Reo, and Maxwell-Briscoe, were building as many cars as all the others combined. Ultimately, Thomas spent nearly one hundred thousand dollars on the race, the equivalent of more than $1 million in present-day dollars.[37]

Many auto makers also feared that the cars would get stuck somewhere in Alaska or Siberia and that the whole project would end in failure, driving them out of business instead of into the history books. In Alaska, newspapers editors and government officials praised the race plan, but skeptical prospectors and dog mushers said they expected to be able to acquire automobiles at bargain prices after the snowdrifts melted in the spring.

Despite all the uncertainties of the road ahead, the French, German, Italian, and American teams agreed to take their chances on what one *Times* reporter called "the longest and most perilous trip ever undertaken by man." As Luigi Barzini had said of the drive from Peking to Paris, "In great or original undertakings, many points must be left to chance."

TWO

THE ROAD TO PARIS

A MAJOR AMERICAN auto magazine described Eugene Lelouvier as "the hero of a thousand adventures" and a "man who had passed his life playing with death."[1] Others described him as a professional blowhard who had passed his life playing with the truth. Both camps agreed that by leaving New York one day in advance of everyone else, the Sporting Anarchist had scored an early publicity victory in his war with the Commissionaire General.

In New York, Lelouvier entertained reporters with tales of his bravery and endurance. He said he had been shipwrecked twice in the English Channel, on one occasion saving all of his shipmates. He said he later set off on a walk around the world, only to collapse from exhaustion in Siberia. A passing caravan of tribesmen found him unconscious, and the daughter of the governor of Irkutsk nursed him back to health.

"After his recovery," the *New York Times* reported, "he insisted on completing his journey and, though weak and scarcely able to walk at the finish, his determination carried him through. After reaching France he returned to Irkutsk and sought the hand of his nurse, and after a brief courtship they were married. She is now in Siberia in her husband's interest, arranging to have gasoline supplies shipped along the trail to him."[2]

Eugene Lelouvier at the wheel of the Werner before leaving New York City.
(UNIVERSITY OF MICHIGAN LIBRARY)

Lelouvier could also go on at length about the time he nearly died after a direct hit from a poison blow dart in the Congo and the time he had crossed the Gobi Desert disguised as a Chinese villager to plot the route of the 1907 drive from Peking to Paris. He found himself unemployed after he got to Peking, however. Refusing to take a back seat to anyone, he had been fired by the driver.

His fortunes had improved by the time he was ready to leave New York, thanks in part to the *New York World*, which stepped in to give him a big send-off. The *New York Times* had pumped up the race to Paris as the biggest event in the brief history of the automobile. For three months the race had received front-page treatment in the *Times*. The city's other papers paid little attention, preferring instead to cover such stories as the new ordinance that banned cigarette smoking by women in public places in New York or the prediction by the Rockefeller

Institute that doctors would one day be able to transplant human organs.

But as worldwide debate about the race intensified, the *World* attempted to share the spotlight by giving aid to Lelouvier. The newspaper that had sponsored Nellie Bly nineteen years earlier organized a celebration for Lelouvier on Park Row, home to many of the city's newspapers. Patrick McGowan, president of New York's Board of Aldermen, presided at the starting ceremony. The *World* arranged for twenty chorus girls from the show *A Knight for a Day* to present flowers to Lelouvier and his two companions, Maurice Drieghe and Max Hohmann. A *World* reporter also rode in the car at the start.

The occasion made for dramatic reading in the pages of the *World*, a newspaper that, in the words of one historian, covered the planet "As if it had been minted fresh the day before, its happenings deserving to be writ large, displayed lavishly, narrated breathlessly."[3] The *World* boasted that more than twenty thousand people jammed the approach to the Brooklyn Bridge to watch the show.

The world travelers, who wore knitted woolen caps and leather coats, sat proudly in a fifteen-horsepower Werner packed with spare tires, tools, camping equipment, and sixty gallons of gas. The French tricolor and the Stars and Stripes flew next to the headlights. "Send me a cake of ice from Siberia," one spectator shouted. "See you in Paris in September," said another.[4]

At that time, when most Americans had yet to ride in a car, the machine would have attracted a crowd if its destination had been around the block instead of around the world. Seventy-five policemen held back the throng as the alderman from Tammany Hall delivered a sermon. "You are about to undertake a journey of twenty-two thousand miles in the interests of progress. You are to blaze the way for the coming railroads that will eventually carry the people of America to France and those of France to America via the overland route," McGowan said, referring to the idea of putting a rail line through the Bering Strait. "From the land whose flag is the red, white, and blue to the land where waves the tricolor of France, I give you a message of liberty, equality, and fraternity."

A mechanic cranked the car and the motor sprang to life at 1:31 p.m. "Then the little gray car puffed and leaped forward as if restive at the delay in setting forth on the world dash," the *World* reported. Lelouvier followed a squad of fifteen mounted policemen who cleared a path through the spectators. The car stalled after a few blocks, but the motorists coaxed it aboard the Staten Island Ferry.

While Lelouvier rolled toward Philadelphia, the men who planned to beat him to Paris gathered for an elaborate farewell dinner at the West Fifty-fourth Street clubhouse of the Automobile Club of America, the home of New York's automotive elite. Formed in 1899 to campaign for the legalization of automobiles in Central Park, the organization included names such as Vanderbilt, Astor, Harriman, and Rockefeller among its members. One magazine described the club founders as an "ultrafashionable coterie of millionaires."

The group's eight-story New York clubhouse had a spacious garage where the chauffeurs parked and a luxurious dining room. Jefferson DeMont Thompson, a club official and chairman of the American Automobile Association's Racing Board, offered $1,000 in gold to the first man to reach Paris with the United States flag. "I will bring back that flag and get that $1,000," Captain Hans Hansen said.[5]

The captain, who had proposed the idea of hoisting sail in Siberia, was a Norwegian soldier of fortune whose handlebar mustache gave him the look of a jovial walrus. He was the navigator on the de Dion,

The French de Dion car before the start. The third man on the car rode on a seat in the middle of the spare tires. This was one of the cars that carried enough extra gear to "build another car or start an iron foundry," a reporter joked. (*AUTOCAR*)

St. Chaffray's car. Hansen listed his occupation as explorer and said he had lived in Siberia for about five of his forty-three years. He had first visited the region while searching for Andrée, the Norwegian balloonist who disappeared on an 1897 flight to the North Pole. Hansen had blue eyes, light brown hair, high cheekbones, and a well-deserved reputation as a colorful character. He always had a story to tell, which made him a favorite with newspaper reporters. On special occasions he wore a uniform with gold braid that he said he had acquired during a short stint with the Argentine Navy in the 1890s. He smoked a pipe with an eight-inch stem.

Hansen said he had placed a five thousand dollar bet in Russia that he could complete the trip to Paris in less than four months.[6] Hansen, who had worked on railroads in Mexico and South America, claimed to be fluent in Norwegian, Russian, German, English, Spanish,

Captain Hans Hansen said he and his companions would reach Paris or "our bodies will be found beside the car." (COURTESY OF GEORGE T. MACADAM)

Chinese, and "one or two Siberian dialects." On more than one occasion, Hansen spoke of how he had sailed a replica of an ancient Norwegian ship to the 1893 Chicago's World Fair. A group of Norwegian seamen did travel to the fair, but the record shows that none of them was named Hansen. It also turned out that Hansen did not know how to drive a car, but his experience in Siberia and his skill with a snow shovel made up for whatever embellishments the captain made to his resume. He was a hard worker who predicted that the real race to Paris would not begin until the drivers had put the Bering Strait behind them.

"My plan is to jog along over the United States in an easy manner," Hansen said. "I shall not race if every automobile in America urges me on. It is when we get to East Cape that the struggle will begin and we shall need all our strength. For an entire month there will not be a moment's rest for man or machine, for I intend to run continuously."[7]

Unlike Hansen, Lt. Hans Koeppen had never been to the Siberian arctic. Koeppen said he knew what to expect, however, because he had read every book he could find on the subject. Koeppen, thirty-one, had taken a leave of absence from the Fifteenth Prussian Infantry to go around the world in the Protos, the German car. A year earlier he had been named to the General Staff, recognition given to the German army's leading officers. An accomplished horseman, marksman, and tennis player, Koeppen weighed 195 pounds and was probably the most athletic of the contestants, but he admitted that he knew as little about driving a car as steering a dirigible. He expected to learn by watching his two companions: army engineer Hans Knape and motor-cyclist Ernest Maas. The three men had met a few weeks earlier, after each had written to German car makers trying to interest a manufac-turerer in entering the race.

The Berlin newspaper, *Zeitung am Mittag*, put up fifteen hundred dollars, the Protos Company invested an equal amount, and the three men provided three thousand dollars each to launch the venture.[8] Six hundred workers in the Berlin factory built the forty-horsepower car in sixteen days. The Protos carried 178 gallons of gas and weighed more than three tons. Koeppen had a reputation for being polite and courteous, but there were limits to his patience. His vehicle had been damaged slightly while it was being taken to the American customs office by horse-drawn cart. A reporter said the six-foot-two-inch Koeppen reacted as if he "would like to attend to the immediate execution of all the truckmen in New York."

Antonio Scarfoglio, the twenty-one-year old Italian journalist, who told his father that if he was not permitted to join the race to Paris, he would try racing a motorboat across the Atlantic. (*ROUND THE WORLD IN A MOTORCAR*)

Koeppen carried a letter of greeting from his commander in chief, Kaiser Wilhelm, who six years later would order German troops to "Let your hearts beat for God and your fists on the enemy." The kaiser's letter was harmless enough. It said simply that the race would allow the people of Germany and America to know each other better and increase trade.[9] The German leader didn't mention military benefits of the race, but Koeppen commented that the contest would show the German hierarchy that the automobile could play a part in modern warfare.

Another man in the dining room that night was far more interested in adventure than the military applications of the auto or anything else. He was a twenty-one-year-old Italian named Antonio Scarfoglio who looked and acted like a wealthy college student out on a lark. His father, a prominent Italian writer and newspaper editor from Naples, had objected to his son's plan to enter the car race. The younger Scarfoglio countered that if he did not get his way, he was going to try something else, perhaps driving a motorboat across the Atlantic Ocean.[10] The father gave in and his son arrived in New York, an instant hero with the city's six hundred thousand Italian immigrants. Scarfoglio represented his father's newspaper, the *Naples Mattina*, as well as the *London Daily Mail* and *La Stampa Sportiva*.

An earlier gathering in Scarfoglio's honor had featured the editors of New York's six major Italian newspapers, the Italian vice consul, and one hundred others. "The horn of the Angel Gabriel would not be too great to sound a paean of praise for the winners of this race," said one speaker. Scarfoglio had brown eyes, thick brown hair, and a penchant for finding fault with people and places that didn't measure up to his homeland. In his 1909 book on the race, *Round the World in a Motor-Car*, the young Italian interpreted his reception in New York as evidence that Italians grew far more patriotic and emotional about Italy when they moved beyond its boundaries. "The enthusiasm of the Italians here is, therefore, not for us personally, it is not our good or bad fortune which moves and interests them. No, it is the name of Italy arrayed in battle against the others."[11]

The Norwegian captain, the German lieutenant, and the Italian journalist had arrived in New York several days before the race began with a dozen other European drivers and mechanics. The ten-day trip to New York was uneventful, Scarfoglio said. "The ladies are ill, the cooking is monotonous and the sea is invisible, owing to the rain."

Arriving in New York, most of the motorists posed for publicity photos wearing the furs they expected to need in the arctic. Thompson, the auto club official, had hoped to greet the racers at the dock, but his chauffeur-driven car had been pulled over by one of New York's bicycle police for exceeding the ten-mile-per-hour speed limit. Thompson had to be content to welcome the racers by phone.

There were delays in getting the cars cleared by customs, but during their time in New York, the motorists saw more red carpet than red tape. Stephane Lauzanne, editor of *Le Matin*, was particularly impressed with the Brooklyn Bridge, which had already spanned the East River for a quarter century. If the French had built the bridge, he said, they would have started with a small footbridge for pedestrians and gradually expanded it over many decades. The massive stone towers of the great bridge testified that progress advanced with giant steps in America, Lauzanne concluded.[12]

Lauzanne also found it curious that New Yorkers could walk on crowded streets without bumping into one another: "People go about with alert and busy steps, eyes straight before them, as if eternally running toward an invisible goal. They are indifferent to all eccentricities, averse to all idleness."

Lauzanne and the other visitors attended numerous luncheons and banquets in New York, including one affair on the twenty-second floor of the Times Tower in Times Square, where the entertainment included a series of phony telegrams purporting to describe conditions the racers found in Alaska. A message from "Chillville, Alaska" said: "Busy trying to make gasoline out of whale oil. Tried it yesterday. Result, machine immediately spouted and dived through hole in ice. Chauffeur had to harpoon it to get it ashore." Another message reported that a driver had been arrested for "exceeding the upper Alaskan speed limit of one mile in 60 hours."[13]

During a break from the banquet routine, the racers buttoned their fur coats and pulled on woolen caps for a fifty-mile tour of New York. It had been cold enough to begin cutting the city's ice supply upstream on the Hudson River, so the arctic costumes were not inappropriate. Five touring cars driven by volunteers carried placards advertising the start of the race. With chains on the rear tires for traction, the cars drove north. A storm had hit the city several days earlier and although twenty-two hundred laborers had found work clearing Manhattan by hand, snow still covered the streets. The tour took them past Grant's Tomb. "He was the Napoleon of the United States," one of the Frenchmen said. The motorists passed scores of sleighing parties all the way through Yonkers.

At the Maplewood Inn near Dobbs Ferry, the men heard "La Marseillaise" on the piano and learned that they had seen a fair sampling of the roads to Albany. A reporter wrote: "The few bicycle policemen who lined the road held up no warning hand, preferring in several instances to salute the cars as they flew over the snowy surface at a good pace."

As the cars slowed to allow a trolley to pass, a small boy shouted: "Will you ever get to Paris?" Charles Godard, the driver of the Motobloc, replied, "Sure." Godard's companions, aware of his limited command of the king's English, congratulated him for quick thinking in an emergency.[14] Godard was a resourceful man.

The year before, the thirty-one-year-old Godard had nearly died while driving from Peking to Paris when his car broke down in the Gobi Desert, but his greatest accomplishment was not in beating the elements: he had conned other people into paying his way. The previous summer Godard had set off with no money to ship his car to Peking or to buy gasoline or other necessities.

The one-time motorcycle stunt rider, who had starred in a Paris fairground attraction known as the Wall of Death, had sweet-talked or swindled others into footing the bill. Now, Godard had persuaded a French auto company to sponsor him in the New York–Paris race. His enemies in France alleged that Godard would be in no hurry to get to Paris because upon his return he was facing an eight-month jail term and a fine of five thousand francs for acquiring funds under false

Charles Godard behind the wheel of the Motobloc. He was so confident he said he placed all of the race instructions in a sealed bag and never looked at them. (UNIVERSITY OF MICHIGAN LIBRARY)

pretenses. His defenders said that Godard was simply at odds with the management of *Le Matin* and that the newspaper had attempted to destroy his reputation.[15]

While Godard and the others acquainted themselves with New York, the lone American entry headed east aboard an express train from Buffalo. E. R. Thomas had given the go-ahead so late that the car rolled off the factory floor with few modifications.

Montague Roberts took the car for a test drive after its arrival in New York and said both he and the machine were ready to go. Though still in his mid-twenties, Roberts had made a name for himself in racing circles since leaving the Army, where he had served in the ordnance department and tested the first artillery truck. As a demonstrator for the New York Thomas dealer, Roberts also introduced customers to the ways of the automobile. Three or four years before the race, he had delivered a car to the Roosevelts at Hyde Park and taught Franklin Delano Roosevelt how to drive it.[16]

Roberts hoped to average thirty miles per hour in the Flyer, considerably above the twenty-mile-per-hour speed limit that applied in most states. He predicted he would reach Albany in one day, Chicago in seven, and Cheyenne, Wyoming, in a month. He had a commitment to compete in the Briarcliff Cup race in Westchester County on April 24 so he planned to turn over the wheel of the Flyer in Wyoming to a relief driver.

The equipment on the car included two shovels, picks, axes, lanterns, three searchlights, extra springs, five hundred feet of rope, a rifle, and revolvers. The racers also stowed away fur coats, woolen underwear, two pairs of plain goggles and two pairs of snow goggles for each man, ponchos, rubber boots, a coffee pot, water pail, tire chains, Thermos bottles, four spare tires, and a foot-powered air pump to inflate tires.

Joining Roberts on the American crew was T. Walter Williams, a former English seaman now working as a *New York Times* correspondent. Williams provided daily dispatches for the newspaper, which covered the race almost as thoroughly as the presidential campaign of William Howard Taft. A third man in the car was to be thirty-five-year-old George Schuster, a stocky company driver and mechanic chosen at the last minute. Schuster, a former bicycle mechanic and racer, had worked with automobiles since the turn of the century, As the chief road tester for the Thomas firm, he knew the highways of New York as well as any man alive. The company doubled his salary to fifty dollars a week for the duration.

Schuster began to earn his bigger paycheck on February 12, 1908, a mild and sunny day in the city of four million. Above a sea of black

The cars line up just before the start of the race in Times Square, as seen from one of the upper floors in the Times building. (*AUTOMOBILE*)

derbies, Times Square and a long stretch of Broadway were awash in forty-five-star American flags. Oklahoma had entered the union three months earlier, but the forty-six-star flag wasn't in circulation, As the cars pulled onto Broadway from Forty-third Street to prepare for the start, a huge American flag unfurled from above, releasing a confetti storm of tiny American, French, German, and Italian flags.

From Times Square to Seventy-second Street, known in that day as Automobile Row, car dealerships and showrooms overflowed with flags and streamers. A large banner outside the garage of the Thomas dealership expressed the nationalistic overtones of the contest. It said: "America Against the World."

This portion of Broadway was popular with automobile drivers, who normally competed for space on the streets with what some of them referred to disdainfully as the "four-legged hay motor." In addition to the race cars, more than two hundred other automobiles gathered along Broadway and side streets for the occasion, one of the largest collections of autos ever seen on the streets of New York.

Sixty Thomas cars took part in the procession along with one Ford, one Oldsmobile, two Studebakers, and forty other models now long departed from the American highway. Parking assignments somehow got confused, despite elaborate instructions in the *Times*, and dozens of the guest drivers and their passengers found themselves trapped in one of Manhattan's first automobile traffic jams.[17]

Looming over the traffic tieup was the twenty-five-story Times Tower. The building, now known as I Times Square Plaza, had been the second tallest building in New York when it opened for business three years earlier. By 1908 it had dropped to fourth, behind the Metropolitan Tower, the Singer Building, and the Park Row Building. Reporters and editors in the *Times* newsroom on the seventeenth floor had a good vantage point to watch what unfolded below in one of the most famous sections of the city. The subway system had opened in 1904, an underground marvel that changed the neighborhood. The area had been a center for carriage makers and blacksmith shops. Now that it could be reached by anyone with a nickel subway fare, Times Square began to develop into the city's most important theater district.

On an average day nearly seventy-five thousand people used the Times Square subway station, many of them unaware that the rumbling one-hundred-ton presses of the newspaper rested on bedrock twenty-five feet below the tracks. Above ground, the ornate Astor Hotel dominated the west side of the square. A large sign on the four-story building next to the hotel advertised the services of Levey the Cleanser.

The race begins in Times Square as the cars head up Broadway. The Times Tower is at the left. The Astor Hotel is on the right. (COURTESY OF HENRY AUSTIN CLARK JR.)

"Gloves cleansed. All lengths. 5 cents a pair." It would be decades before the neon signs of cascading waterfalls and giant beer bottles turned night into day in Times Square, but thanks to an advertising man, the words *Great White Way* had already entered the language. The straight rows of incandescent lights that ran along the theater signs and store fronts lit the neighborhood.

Vaudeville performers mentioned the auto contest in shows such as "The Talk of New York" and "Miss Hook of Holland." In their comedy act at the Criterion Theater, Mr. Wise drunkenly asked his partner Mr. West: "Does this automobile race from New York to Paris meet with your approval?" Mr. West replied: "It's surely up to the *Times*."[18] A short film taken by the American Vitagraph Company of the start of the race soon topped the hill at Hammerstein's Victoria Theatre of Varieties, one of a dozen theaters in the square.

Adding to the festive air on race day were bands playing national anthems of the United States, Germany, France, and Italy. With nearly two hundred thousand immigrants settling in New York each year, every car had its vocal partisans in Times Square. About three hundred policemen struggled to hold back what the *Times* described as "one of the greatest throngs that ever crowded into a small space." Some of those who got in close tried to share the fame of the adventure in a small way by writing their names on the cars. In the months ahead the original colors of the cars would disappear under names from across the globe.

The bystanders included people who fed their families on fifteen dollars a week as well as some of the richest men in the world. Among the latter was Col. John Jacob Astor, who had built the Astoria portion of the Waldorf-Astoria. A mechanically minded man, Astor had invented a bicycle brake and various other gadgets, and he owned seventeen cars. He said the contest was the "most stupendous automobile achievement ever conceived" and that it would prove the practical value of the car to skeptics. Astor believed that one day it would be against the law to keep horses in large cities and that streets would be smooth and easily cleaned, with no manure to threaten pedestrians. Astor didn't live to see the disappearance of the horse: Four years later he was the richest man to go down on the *Titanic*.

The German Protos on the starting line in New York City. (COURTESY OF THE
WILLIAM F. HARRAH FOUNDATION NATIONAL AUTOMOBILE MUSEUM)

Astor's vision of America's motoring future seemed a distant dream
to those at the starting line for the race to Paris. Bad roads were a
common hazard in the United States, and the drivers said they worried
the most about tire trouble. Under normal conditions a set of tires
might only last for one thousand or two thousand miles. These weren't
normal conditions. St. Chaffray, who carried a bouquet of red and
white carnations, said he didn't fear Alaska or Siberia. "The only part
of the journey that I dread is from New York to Buffalo and from
there to Erie, where, I hear, the ice and snow is eight feet deep and
the roads almost impassable."

Before the cars began to bounce off to Buffalo, one bystander told
a friend that none of the motorists would ever make it to Paris. "I've

been through the Alaskan country and know what I'm talking about," novelist Rex Beach said to theatrical manager Frederic Thompson. Thompson offered to bet one thousand dollars that Beach was mistaken. Beach, whose writing about Alaska described adventures in some of the toughest territory on earth, immediately shook on the wager.[19]

Had there been a vote among those who watched the start of the race, Beach's position would have won the day. New Yorkers knew how hard it was to get anywhere in their part of the country. They could only imagine what Siberia was like. With horses still drawing some of Manhattan's streetcars, slow travel and congested streets were a way of life. No doubt New York Mayor George McClellan had time to reflect on that aspect of city life as he tried to get to Times Square from his home in Washington Square. McClellan, the son of the famous Civil War general, was supposed to fire the starting gun, but he had been given the wrong starting time. He didn't leave home until after 11:00 a.m. The mayor was a popular figure with the automobile lobby, which liked his plan to require mufflers in the city and his proposed ban on the use of sirens except by the fire department. Delayed by the heavy traffic, all the mayor saw of the race was the exhaust smoke from the cars as they headed toward Yonkers.

In the mayor's absence, Colgate Hoyt, president of the Automobile Club of America, looked at his watch and decided that Paris was calling. He rose from his seat in the grandstand, lifted his hand to call attention, and at 11:15 a.m. fired a shot from a gold-plated .22-caliber pistol. Hoyt said the crowd's reaction was "the finest automobile ovation that I ever witnessed."[20]

The cheering spectators lined Broadway for eight miles. Professors at Barnard College and Columbia University dismissed classes to allow their students to watch. A Columbia Latin professor said it was the chance of a lifetime. The *Times* said 250,000 people turned out that day in the city and nearby towns along the route. The noise overwhelmed the men in the cars. Scarfoglio, the young Italian journalist, said he didn't remember much of the start except they moved forward "between two thick hedges of extended hands amidst a roar as of a falling torrent."[21]

THREE

SNOWBOUND

THE FIRST PEOPLE to drive across the United States did it to settle a fifty-dollar bet. Dr. Horatio Nelson Jackson, a wealthy Vermont surgeon, and mechanic Sewell K. Crocker rode from San Francisco to New York in the summer of 1903. They traveled most of the way with a bulldog named Bud. Jackson said the canine watched the road as closely as his masters, bracing himself when he saw a bump or a rock. Bud's eyes soon became bloodshot from the dust, however, and Jackson bought the dog a pair of goggles. Before long, Bud refused to move in the morning until his eyewear was in place.[1]

It took Jackson, Crocker, and Bud sixty-three days to cross the continent in their twenty-horsepower Winton. They meandered nearly six thousand miles, taking many detours to avoid impassable trails and flooded areas. The men went without food once for thirty-six hours and on numerous occasions they had to use a block and tackle to haul the car out of deep mud. The trip cost the doctor thousands, but he won the $50.

By the time the racers departed for Paris, other adventurers and professional drivers had completed about a dozen trips across the American continent. The longest expedition had taken nearly seven months. L. L. Whitman completed the fastest journey in a little more than fifteen days. "We roasted, shivered, fasted, thirsted most mightily," Whitman said.[2]

Few of the 63,500 American cars sold in 1908 strayed far from home. In many states horses still had the right of way over cars, and bad roads made any long-distance trip an expedition into the unknown, especially in winter.

Everyone knew that the weather might create insurmountable obstacles on the way to Paris, especially in Alaska or Siberia. No one expected that the first casualty would be laid low by the good road to Philadelphia. Eugene Lelouvier, who had departed a day before the official race began, ran into trouble as soon as he was beyond the cheering crowds and the politicians' speeches.

Lelouvier collided with a horse-drawn cart soon after leaving the ferry terminal on Staten Island. At Perth Amboy, he hit a cart loaded with food and complained loudly that the car's brakes had failed. He stopped for repairs five times between New Brunswick and Trenton, hardly missing a ditch or a snowbank. At 10:15 p.m., he slid off the road at twenty miles per hour and stayed stuck for three hours before two other cars showed up and towed his car toward the City of Brotherly Love.

The Werner was set free on one occasion, but Lelouvier, who refused to give up the wheel, slammed into another snowbank. After pulling him out again, the men who stopped to help said they could stand no more. They drove on, leaving Lelouvier to find his way alone down Broad Street at 5:30 a.m.[3]

Members of the Quaker City Motor Club had turned out in force the night before to welcome the Frenchmen; all but one went home at 2:00 a.m. The sentry greeted the cold and grumpy motorists at 6:00 a.m., loaded them into his car, and dropped them off at the Rittenhouse

Hotel. Lelouvier had managed an average speed of six miles per hour on the first day's sixteen-hour run.

The *New York World* summed up the situation with a small story under a charitable headline: "BAD ROADS DELAY THE WERNER CAR." A *World* reporter had accompanied Lelouvier long enough, however, to understand that the real problem was not beneath the tires, but behind the wheel.

It took a couple of days for the Quaker City Automobile Company to ready the battered car for the road. When the Werner left Philadelphia for points west, Lelouvier was no longer at the wheel. After his two companions, Maurice Drieghe and Max Hohmann, had demanded that he leave the driving to them, Lelouvier walked off in a huff. He boarded a train to New York and said that his wife in Siberia would see to it that his former friends would be unable to buy a drop of fuel in the frozen north. Drieghe, with gestures and shrugs, said the experience had proven that even a French daredevil might not know how to drive a car.[4]

Drieghe and Hohmann promised to keep going and they did. It took them two months to reach Seattle, where they received a hero's welcome. They told a newspaper reporter that they had driven the entire way. "It is not so difficult to travel through the snow in an automobile as one would imagine," Drieghe told the *Seattle Post-Intelligencer*, "And the only serious trouble we had with snow was in the Allegheny Mountains."

Drieghe, who posed for pictures in front of the *Post-Intelligencer* building, said that they had traveled without a guide and that their only map had blown out of the car in Wyoming. "The trip through the Rockies was not difficult. We had good roads, that is, they were dry and hard all the way," he said.

A competing Seattle newspaper found reason to suspect Drieghe's story. Witnesses in Oregon City, Oregon, told the *Seattle Times* that the two men and their car arrived in their town in a boxcar after crossing much of the continent by train. "The machine broke down at Columbus, Ohio, and was shipped on a flat car to St. Louis and there transferred to a box car, where it could not be seen," the *Times* said. The men, who would only tell the townspeople that they were with a "moving picture outfit," took the car off the train in Oregon City and drove to Portland, where they told tales about a difficult drive through the sands of eastern Oregon.

Challenged on his story, Drieghe said it was immaterial whether he had taken a train because "the public has no interest in our affairs."[5] After this debacle hit the papers, he was right.

In addition to deceiving the public about how they reached the West Coast, Drieghe and Hohmann also kept silent about the train trip they had taken across the Allegheny Mountains in Pennsylvania.[6] The snow in the mountains made travel difficult, if not impossible, and most experienced cross-country travelers avoided the Alleghenies altogether. Drieghe and Hohmann had dared to be different, but the snow stopped them cold.

In the first years of the century, the most popular way to the west was a northerly "water level route" through upstate New York that ran parallel to the Erie Canal and the New York Central Railroad.[7] The *New York Times* recommended that route and the six official entrants in the race to Paris followed it. It was not until the completion of Interstate 80 in the early 1970s that a major road headed directly west out of New York City.

The race organizers predicted that the cars could make at least 150 miles a day in the East, but the drivers received stern warnings to ease up on the accelerator. "Between New York and Chicago, there will be no daredevil pacing along the public roads," the *Times* said. "This section of the country is too thickly populated to permit driving at a dangerous pace." In New York, a "dangerous pace" meant more than twenty miles per hour in the country, ten miles per hour in business districts, and four miles per hour on steep curves and hills. One auto expert said the drivers should be on the lookout for the "occasional overzealous constable who shares in the fines levied on automobilists violating the speed laws of his particular village."[8]

The racers received detailed route information listing cemeteries, railroad crossings, churches, and other landmarks. There were no major long-distance roads in America then, only dirt trails that connected one place to another in a jumbled pattern that owed much to chance and tradition. Even trips between larger towns could be complicated. Here's what it took to get from Albany to Schenectady: "Make right bend around Capitol into Washington Avenue to one block beyond Tenth Battalion Armory, turn right onto Knox Street and over high viaduct into Northern Boulevard. Continue on Boulevard, making left curve, and then easy right over viaduct over New York Central Railroad. Go past first four corners and turn left at second four corners, direct to Latham Corners. Cross trolley tracks in front of power house and turn left, direct ahead to Schenectady."[9]

West of Chicago, the *Times* said, "There is less necessity for detailed directions as the road from place to place is not confused by a multiplicity of directions." To help the drivers keep on track, members of some auto clubs pledged to mark the way with a plan right out of Hansel and Gretel. Instead of bread crumbs though, the auto clubs said they would use trails of confetti to show the route from town to town.[10]

As it turned out, the trip to Chicago did become a speed contest of sorts, but it was the rate at which the men could shovel snow and extricate their cars from the drifts that really mattered. Though warned about speed limits and overzealous constables, no one cautioned the racers about what Scarfoglio, the young Italian journalist, described as "the soft enemy."

The enemy was everywhere. One headline describing the first day of racing could have been repeated almost anytime during the first month: "AUTOS FIGHT SNOW DRIFTS, ALL THE LEADERS STUCK."[11] The combination of snow and slush made for such rough going that August Pons, driver of the one-cylinder Sizaire-Naudin, dropped out of the race after ninety-six miles. He couldn't repair the car's broken differential. Pons had faced similar misfortune the year before when he was knocked out of the Peking-Paris trip. Years later, designer Maurice Sizaire said he believed one of his rivals had placed a pebble in the rear axle in New York, causing the breakdown. Nothing was said of this suspicion at the time of the race, however, and the focus quickly shifted to the five other competitors.

The remaining cars and their crews were as follows: The French de Dion, driven by M. Autran and St. Chaffray, with Hansen providing navigational help; the Italian Zust, commanded by Scarfoglio, driven by Emilio Sirtori, and kept in running order by Henri Haaga, a German mechanic; the French Motobloc, driven by Godard with the assistance of Maurice Livier and mechanic Arthur Hue; the German Protos, driven by Hans Knape and Ernest Maas, with the aid of Koeppen; and the American Thomas Flyer, driven by Montague Roberts with mechanic George Schuster. Mechanic George Miller joined the car in Buffalo. Passenger Skipper Williams represented the *New York Times*.

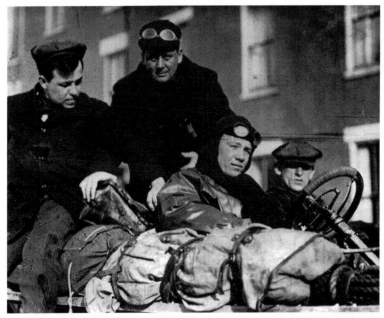

The crew of the Thomas Flyer. From left, mechanic George Miller, correspondent Skipper Williams, driver Montague Roberts and mechanic George Schuster. (COURTESY OF THE WILLIAM F. HARRAH FOUNDATION NATIONAL AUTOMOBILE MUSEUM)

Outside of New York City, the Thomas Flyer, the de Dion, and the Zust quickly emerged as the leaders. Koeppen's Protos and Godard's Motobloc brought up the rear. Godard said he would live by the proverb "Who goes slowly, goes far." He was in no hurry, it was said, because he expected that St. Chaffray would soon give up the idea of crossing the United States in winter. Godard thought the drivers would be allowed to ship the cars to Seattle, which would guarantee that the racers would arrive in Alaska before the spring thaw.

Leaving Hudson, New York, on the second day, the cars plowed through foot-deep snow in single file. Schuster walked in front of the Thomas Flyer with a long stick he used to check the snow depth. The snow was shallower in the fields, so the drivers went cross-country, bumping over the hidden furrows. In the deepest spots they dug through the snow and put down planks to get traction. "We literally fought our way, inch-by-inch and foot-by-foot over the 22 miles between Albany and Hudson," Scarfoglio wrote. "If the landscape which surrounded us had not been so uniformly sad under its white blanket which reduced everything to the same level, I believe that we should be able to remember every stone of this cruel road."[12]

The Albany Automobile Club sent fourteen cars to greet the leaders five miles outside the state capital and escorted them to a luncheon with Gov. Charles Hughes at the Ten Eyck Hotel. Then it was on to Schenectady and the seventy-year-old towpath of the Erie Canal. Thousands of mules pulling canal boats from Albany to Buffalo had packed down the fifteen- to thirty-foot-wide trail next to the canal.

With competition from the railroads, freight traffic on the canal had dwindled to less than half of what it had been a generation earlier, and there was even talk of turning the towpath or the canal into a 325-mile highway across New York. But as the *Buffalo Express* reported, the towpath was not ideal for automobiles. "Few drivers would enjoy the job of driving during this weather on the perilous path, much trod of mules during the summer. Danger lurks near always. A slip of the wheel and zip—you are in the canal bed and probably dead with the machine on top of you. But the towpath, dangerous as it is, is much better than the highways. It is at least fairly clear of snow."[13]

One of the cars escorting the racers did fall into the canal, injuring two men. That didn't stop the Italians from driving forty-five miles per hour on the path. Hansen said he would have none of that: "Life is too short to go at that pace in such a dangerous spot, and our car will take things more calmly."

In every town along the canal, the race was the prime topic of conversation and the subject of countless wagers in barbershops and hotel lobbies. In Utica, the motorists couldn't even examine their cars because so many people had followed them into the garage. Lawyer Harvey Ferris solved the problem by climbing on top a parked car, pointing down a corridor and borrowing a line from P. T. Barnum. "This way to the egress. Don't miss the egress," Ferris said. Many people rushed out to see what kind of strange animal was called an "egress."[14]

The racers soon developed a regular routine. Most rose at 5:00 a.m. and kept going until 7:00 or 8:00 p.m. They drained their radiators at night to keep them from freezing, and the mechanics tinkered with the machines until midnight. Every car had mechanical and tire problems that ranged from cracks in the chassis to broken tire chains.

The weather warmed a little and the cars had to leave the towpath at Syracuse because of rising water on the Mohawk River. The trail out of Auburn, which the *Times* described as the worst road in the United States, lived up to its reputation, and the race rolled to a dead stop at Dismal Hollow, a place in the Montezuma Swamp. A drift from two to nine feet deep stretched two hundred feet in front of the cars. The men prepared to camp for the night, but an American guide hired by the Italians appeared with six horses and pulled the cars through.

"The roads upstate are simply atrocious and all the drivers are disgusted," Roberts said.[15] He said that even main roads had drifts from ten to twelve feet deep. Sirtori, the twenty-six-year-old driver of Scarfoglio's Zust, said: "My heart is full of evil thoughts about the men who make the roads." He said Italy was a poor country, but at least there were good roads in all directions and road signs. "Perhaps the roads in New York are not marked like that because the officials are ashamed to call them roads."

Farmers along the way blamed state officials for not keeping the roads up to par, but others criticized the farmers. "The farmers will not pay their quota toward the repairing of the roads because they contend it is for the benefit of millionaire automobilists," said Dr. Charles D. Vale of Hobart College in Geneva. "In their eyes no one but a millionaire can own an automobile. They use their light wagons that can go over the fields as easily as the roads and when the snow is too deep they use sleighs."[16]

A new law under which the state and counties split the cost of road work had not yet made much of a difference. The bicycle boom of the late 1800s had sparked a Good Roads movement, but the political pressure for better highways took time to pay dividends in rural America. Since the Civil War, road building had been entirely in local hands. Residents had paid their road taxes by moving dirt with horse-drawn equipment and hand tools. The work was notoriously shabby and farmers had little incentive to do more than the minimum. Their horizons were shaped by the limits of a horse and buggy and by the knowledge that the railroad was the only reliable means of long-distance transportation.[17]

Nothing symbolized the power of the railroad quite like the Twentieth Century Limited, an express train that combined luxury and speed on its twenty-hour run from New York to Chicago along the route followed by the auto racers. The train compiled a daily "sailing list" of passengers, comparing the service to that of an ocean liner. Some Twentieth Century Limited advertisements in February made mention of the auto race. Few people would have believed that in less than a generation the automobile would knock the railroad from its exalted position in the American consciousness.

The horseless carriage was not yet a serious threat to the iron horse, but the revolt began while the Paris racers were crossing the United States: the first flyers advertising Henry Ford's new Model T had appeared in dealerships and produced an instant response. "It is without doubt the greatest creation in automobiies ever placed before a people," a Ford dealer from Pennsylvania reported to company headquarters in Detroit, "and it means that this circular alone will flood your factory with orders."[18]

Introduced in the fall of 1908, the car that Ford and his engineers called "the family horse" converted millions of Americans to the automobile and became the world's most popular car. The Model T was light, powerful, and built for bad roads. It featured several mechanical innovations, such as its improved planetary transmission, which came in handy for rocking it out of mudholes. "The Fords were obviously conceived in madness," essayist E. B. White once wrote. "Any car which was capable of going from forward into reverse without any perceptible mechanical hiatus was bound to be a mighty challenging thing to the human imagination." In many ways, the rugged Model T would have been the ideal car for the race to Paris, but it was several months away from production. The Thomas Flyer that participated in the Paris race was used as a pilot car the next year to plot a route through the Pacific Northwest on a race to Seattle that was won by a Model T.

In 1907, Ford had told E. R. Thomas, the owner of the Thomas Flyer, of his plan to increase Ford production and decrease prices by building a four-cylinder car and sticking to a basic design.[19] The world would never be the same.

While Ford envisioned a new mass market, E. R. Thomas continued to direct his efforts at the upper-class market, which was already near the saturation point. The Model T carried an $850 pricetag when it was introduced. The Thomas Flyer cost $4,000, the equivalent of five years' pay for an average laborer.

Thomas, fifty-seven, was a former steamboat captain who had entered the car business the way many of his generation did, via the bicycle. He built Cleveland Bicycles in Ohio and Toronto before switching to motorized vehicles in 1900. "Uncle Ed," as he was known in later years, never learned how to drive, but he said it was his ambition to produce the best car in the world. "Since the dawn of civilization," he once said, "there have been means of travel other than walking to which one aspired. The ambition to possess an automobile is therefore innate in every human being."[20]

When the leading racers arrived in Buffalo, home of the Thomas Flyer, the city showed its innate enthusiasm for Uncle Ed's favorite car. "Thomas Flyer scorches across Western New York at Express Train Speed and leads nearest Competitor by 2½ Hours into Buffalo," said the headline in the *Buffalo Express*.[21]

A small band packed in an automobile played "Hail Columbia" until a mounted policeman threatened the musicians with arrest for disturbing the Sabbath. About five thousand people met the Thomas outside the Iroquois Hotel. As Schuster went off to visit his wife at his south Buffalo home, Roberts and Williams rested. Despite a brief fling at forty-five miles per hour just outside of Buffalo, they had averaged eight miles per hour so far, covering 471 miles in five days, somewhat short of express train speed.

Thomas said he was glad that Roberts had talked him into entering a car. "I consider it would be a disgrace and reflection upon the

E. R. Thomas, owner of the Thomas Flyer. (COURTESY OF THE *BUFFALO NEWS*)

With the American flag flying, the Thomas Flyer enters Buffalo, escorted by several Buffalo drivers. The Thomas was built in Buffalo. (COURTESY OF HENRY AUSTIN CLARK JR.)

American manufacturers if our country was not represented in the race, which is the greatest event that has ever happened in the history of the automobile industry or any other sport," he said.[22]

The Thomas factory on Niagara Street employed fourteen hundred people, most of whom earned twenty-five to thirty-five cents an hour, about three times what car workers earned in Europe, as Thomas was proud of pointing out. Thomas also liked to say that European cars could handle the "billiard table" roads of France and England, but the rugged cars in America had to face gullies, rocks, and washouts on every corner.[23]

The Thomas factory was one of two noteworthy auto plants in Buffalo, an emerging industrial center drawing its power from electricity generated at Niagara Falls. The other was run by George Pierce, another veteran of the bicycle business. Pierce built his first car in 1901, the predecessor of the Pierce-Arrow, the most famous of the thirty makes of cars built over the years in Buffalo. Pierce opened the doors of his factory to St. Chaffray, who took the de Dion there for repairs.

The visitors to Buffalo found broad paved streets and a new monument in the city center that served as a mute reminder of the highest and lowest points in the city's recent past. The monument honored President McKinley, who had been assassinated in 1901 while attending Buffalo's Pan-American Exposition.

St. Chaffray said people in France expected the racers would find buffalo in Buffalo, but all he discovered was an excellent hotel worthy of a medal from the Automobile Club of France. St. Chaffray was not nearly so generous in complimenting his racing crew. St. Chaffray and Hansen had two loud arguments in the Iroquois Hotel, in "which fried eggs threatened to be wasted," as one witness put it.[24] Hansen, who had been knocked out of the car at least once by St. Chaffray's poor driving, said he would put the Commissionaire General "in the gasoline tank" if he didn't stop running off the road two or three times a day.

The captain also complained that St. Chaffray sat in the driver's seat smoking cigarettes and giving orders every time the car got stuck, while Hansen and Autran dug it out. It was St. Chaffray who boasted in a newspaper dispatch that he had been working so hard and his muscles were getting so big that he feared his coat soon wouldn't fit. His tailor had no need to worry.

While Hansen did most of the working, St. Chaffray did most of the talking. "I am the nephew of the Marquis de Dion who makes this car," St. Chaffray told Hansen in Buffalo, "and when I tell you to get out and push, you shall do so."[25]

Hansen wanted to quit the race right then, but others intervened and St. Chaffray promised to take his turn with a snow shovel. Hansen agreed to a truce and declared that he was ready to proceed: "We will either reach Paris or our bodies will be found beside the car," he said.[26]

E. R. Thomas, the mayor of Buffalo, and other leading residents scheduled a banquet for the next evening, but the guests of honor left town before the celebration could begin. The Italians had been more than twelve hours behind the leaders, but the Zust caught up with the Thomas and the de Dion after an all-night drive from Rochester. The Italians refused to stop in Buffalo and took the lead while the others prepared for the banquet.

"It seems ridiculous to confess it, but in this race we are living only with and for the desire or the hope of the day. To be first, to be ahead of the others today—that is enough," Scarfoglio said.[27] When St. Chaffray learned the Italians had shuffled through Buffalo, he quickly prepared his car and took off after them without telling the

Americans. In his car was a "sad-faced Hansen," who had been eagerly looking forward to the night's entertainment, a reporter said.

Roberts, Schuster, and Williams didn't get the word until sometime later that morning. They roared out of Buffalo 3½ hours behind St. Chaffray, running hard along the eastern shore of frozen Lake Erie. Annoyed at the French and the Italians for trying to sneak off, Roberts passed Scarfoglio close to the Pennsylvania border, where the Zust had stopped with tire trouble. The Americans then surprised St. Chaffray and stopped for the night at the same hotel in Erie, Pennsylvania.

At dinner that night, St. Chaffray made some sarcastic remarks to Roberts. "When you wish to go into a city ahead, you ask me," St. Chaffray said. The Frenchman may have given himself the grand title of Commissionaire General, but Roberts had no intention of listening to any orders from St. Chaffray. "From now on you will know this is a race," Roberts said.[28] According to Hansen's account, St. Chaffray then demanded that Roberts leave the room, but the Norwegian rose to the American's defense, saying it was a public restaurant.

For the first few days, the motorists had cooperated with each other and had taken turns breaking trail. Now, an atmosphere of international ill will took hold. The racers deluded themselves into thinking that an hour or two might really make a difference in a six-month race. They grew paranoid that their opponents might try to sneak off into the night. The Americans rose at 3:00 a.m. the next morning because of a false report that the Italians were back on the road to Cleveland.

As the race took on a more competitive tone, a worldwide audience followed the dueling motorists through newspaper and magazine dispatches. In towns along the route, newspapers gave it front-page treatment. Throughout America, the race remained one of the major news events of the winter, an oddity unmatched by anything except perhaps the story of the Texas woman who took over the Alamo for three days in a dispute over the monument's future, or the report by astronomer Percival Lowell that canals on Mars were ancient artificial waterways that proved the existence of intelligent life on that planet.

In Johnstown, Pennsylvania, lumber merchant Jacob Murdock eagerly read all he could about the race. Murdock made several train trips that winter from Pennsylvania to California. He said he used to sit for many hours, gazing out of the train "dreaming dreams of making the journey home some day in my automobile." Inspired by the racers, Murdock became the first man to drive from coast to coast with his family. He did it that spring, fighting mud in the Midwest and dust in the desert while trying to keep three children entertained for thirty-two days.[29] He averaged more than one hundred miles a day. Murdock advised other drivers to follow his example and start on the West Coast and head east, "For the prevailing winds are from west to east, and they can keep or retard one a lot."

In New York City the public school system added the race to the curriculum to heighten interest in geography. Preachers found meaning in the undertaking as well. "In this great automobile race," the president of the National Bible Institute said, "the reward will come to the men who patiently persevere in the face of gigantic obstacles. This quality is essential also in the running of the race of life."[30]

Other New Yorkers tracked the cars on a big bulletin board at the offices of the *New York Times*, a precursor of the electric sign that would one day flash headlines around the building in the center of Times Square. On a map inside the front window, a card and flag showed the location of each car. People gathered there at all hours,

There was no telling how far men could go by automobile, as shown in this advertisement for the Goodrich Rubber Co., "Akron to Mars." (*AUTOMOBILE*)

checking the pocket maps on which they plotted the racers' progress. The *Times* reported that immigrants from Norway, Ireland, Italy, Germany, and France would argue with lifelong New Yorkers over which car was going to win. A *Times* reporter stood by as a Swede and an Irishman debated the question. An Italian broke in to speak up for his country's car.

"'What you talk? Mucha plenty time yet. Bigga man what take-a-de front seat he getta to resh, mebbe he take-a de back seat. Italiana car he make-a dem all look like thirty cent.'

" 'Back to Mulberry for yours!' chimed in a newsboy. 'De Thomas'll put it inter dem so deep it'll take e rest ten years to dig it out.'

" 'Pooty soon mebbe ve see dot Protos car mit rubber tiders vhat can't break,' said a German. 'Den look oudt! Dot's all.' "[31]

In the early stages of the race, the *Times* ran daily accounts of the racers' progress in the far right column of the front page, the slot reserved for the most important news of the day. Other newspapers didn't have a race to Paris, but they kept trying stunts of their own. One week into the race, the editors of Hearst's *New York American* launched a Studebaker on a trip from New York to Fort Leavenworth, Kansas. Three shifts of drivers, who shuttled ahead by railroad, took turns at the wheel. The stated purpose of the sixteen-hundred-mile trip was to carry a message to Leavenworth from Maj. Gen. Frederick Grant, to show that the automobile could be used to carry dispatches great distances in wartime.[32]

Somehow, the trip to Kansas didn't match the drama in the reports on the race to Paris provided by Skipper Williams, the *Times* correspondent on the Thomas Flyer. He seemed the right man for the job. Williams had left his home in England at fifteen and spent nearly two decades on the high seas. He went ashore at various times to look for gold on the Orinoco in South America, to work as a foreman on the Panama Canal, or to install lightning rods in Central America. He went to Alaska in 1897 as the third mate on the S.S. *Ninchow* and traveled inland to investigate the Klondike. Returning home, he gave illustrated lectures on the gold fields at Albert Hall in London. He entered journalism in 1899 and covered the Boer War alongside Winston Churchill, Rudyard Kipling, H. G. Wells, and Arthur Conan Doyle. Williams was a "typical John Bull in appearance," a friend recalled, "pink, plump and personable."[33]

Skipper Williams, who
became a legend in the
newsroom of the *New York
Times* and on the city's
waterfront, covered the
early portion of the race to
Paris. (COURTESY OF THE
NEW YORK TIMES
ARCHIVES)

On an assignment in New York in 1905, Williams met *Times*
publisher Adolph Ochs, who offered him a job. Williams stayed with
the *Times* until his death in 1942. Though he would soon become
famous on the docks of New York as the ship news reporter for the
Times, the Skipper labored largely in anonymity on the 1908 race.
The newspaper almost never put bylines on reporters' stories in those
days. "The *Times* is not running a reporters' directory," managing
editor Carr Van Anda would say.[34]

Williams often injected humor into his unsigned reports, sometimes making fun of himself. His attempts to climb over the shovels,
baggage, and spare tires to reach his back-seat on the Thomas never
failed to amuse a crowd. Bystanders shouted "Bravo, fatty" and "You'll
lose that in Siberia" as they watched him struggle aboard. Williams
said for a time his seat was hanging "like the sword of Damocles"
because a severe jolt had loosened its moorings. Schuster said if Williams
feared he was about to fall out of the car, he should grab Schuster's

hand and hang on. Williams said he chose instead to cling tightly to the front seat at all times.

Williams never smoked while riding in the Thomas. Gas bubbled out of the tank beneath his feet whenever the car hit a bump. He also didn't like to see anyone approach the car with a cigarette because with one wayward spark, "the car and its occupants would take an aerial course far out of the route from New York to Paris."[35]

The reporter took note of many bizarre events along the way, such as the impromptu salute given the Thomas Flyer by a "commanding-looking" woman who stepped to the front porch of her farm house with her four children and fired her rifle into the air.

The correspondent kept in touch with the home office by telegraph. The *Times* was experimenting with transatlantic wireless transmission, but the telegraph remained the newspaper's major means of communication with the world beyond its doorstep. Williams sometimes had trouble sending his reports to New York in a timely fashion. In Corunna, Indiana, he wrote sarcastically that the telegrapher was so slow it would take him at least a week to send two thousand words to New York. "The lonely operator who was the agent and the general Pooh-bah of this out-of-the-way station was more than an hour trying to get Toledo on the wire," Williams reported. The correspondent said the Lake Shore Railroad ran only two trains a day through Corunna because "no one wants to go there and it does not care to encourage the natives to leave."[36]

Williams's reports were transcribed on the eighteenth floor of the Times Tower, just above the newsroom. A dozen telegraph operators worked there, each sitting next to a small wooden sounding box and a typewriter. The operators took down cable reports at twenty-five to thirty-five words a minute. After receiving a dispatch, the operator would send it down a chute to the main editorial offices on the floor below. A large U-shaped desk was divided into two sections, one for the night city editor and his assistants who handled local news and the other for the telegraph editor and his staff. They wrote the headlines, edited the stories, and sent them down one floor by pneumatic chute to the sixteenth-floor composing room.[37]

When a major story broke, one of the first people to check on the details was Carr Van Anda, who had the mind of a mathematician and the skills of a field general. Known to his employees as V.A., he was respected for his abilities, but "he seemed to have no more warmth than a deep-sea fish," *Times* historian Meyer Berger once wrote. In later years, reporters spoke of the "Van Anda death ray" that could be focused upon a wayward journalist. Like Ochs, Van Anda shunned publicity about himself and devoted his energy to the daily creation of what was to become the most influential newspaper in the world.

After leaving the *New York Sun* in 1904 to join the *Times*, Van Anda established a routine that remained the same for more than twenty years. He arrived at the office seven days a week at about 1:00 p.m. He read the telegraphic dispatches at the same time as the copy editors. "Well, there's going to be big news tonight," he would say on occasion, rubbing his hands together. He was a well-educated man, although he had attended college for only two years. He independently pursued the study of such diverse fields as physics, astronomy, Egyptian hieroglyphics, and horse racing. Above all, he had a passion for news.

On any important story, he took pride in offering the most comprehensive coverage in the city. To round out the reports from Williams about his backseat travels across America, the *Times* also printed first-person accounts from the European contestants. The racers often strayed from the subject at hand. In one treatise, St. Chaffray ventured forth on the status of American farmers. He said they were well-off compared to their European counterparts and some even had telephones.

"All here is republican," he said. "It means that everybody looks to be of the same class. If one has only a dollar in his pocket he looks as rich as the wealthiest man."[38]

While St. Chaffray was generally diplomatic in his dispatches from the field, Scarfoglio relied on sarcasm, humor, and snide remarks. Scarfoglio repeated much of his work in *Round the World in a Motor-Car*, a book published the year after the race. He complained bitterly about most of the countries visited on the world tour. To the eyes of this twenty-one-year-old, the cities of the United States were ugly and pompous, the landscape was monotonous, the roads were terrible, and the people were irritating. In the flowery style then in favor among Italian journalists, he wrote that the American practice of "stealing" names of cities from the old world was particularly annoying.

"They are rich in names which have been plundered from the geography and history of the world: stifled with stucco and gilding and colonnades; their 'capitols,' 'pantheons,' 'coliseums,' are grotesque miscarriages of magnificence," he wrote.[39]

He criticized Americans as culturally deprived and primitive, but his objections seemed to be based more on the lack of a rigid class society than anything else. "I do not like the Americans as a whole, just as I do not like the cheesemonger whom a prize in a lottery or a sudden rise in the price of potatoes has made wealthy. There is still too much of the herdsman about them and their clothes are still permeated by the smell of the soil. Riches alone do not justify everything. The opulence of others is always irritating, but that of the Americans is particularly so, because it is paraded, thrown proudly in your face, and shown about as the only true sign of greatness."[40]

Part of Scarfoglio's problem stemmed from the difficulty of communications. Until he bought a typewriter in the Midwest, many telegraph operators said they couldn't send his dispatches because they couldn't read his writing. Those who could read his accounts were treated to a style of writing described by one historian as an "almost incomprehensible wrought-iron masterpiece, encrusted with jewel-like adjectives and archaic verbs."[41]

Scarfoglio said that Americans trusted providence and the weather for the making and maintenance of highways, but that these were the worst possible contractors. Those contractors proved him correct when the race shifted to Ohio and Indiana. The day after Roberts argued in Erie with St. Chaffray, the American made good on his pledge to take the lead. By nightfall, he was in Toledo, 29 miles ahead of St. Chaffray, 120 miles in front of Scarfoglio, 220 miles ahead of Koeppen, and 300 miles ahead of Godard.

The racers awoke the next morning to learn that heavy snow had fallen through the night over Ohio, Indiana, and Illinois. The storm cut telegraph service outside of Chicago and stalled the Chicago-Denver Express on the Rock Island Line. The *Chicago Tribune* could find only one good thing to say about the thirteen inches of snow that covered the city: "It stops the mouths of the older people who are in the habit of saying that there are no such snow storms in this degenerate age as there were when they as boys had to fight their way through 10-foot drifts."[42]

The lack of horse-drawn wagons in Chicago hampered efforts to clear the streets. After the financial panic the previous fall, businesses had unloaded thousands of horses because they could not afford to feed them. Hundreds of unemployed men sought temporary work at

$1.50 a day shoveling snow. For the first time since 1895, the public schools had to shut down.[43]

In Indiana and Ohio, the roads were clear of everything but snow. Winds of thirty-five miles per hour kicked up drifts that even horses couldn't get through. Anyone with any sense stayed inside, curled up by the fire, waiting for it to blow over. The Paris racers refused to wait for better conditions. On the way out of Toledo, the Thomas fought through eighteen inches of snow, following a car driven by Jack Spurrier of Cleveland, the only man they could find who dared to be a pilot driver. The driving conditions in western Ohio and Indiana were "much worse than they will be in Alaska," the *Times* said confidently.[44]

While the wind howled in the telegraph wires, the men sat close to one another to keep warm. They held on tight to keep from getting tossed out of the cars. Hats, gloves, and scarves had to be replaced frequently because they kept blowing away. The Italians said the thermometer on the side of their car registered about ten degrees. They broke pieces of corned beef with a hammer and chisel and put pieces of meat on the radiator to warm them up. It wasn't snow that fell from the sky on Scarfoglio, but "fragments of glass, needles and pins which penetrate our insufficiently covered faces and wound us."[45]

In the days after the storm, farmers in northern Indiana discovered a new chore for their idle horses: pulling cars in the snow. As many as ten horses at a time hauled the Thomas through the drifts. The sixty-four miles from South Bend to Hobart cost the company eight hundred dollars. All told, the racers spent twenty-five hundred dollars on borrowed horsepower in Indiana, a windfall that disproved the theory advanced by some farmers that the automobile was of no practical value. Crossing Indiana, the Americans covered only ten to thirty miles a day.

Williams asked one of the farmers who hitched his team to the Thomas Flyer if he and his neighbors traveled much. The man replied that he had taken his family ten miles to Kendallville six months earlier and that as a boy his dad had taken him twenty miles to Goshen to see the circus. "Then he asked the *New York Times* reporter why the automobiles were traveling from New York in the deep snow to Paris, Indiana, when there are so many fine cities in the East," Williams wrote.[46]

Once, while waiting for a team of horses to pull the car out of a drift, Roberts amused himself by taking target practice with his pistol. He had learned to handle a gun in the army and he offered to bet one dollar that he could hit a post at two hundred feet with his .45-caliber revolver. Mason Hatch, a Thomas company employee from Buffalo traveling with a pilot car, took the bet and watched Roberts put two bullets through the post. Hatch had the reputation of being one of Buffalo's best-dressed men, but Williams said that the toil in Indiana made him look like he belonged on the list of "Who's Who Among the Park Row Derelicts."

Williams said none of the men could think of anything but the race. They collapsed in their hotels at night and had bellboys read them the latest news dispatches on the race. Mechanic George Schuster refused to carry any coins, Williams claimed, because he didn't want to add unnecessary weight to the car. In Indiana, Roberts lost twenty pounds and, Mason Hatch from the pilot car "nearly lost his mind," Williams said.

There was some talk of putting rotary plows on the cars. Back in Buffalo, E. R. Thomas said such a machine could be placed on a car,

Deep snow turned the drive through Indiana into a far more difficult chore than anyone had imagined. The cars made only ten to twenty miles a day in some areas. Here, the Italian Zust, second from right, follows a pilot car in the snow. (COURTESY OF HENRY AUSTIN CLARK JR.)

but there was no need for it. "The weather is the worst in years," he said. "Yet for one reason we are glad that it has come at this time. It gives the Thomas Flyer, which is defending America, an opportunity to demonstrate its ability to overcome the worst possible conditions found upon American roads."[47]

No one else found much to be glad about in the snowdrifts of Indiana. When Hansen joined Roberts and Williams at a cafe for what the *Times* reporter described as "boiler plate steak," the explorer tried to make small talk with the waitress, "We have had a long, cold journey today madam," Hansen said. The waitress snapped back: "Well, what did you come for?" Hansen said no more, but murmured that he'd wait until he got to Yakutsk where the women were more sympathetic before trying to reopen communications with the opposite sex.

Siberia was often on the captain's mind as he smoked his pipe and reflected on the difficulties of car travel. A broken gear shaft in Kendallville, Indiana, forced Hansen and Autran to go to Chicago by train to get a new one. Hansen told the Chicago papers that the contestants could look forward to easier traveling in Siberia.

"In Siberia there are level plains and it is so cold that there always is a crust on the snow, so it is possible to make good progress. But between here and New York it is far different. There are drifts that look as big as mountains and it is a case of dig most of the time. All of us have become experts with snow shovels and I guess we will become more so before we get across the American continent. I feel confident that once we get into Siberia we will make much faster progress and our troubles will be over, comparatively speaking."[48]

Hansen had more trouble than most men. He said he was jumped in one Indiana town by a Swede who, as Williams put it, "mistook the gallant captain for a Norwegian sewing machine agent who had visited the village 10 years ago and separated the Swede, among other farmers, from certain sums of money."

Hansen and the Swede fought and fell into a snowbank, where "Hansen got the upper hand by a back hitch he had acquired in the mines at Umtilikavitch, Siberia," Williams said.[49]

Despite Hansen's battles and the de Dion's breakdown, the Americans didn't build much of a lead because the Thomas Flyer flew across Indiana at about two miles an hour. On the worst day, the Thomas covered eight miles in twenty-two hours. Since there was no other traffic on the roads—horse-drawn or otherwise—it was impossible to get good information about conditions outside of each town.

With one exception there were no sign boards or anything to show how far it was to the next settlement. In northeastern Indiana, the men on the Thomas spotted a sign that said: "You are now 50 miles from Buggins' famous shoe emporium. Keep straight on." Two-and-a-half miles farther on they spotted a sign that said the emporium was now 47½ miles off. Signs followed at regular intervals and the American crew began to take an interest in Buggins. When they drove up to the emporium, Roberts stopped and called out to a prosperous man standing by the door: "Are you Buggins?" The man nodded and Roberts waved. "That's good enough old man. We just wanted to see you. That's all."[50]

The two cars at the rear, the German Protos and the French Motobloc, went through Indiana some days after the leaders, but the road conditions remained the same. The Frenchman Godard spoke of the Gobi Desert with longing and said that on the Peking-Paris run, at least he was able to make steady progress. "Here the snowdrifts are endless and we go on and on and get nowhere," Godard said.[51]

Godard, who was now asking people to address him as "Baron," claimed that he suffered at the hands of the "peasants" in Indiana. The trouble began when he stopped for the night in Wawaka, Indiana, a village of three hundred. As Godard slept in a hotel, someone broke into the barn where the car was parked and took a movie camera, film, guns, tools, and clothing.

Later, after getting slapped with a bill for sixty dollars from a man who had used two horses to tow the Motobloc, Godard refused to pay. He drove away, but the farmer notified a policeman in Michigan City, Indiana, who set off by railroad to apprehend the Baron. Godard was arrested and forced to pay the bill plus a twenty-five dollar fine.[52]

"These Indiana people are like a pack of wolves," he said through an interpreter. The charges in the hotels and restaurants amounted to highway robbery, in his view, and he claimed he paid five dollars for a one-dollar room, "If I must pay to sleep on the ground, I will buy one lot for five hundred dollars in the cemetery and I can sleep on the ground for always."

Godard wired the editor of the *New York Times*, complaining about the behavior of the Indiana farmers. He said they charged him three dollars a mile for horses, and worst of all, they piled snow on cleared roads to squeeze more money out of him. "We are disgusted. Want you to intervene to our protection," Godard told the newspaper. The *Times* said it would investigate.[53]

Godard's main problem was that no one on his car was conversant in English and that hand signals were a poor way to bargain for horses or hotels. All the racers paid what they claimed were exorbitant rates to the innkeepers across the country. "All men, including drivers, engineers, and reporters who ride in motor cars are assumed to be millionaires," said Skipper Williams.

The *Times* said that some of the accusations against the people of Indiana were unjustified: for instance, no one in his right mind would shovel snow onto a road. The newspaper said there was sufficient evidence, however, that all the racers were being overcharged by the merchants and farmers, "Rustic greed has manifested itself in a way to bring humiliation upon us all," the newspaper said.[54]

James Graves, the mayor of Kendallville, said the people of Indiana would try to help all the racers, "but you bet we Indiana boys want to see the American flag always to the front right away from Kendallville to Paris." The mayor waited up until 4:00 a.m. to see the first car arrive and said he could not remember any event that had created so much interest among the local people.[55] It was apparent to everyone by now that the race began at the wrong time of year. It would have made much more sense to start in late summer or fall, but what Collier's magazine labeled "journalistic impatience" required that the contest start in midwinter. From their cars, the men saw a countryside that seemed bleak and desolate under its winter cover. The storm had kept many people indoors, and abandoned sleighs littered the trails. Rural mail delivery had been halted. Williams said all he saw was snow, fences, and "occasional bunches of bare trees that look as if they resented growing in such a lonesome place. The few inhabitants who live outside the towns hibernate like bears during the winter and lose all touch with the ordinary world."[56]

The *Chicago Tribune* sent a photographer out with a horse-drawn sleigh to bring back pictures of the racers. The sleigh tipped over twice. The second time, the photographer lost a bottle of chemicals used for developing film. He returned to Chicago and wrote a story under the byline "FROZEN STIFF PHOTOGRAPHER."[57]

With the roads still drifted shut four days after the blizzard, the Indiana Railway Company offered the use of its tracks to the American car on the thirty miles between Goshen and South Bend. Roberts followed the general manager's special car on the tracks, bouncing along on the uncovered railroad ties. The tracks ran next to the Lake Shore Railroad, and many train passengers waved handkerchiefs at Roberts and his crew. The car covered the thirty miles in three hours; then it was back to bucking snowdrifts.

C. A. Coey, a Thomas dealer from Chicago, and the man credited with first suggesting the name Thomas Flyer, showed up at South Bend with two sleighs filled with snow shovelers. Coey, who at the time was building an airship that could carry six passengers, may have

The Thomas Flyer bounces along the tracks of the Indiana Railway Co. near South Bend. A bad winter storm had made the roads impassable. (COURTESY OF HENRY AUSTIN CLARK JR.)

wished for some aerial help. The car moved along at a pedestrian's pace and kept sliding off the road, which was peaked in the center.

It was a three-day trip from South Bend to Chicago. The Thomas Flyer arrived on Chicago's Michigan Avenue with its crew "weather beaten, chilled by the rain and exhausted by fifty-three hours constant labor," Williams said. About one hundred of Chicago's motorists showed up to welcome the leaders in the sleet and rain. Their cars bore the blue-and-yellow pennants of the Chicago Auto Club, and a band played "See the Conquering Hero Comes." The racers were worn out, but Schuster had enough energy to bolt out of the car and chase some teenagers for three blocks after they pelted him with hard snow- balls. The Thomas car reminded a *Chicago Tribune* reporter of the "deck of a ship in a hurricane with the crew in drenched oil skins clinging to the sides."[58]

There was talk that the Americans had violated the rules of good sportsmanship and the race by riding on the train tracks and using horses on the snow-dogged roads. News that the Italians, French, and Germans were hiring extra horsepower tempered the debate somewhat, but hard feelings remained among the foreigners. The farmers across Indiana provided their horses to all the racers for a price, regardless of nationality. The Indiana Railway Company, however, refused to allow the foreign motorists on the thirty-mile section of track over which the Thomas had been escorted. Company officials said later that they were not trying to slow down the Europeans, but that no one with the authority to approve the request was available when the motorists asked for permission. The European cars drove on the tracks anyway. When it heard about this, the company issued orders to the trolley operators to watch for the foreign cars and avoid running them down.[59]

About twenty minutes before Roberts pulled into the Chicago Automobile Club, the red Studebaker carrying the military message for Hearst's *New York American* reached Chicago. It had taken the Studebaker eight days to reach Chicago, as opposed to the thirteen days, six hours, and ten minutes consumed by the Thomas, which did not have relief drivers. "The farmers helped us dig through snowdrifts and brought their horses out to assist us through drifted roads where ordinarily a farmer would not ask his horses to go," said one of the men on the Studebaker. He said if farmers were treated like gentlemen, they would not be hostile to people in cars.

Scarfoglio and St. Chaffray arrived in Chicago a day after the Thomas. Since the men on all the cars planned to stay in Chicago for

Arriving in Chicago, the crew of the French de Dion wore heavy winter coats that looked like sleeping bags. Standing from left are: Georges Bourcier de St. Chaffray and Captain Hans Hendrik Hansen. Behind the wheel is M. Autran, a driver from the de Dion factory. The other man is unidentified. (COURTESY OF HENRY AUSTIN CLARK JR.)

a few days, it didn't really matter who arrived first, second, or third, but the relative position of the cars became a matter of national pride. Sirtori, the driver of Scarfoglio's car, said he and St. Chaffray had agreed that the Italians would enter Chicago in front of the de Dion. The Italians had waited more than five hours for the French earlier that day. St. Chaffray apparently decided that the honor of the French auto industry was threatened, however, and he tried to reach the auto club before the Zust.

The two drivers fought for the lead and nearly collided a few times in a mad rush that endangered the lives of pedestrians. Cheering crowds looked on as the cars cut through the dusk, hitting speeds on Michigan Avenue that were probably somewhat under the sixty miles per hour estimated by the *Chicago Tribune*. St. Chaffray darted into the lead for half a block, but Sirtori regained it on State Street. "The cars passed so close that the wheels grated," a witness said. "The Italian made a big racket with his horn and St. Chaffray on his brakes. This gave Sirtori the lead into the club."[60] Bystanders showered the cars with flowers and carried the racers on their shoulders into the auto club. Sirtori rejoiced in his narrow victory over St. Chaffray, but the Commissionaire General refused to concede, saying the cars had arrived at exactly the same moment.

As Koeppen in the Protos and Godard in the Motobloc continued to fight their way through Indiana, St. Chaffray and the others rested and toured the town that Carl Sandburg would soon christen the City of the Big Shoulders. St. Chaffray stopped by the Chicago stockyards, which had gained notoriety two years earlier with the publication of Upton Sinclair's *The Jungle*, and toured the lakefront.

"The Windy City, located on the border of the lake, has realized the astonishing feat of becoming perhaps the greatest port in the world," St. Chaffray said.[61] Even Scarfoglio liked Chicago, the greatest meat-packing and grain-shipping center in the country. "It is not ashamed to be dressed in its working clothes and to spread out its toil-blackened hands," he said. "And Chicago does not give one the sense of repulsion which one experiences at Washington or at Albany, and to a certain extent, all over America. Chicago lives by smoked pig, boasts of it and shows it in its dress like a good laborer."[62]

In this working-class city, a major health concern at the time was the milk supply. The city health commissioner had just announced a plan to organize distribution of the milk produced by the 1,387 cows kept within the city limits. In the days when blocks of ice were the only means of refrigeration, the source of supply had to be close at hand. "While the commissioner does not want to turn the city into a large dairy farm, he is convinced it is entirely practical to maintain enough cows inside the city limits to furnish, if not the entire amount of milk used in it, at least such a large proportion as may feed the babies," the *Chicago Tribune* reported.

The *Tribune* said the commissioner knew of the prejudice felt by the average Chicago resident against the cow. For thirty-seven years, Chicagoans had placed the cow on the list of "undesirable citizens" because of the legend of Mrs. O'Leary's cow, the newspaper said. The cow had allegedly kicked over a kerosene lamp, starting the Great Chicago Fire of 1871. "The commissioner, however, thinks time has largely softened that prejudice, and, besides, there are not nearly as many kerosene lamps as there were in those days," the paper said.[63]

Notwithstanding the commissioner's fondness for milk, the drink of choice for the racers waiting to head west had more kick to it than Mrs. O'Leary's cow. At least one pilot car was to be loaded up in Chicago with tobacco and liquor to fortify the men as they passed through dry portions of the West. Chicago had recently been identified as the worst city in the country by the national chairman of the Prohibition Party. To no one's surprise, the wine flowed freely at a banquet for the racers on the night of February 27. When Captain Hansen rose to respond to a toast, however, he had more than the beverage selection on his mind: "Besides telling you how much I appreciate your hospitality, I have also something serious to say. The truth is bitter to tell and to hear, but I must speak it. I and Mr. St. Chaffray did not agree about the race and the result is I leave the car. Is that not true, Mr. St. Chaffray?"

The Commissionaire General nodded and Hansen went on. "But the race is not finished. It is a long way to Paris and you will hear from me yet before the end of the race."[64] In fact, people were hearing from Hansen before the end of the night. He pulled a yard-long silk American flag out of his pocket and said he would wave it in the streets of Paris or die in the attempt. Earlier, Hansen had sent a wire to the Marquis de Dion telling him he was quitting the French car because St. Chaffray refused to do a fair share of the snow shoveling. The explorer packed up his traps, sleeping bag, compasses, and sextant before boarding a train for a quick trip to Buffalo. He went to meet E. R. Thomas to speak about joining the Arnerican crew. Within a few days he was back in the race, serving as navigator on the Thomas Flyer for one hundred dollars a month.[65]

Before the race began, St. Chaffray had gone on at length about Hansen's abilities and achievements. The story changed as soon as the two parted company. "He is an imposter, a poser as an arctic explorer, when, in fact, he was a wine peddler in Paris before he started on this trip. As soon as we left Buffalo he commenced to act up. He was fond of the girls and was always asking for money. When we looked into the lunch basket for our noonday meal, it was always empty and Hansen always full. Whenever we struck a hard place of road he took the train to the next station," St. Chaffray told a reporter.[66]

The truth about Hansen was somewhere between St. Chaffray's portrait of a compulsive liar and Hansen's self-portrait of a glorious explorer who had conquered the globe. The evidence suggests he was a self-reliant adventurer who could stretch the truth when he had to and do whatever was necessary to survive. Since the Thomas company thought enough of the captain to put him on the payroll, American newspapers treated him with respect and never pestered him with too many questions about his background.

Besides, Hansen was now on the American side. He gave a deposition to a Chicago notary in which he claimed that a Frenchman in Chicago sent out by the automobile club had tried to lead the Thomas Flyer astray. Hansen also said the de Dion and Zust cars had been towed at times with their engines shut down and that St. Chaffray had tried to get the other cars to agree to stay behind his car at all times.[67] St. Chaffray said Hansen was lying. The continued public fighting did nothing to improve the image of the race among critics who called it an idiotic scheme. *Motor*, a prominent English magazine, was headlining its reports "The New York–Paris Farce."[68] The English journal *Autocar* said that instead of creating sympathy for the drivers, the reports of tough going in Indiana reinforced the notion that the race was "a harebrained venture." The magazine said the contestants were getting a good taste of what Alaska would be like, but if they kept going at their present rate, they would probably never see it.[69]

"I sincerely trust that no one in Europe will take this run seriously, in spite of the screaming of the American press," one critic wrote to an English friend. *Autocar* stated that "all American motorists now regard the New York to Paris race as a joke." This prompted a denial from a Buffalo man who wrote to the magazine to say the contest was the "most remarkable race in the history of the world."[70]

Since the start there had been speculation that the motorists would eventually ship their cars to Seattle by rail. By now, all of the Europeans who had struggled through one thousand miles of snow to Chicago hoped that would be the case. The Commissionaire General did not disappoint them. He said the cars could go by train, which would allow them to catch the steamer *Portland* in time for its March 10

THE NEW YORK AND PARIS AUTO RACE—TIRE TROUBLE IN SIBERIA

The race was lampooned by newspaper and magazine cartoonists. This is how an artist for *Life* pictured one scene from Siberia.

MAKING GOOD PROGRESS.—All American motorists now regard the New York-Paris Race as a joke. Our illustration is a reproduction of the recipe of the *Chicago Record Herald* for making good progress.

The English magazine *Autocar* said, "All American motorists now regard the New York–Paris Race as a joke." It reprinted this cartoon from the *Chicago Record-Herald* poking fun at the idea of crossing America by car, aboard a train. (*AUTOCAR*)

departure to Alaska.[71] R. W. Vollmoeller, manufacturer of the Italian Zust, thought it was a splendid idea: "The original plan was to reach Chicago in five days, but over two weeks have been consumed on this part of the journey. What shall we expect next? From Chicago to San Francisco we have yet 2,000 miles to travel and more storms are coming. Shall we not consume six more weeks to get to San Francisco?"[72]

In Buffalo, the home of the Thomas Flyer, critics heaped ridicule on St. Chaffray and the plan to use the railroad. A newsman for the *Buffalo Evening News* penned a poem titled "Motoring a la Chaffray."[73]

"Arouse, brave comrade, Autran:
There's work to do, allons!
Make haste with boards and hammer
To crate the De Dion,
A bas! the frightful highways
That wrought us much dismay!
We tour henceforth by freight car,"
Quoth Bourcier Saint Chaffray.

Before us rise high mountains
Our onward way to bar,
Those Rockies and Sierras
Reject our touring car.
But courage, my brave Autran!
Behold, a better way!
'We'll scale them on a flat car,'
Says Bourcier Saint Chaffray.

"Motoring a la Chaffray" did not mesh with the publicity goals of the E. R. Thomas Motor Company, which wanted to show that its product could conquer the continent. Roberts said the Thomas would continue by road to San Francisco no matter how long it took. Meanwhile, the French backers of the race overruled St. Chaffray. *Le Matin* warned that any driver who tried to ship his car to Seattle would be disqualified.[74]

From then on St. Chaffray said he was not in a position to give advice and he softened his pronouncements on the race rules, but the fighting did not end. Before leaving Chicago, St. Chaffray and the crew of the Zust filed a protest with the *New York Times* and *Le Matin* against the Thomas Flyer. St. Chaffray and Scarfoglio alleged that the Thomas company had rebuilt the Thomas Flyer in Buffalo, that horses towed the car while the engine was shut off, and that the car had traveled on railroad tracks and trolley lines. The Europeans complained that they could no "longer consider the Thomas car on the same footing as the other contestants."

E. R. Thomas said the protesters were trying to excuse their poor showing by making up lies about the American car. "From the time the Thomas car began to take a definite lead, the foreigners started their complaints about one thing or another. I am not surprised at this latest outburst. They are fighting among themselves, while our people are going ahead steadily and surely. The whole truth of the matter seems to be that the foreigners are bad losers."[75]

Thomas said the company made minor repairs at the factory, such as adding new springs and replacing two small gas tanks with one large one. Roberts said the Europeans had used horses as much as he had and that while an electric car preceded the Thomas Flyer on the trolley tracks, the racer ran on its own power. The American driver said he had never heard of a race in which a protest was not filed against the winner.[76]

That may have been true. But with about twenty thousand miles to go, it was too early to claim the title.

FOUR

OF MUD AND MOTORISTS

IN 1839, THE Territory of Iowa hired a man to plow a nearly one-hundred-mile-long furrow in a straight line from Iowa City to Dubuque. With a big plow drawn by five oxen, Lyman Dillon carved a scar in the solid sod. Settlers no longer lost the trail, and the wheels of their white-topped wagons helped beat down a road alongside the furrow.[1]

Road-building efforts in the Hawkeye state had not advanced much by 1908, and Iowa was to shake its reputation as the muddiest state in the union. Iowa boasted rich soil, abundant crops, and six mainline railroads that crossed the state, connecting Chicago and Omaha. But because of a controversial taxing system that put a greater burden on those who lived adjacent to roads, Iowa voters routinely rejected funds to build or improve highways. As a result, on a rainy day, Iowa loomed as a three-hundred-mile mudhole for those who dared to cross it by car.

As late as the 1920s, the guidebook for the transcontinental Lincoln Highway advised motorists that when it rained in Iowa or Nebraska, the driver should stop and wait if "he wishes to save his car, his time, his tires and his temper."[2]

In Chicago, Skipper Williams spoke to a man called Pawnee Bob who said he had carried the mail for the Pony Express in the 1860s.

"Say boys, the snow is at least clean, but the muddy roads of Iowa are too fierce for words," Pawnee said. "If you jump out of the car to shove you will have to wait for a team of farm horses to pull you out."[3]

Paying heed to Pawnee and other experienced westerners, the crew of Thomas Flyer resumed the race on February 28 with a two-piece portable bridge strapped to the sides of the car. The two-hundred-pound bridge was to be used to cross ditches of three to five feet, allowing the car to go cross-country when required. The wooden bridge didn't ride smoothly on the car, however. As the car jolted over the muddy ruts, the bridge swung back and forth, first threatening to knock Schuster off the front of the car and then Williams off the rear. The portable bridge proved to be of little use and it was discarded.

Williams had complained several times of the rough ride in the back of the car. He was bounced about unmercifully and often nearly tossed out. He had little time or energy to write after spending a full day perched above the gas tank, holding on for his life. These daily annoyances finally became too much for him, so after an exchange of messages with his home office, Williams left the car and returned to New York. A photographer and a second correspondent would join the car later, but the newspaper decided it could rely on the daily cables from Schuster or Roberts, the work of local correspondents, and the Associated Press until the Thomas reached the West Coast.

In the days ahead, the news that came across the telegraph wires covered familiar ground: the Americans kept the lead, but found hard traveling all the way. Mechanical problems and language difficulties handicapped the Europeans. Bad roads handicapped everyone.

Few motorists had driven from Chicago to California then, but the race route covered one of the most heavily traveled paths in American history. Western settlers, prospectors who looked for gold in California, and the builders of the first transcontinental railroad had passed this way before. The Paris racers headed due west from Chicago, bound for Iowa, Nebraska, Wyoming, Utah, Nevada, and California. Within a few years, much of the trail they traveled would become part of the first transcontinental road in America—the Lincoln Highway.

The Lincoln Highway was an attempt by businessmen, merchants, and the automobile industry to create a coast-to-coast road in honor of Abraham Lincoln. The idea came from Carl Fisher, founder of the Indianapolis Speedway. Fisher and Henry Joy of Packard, president of the Lincoln Highway Association, lobbied drivers, civic groups, businesses, and governments to help build or finance road work. Individuals who sent in five dollars received a certificate, membership card, and radiator emblem. Certificate number 1 went to Woodrow Wilson.

The Lincoln Highway started as a red line on a map. Critics complained that much of it remained just that. West of the Mississippi, in particular, motorists confronted a rough and muddy dirt trail that had not improved much since Lyman Dillon and his oxen plowed through Iowa. With mixed success, the Lincoln Highway Association worked to raise the nation out of the mud. "The highways of America are built chiefly of politics," Carl Fisher once wrote, "whereas the proper material is crushed rock or concrete."[4]

Not until the 1920s, when the federal government took over the task of building major roads, did the Lincoln Highway emerge as the major east-west thoroughfare envisioned by its founders. By that time, however, at least three dozen long-distance automobile trails appeared on the roadmaps of America. Promoters blessed their routes with names as grand as any carried by the mighty railroads. Thousands of towns fought for a place on the map, longing for the extra commerce and importance that automobile traffic would bring. Many of these competing roads were still "built chiefly of politics" and they looked far better on the map than they did from behind the wheel. Still, the Dixie Highway, the Pikes Peak Ocean to Ocean Highway, the Atlantic-Pacific Highway, the Arrowhead Trail, the Lone Star Route, and the Yellowstone Trail beckoned travelers with names that spoke of faraway places and the romance of the open road.

In many spots in the West, numerous competing roads ran along the same trail. Promoters marked their roads with bright bands painted on barns, trees, fence posts, and telephone poles. The telephone poles looked like totem poles, covered with multicolored highway symbols. The Lincoln Highway Association complained once that a long stretch of road carried the brands of fifteen different highways.[5]

The final solution to the road wars pleased neither the Lincoln Highway Association nor the backers of any of the other named roads. In 1925, the federal government adopted a system that did away with names and substituted numbers. What this plan lacked in romance, it gained in simplicity. The same basic framework exists today: east-west roads carry even numbers, while north-south roads bear odd numbers.

The mass confusion created by road signs in the 1920s was the opposite of the problem faced by the men trying to find their way to Paris in 1908. Skipper Williams said the men never knew their exact location. "There are no road signs in the state of Iowa except the few at various points which point out to the wayfarer that he can save money by purchasing his socks or tea at Podger's Universal Store. A hand points to the direction in which the economical traveler should go, but it does not state whether Podger's Store is located in Cedar

Rapids or Sacramento. The farmers along the route were all kind and meant well, but they knew less of directions or distances than the Hoosiers of Indiana."[6]

"The route books given the contestants give the names of the towns and distances apart, but do not describe the roads to be followed, as no road route from Chicago to San Francisco has ever been compiled," Williams said.

From Chicago to Omaha the Paris racers followed a course that usually ran parallel to the tracks of the Chicago and Northwestern Railway. The railroad instructed all of its operators to help the cars in any way possible and to inform the towns ahead of the racers' progress.

Scarfoglio's Zust and St. Chaffray's de Dion departed Chicago one day behind the Americans. On the de Dion, Hansen's place had been taken by Emmanuel Lascaris of the Chicago Automobile Club. Lascaris was a French attorney who had practiced in Paris and New York.[7] Girls dressed in white stood at the windows of the fifteen-story auto club and waved handkerchiefs. A woman ran up and threw flowers at St. Chaffray. "I would rather have the good wishes of one fair lady than all the wine in France," said the Commissionaire General.

Slowed by mechanical problems, snow, and strife, the Protos and the Motobloc trailed the chivalrous St. Chaffray by five days. The Chicago Automobile Club toasted Koeppen and Godard at a banquet March 4.[8] Godard filed a claim with Chicago detectives for the nine hundred dollars in goods stolen from him in Indiana. The Baron's finances took a slight turn for the better when he went shopping in Chicago. A shoe dealer refused to take payment for some arctic boots. Instead, he asked the Baron to send them back to Chicago after he

completed the race. The merchant planned to display the famous footwear in his store window.[9]

The *Chicago Tribune* poked fun at Baron Godard by remarking that the man who expected to pick his way across glaciers in Alaska and across the steppes of Siberia had gotten lost within the city limits of Chicago while trying to find the auto club. Godard wandered about on the south side until another motorist pointed the way. The headline said: "WORLD RACERS LOST IN CITY" and "Chicago Baffles Frenchmen, Who Conquer 'Polar Indiana.'"[10]

The Germans in the Protos had nearly as many troubles as Godard, but of a different sort. The two men who had accompanied Koeppen from Germany, Hans Knape and Ernest Maas, complained that Koeppen had failed to give them enough credit in his newspaper dispatches. As in the other cars, there were strong personalities at work. The two men delivered an ultimatum: they would quit if Koeppen didn't. The lieutenant refused to drop out of the race, and he wished Knape and Maas a pleasant trip back to Germany.[11] Koeppen, who could speak a smattering of English, said the race would put him ten thousand dollars in debt, but he would go on no matter what the cost. He hired O. W. Schneider, a German immigrant who had served in the kaiser's army, to drive the car.

The Protos needed repairs in Chicago, and Koeppen searched for some spare parts. A joint in the steering system had broken and he went into a pawn shop looking for a replacement. "I have broke my knuckle. Can you not sell me one?" he asked. The man behind the counter produced a set of four-ounce boxing gloves. Koeppen shook his head and said he needed some steel. The man dug through his shop and handed over a pair of brass knuckles. At that, Koeppen returned to the Chicago Automobile Club and found a mechanic.[12]

The men on the Thomas Flyer could usually scrounge parts from Thomas dealers or order replacement parts from Buffalo. The foreigners had to improvise or wait until spare parts could be shipped from wherever they had been stored. Koeppen had sent his load of spare parts to Seattle and had to wait on several occasions while parts returned by rail.

As the motorists chugged through Illinois and Iowa, they passed grain fields, white farmhouses, red barns, and cattle. In small towns along the railroad tracks, grain elevators and church spires etched a small notch in the open skies. Outside of the towns, entire families came to wave and look at the cars when the motorists came within hailing distance of a farmhouse. Squealing pigs wandered in the mud.[13]

Upon crossing the Mississippi, St. Chaffray said it didn't appear to be a river at all. "The Mississippi is a frozen field, and workmen saw the precious pieces, which Chicagoans may drink in their glasses. The ice is clear and fine, but how black and chilly is the mud we then have to face."

A couple of days later, St. Chaffray pulled into Cedar Rapids, Iowa, and said his first impression was that everyone there must have been a millionaire because the houses were so nice. He was astonished to learn that people could get a 5-percent mortgage to build a new home in a housing development. "You pay year-by-year the $3,000 to $5,000 with a smaller rent than you would pay for a very common flat in Paris, and you remain landlord of the well-built house." He explained to his countrymen that in the United States, developers could buy large tracts of land and create new neighborhoods.[14]

The Commissionaire General had time to analyze the housing market because his car was broken down again, this time with a damaged steering gear that took several days to repair. He also had time

to inspect the Quaker Oats factory. He couldn't get over the idea that Americans had invented a way to make good food out of oats, which he had considered fit only for horses. The taste of oatmeal with sugar and milk and the sight of thousands of acres of Iowa grain fields convinced him that "human art has no limit when it can convert such a thing as oats into an eatable meal for the best dining rooms."[15] He marveled at the creation of puffed rice and provided a detailed description of the guns from which the rice was fired. "After a few moments the guns were opened and the rice went out at top speed in a big room, with a big noise, having changed its nature."

Forced to provide something in his dispatches other than accounts of his lack of progress, the Commissionaire General also dipped into local politics. He said that the best candidate in the Cedar Rapids mayor's race did not despoil the community with posters that made the town look "like a low-class fair," but instead passed out cards with his picture on them.[16]

When the Commissionaire General began to roll once more, the mud continued to make his life miserable. St. Chaffray announced he had found Dante's Inferno in Iowa. "The crew of the De Dion car have spent a second night in the fields without sleep, wet and cold in damp mud. The hell of Dante is situated between Logan and Crescent, Iowa. It is not a river which conducts to the hell, but an ascent, narrow in every part, round like an egg, slippery as a soaped pig."[17]

The cars traveled slower than ten miles per hour across most of Iowa, encountering long stretches of the wet, sticky mud known as gumbo that ranged from two inches to two feet deep. "No French dog would consent to put his feet on such paths," St. Chaffray said of Iowa's roads. "He would prefer to never go outside."[18]

A few days later Scarfoglio found himself stopped by heavy rain in Denison, Iowa. He thought it strange that farmers in the hotel with mud on their boots would simply puff their pipes in resignation as they watched the rain flood the land. To him, it was evidence of a character flaw.

"The American, as a rule, does not love the land; he does not care for the wealth which is acquired by slow, regular labor. He is a man of adventure, a man of the sudden, of the unexpected. He is a gold-seeker today as he was a hundred years ago and his joy is in the mine discovered by chance, conquered in a day, worked out in a month, exhausted in a year. Gold, coal, petroleum, it does not matter what, so long as it is a fortune which bursts from the rock at the lucky blow of a hammer," he said.[19]

Mud and mechanical problems slowed all the racers somewhat, but the Americans still managed to extend their lead because they had fewer breakdowns. Schuster, the man chiefly responsible for keeping the Thomas Flyer running, was pleased with the performance. "We have had two blowouts and one tire puncture so far and no other trouble to speak of," he said in Omaha.

Roberts grew tired of answering questions about the Bering Strait and the protest from the Italians and St. Chaffray. Whenever someone said "protest," he replied: "Oh you mean the Protos car; they are way behind."

As the Thomas reached Omaha, a crowd estimated at eighteen thousand swarmed into the streets. "Outside of a lynching, this is the biggest spontaneous showing ever made in the city," the Omaha World-Herald reported.[20] Every whistle in the town sounded, fire bells rang, cannons fired, and a huge siren wailed for an hour. Town officials declared a holiday on the west bank of the Missouri River, and police

cleared a path to the garage of H. E. Fredrickson, the Thomas dealer in Omaha.

When Scarfoglio reached the city, he said it reminded him of a spacious Italian town, except for the ugly buildings. "It appears to have been built for the consolation of men who reach the last stage of their journey before plunging into the unknown," he said.[21] The city had been the construction headquarters for the Union Pacific, the first transcontinental railroad, so in that sense the Italian was right. More than one observer said that for many years people in Omaha never lost their sense of surprise that the town had become a city.

The Thomas picked up a new passenger in Omaha. Captain Hansen threw his bags in with Roberts, Schuster, and Miller. Charlie Duprez, a photographer from New York assigned to take pictures for the *Times* and the Thomas company, would ride in the pilot car.

Hansen pulled out his wallet and produced a tiny silk American flag, a gift from a woman in New York. "Our car will win and I will present this little piece of silk to the American consul in Paris before the nearest car is within one hundred miles of us," the captain told reporters.[22] He now pledged his allegiance to the American flag, but the captain's rhetoric had stayed the same. He spoke of Siberia and boasted of his fearlessness. "The most pleasant way to die I know of is to freeze to death."[23]

After being out of the limelight for a few days, Hansen wasted no time climbing back on center stage. Addressing a banquet crowd that night at the Rome Hotel, he told of his sour experiences with St. Chaffray and what it would take to cross Siberia. He said he could travel blindfolded through the arctic if necessary and that he knew how to compensate for the way a car would distort compass readings. Following the banquet, Hansen and Roberts strapped on

Captain Hansen talks of his adventures with Montague Roberts, driver of the American car, in the Rome Hotel in Omaha, Nebraska. The captain had just signed on with the Americans after his falling out with St. Chaffray. (COURTESY OF HENRY AUSTIN CLARK JR.)

roller skates and raced around an auditorium. Hansen may have won honors for oratory, but Roberts whipped him at roller skating.[24]

That the swashbuckling Hansen had chosen to resurrect himself in Omaha was appropriate considering that Col. William F. Cody, a master showman, had helped organize the reception for the racers in the city. A one-time Pony Express rider, guide, scout, and the hero of dime novels, Buffalo Bill bought drinks in Omaha and invited the racers to visit his ranch in western Nebraska. He was in his sixties now and near the end of a career that had made him one of the most famous men in America. Cody was a legend on horseback, but he knew the automobile's status as a curiosity in the West. Three years earlier he

The American crew took time out to visit Buffalo Bill's house outside of North Platte. Buffalo Bill was across the state in Omaha, where he served on a welcoming committee for the racers. (COURTESY OF HENRY AUSTIN CLARK JR.)

had been photographed behind the wheel of a Ford Model K on the steps of the state capitol in Denver.

Buffalo Bill did not travel to North Platte to play host for Roberts and the others, because he was estranged from his wife. The men on the Thomas Flyer spent little time sightseeing on their way across America, but because of the Cody name, they made an exception in North Platte. Buffalo Bill's grandson, twelve-year-old Cody Boal, rode his pony down Dewey Street in front of the car. After lunch, Roberts was photographed on the boy's pony. Later, the men toured Scout's Rest, the family ranch outside of town, where Buffalo Bill had entertained characters such as Kit Carson and Death Valley Scottie.

Years later, North Platte erected an arch across the pavement at the west edge of town that featured a larger-than-life portrait of Buffalo Bill and the words "Buffalo Bill's Home Town. Drive Safely."[25]

The route across Nebraska was familiar ground to Buffalo Bill, a route still known to some as the Mormon Trail. A half-century earlier, the followers of Joseph Smith had been driven out of Nauvoo, Illinois. From 1846 to 1869, sixty thousand Mormons trekked to Utah. Brigham Young led the faithful up the Platte River and across the mountains to the promised land.

Across most of Nebraska the Mormons traveled along the north bank of the Platte and its broad, flat floodplain. Young selected a route on the north side of the Platte to keep away from potential enemies on the south side along the Oregon Trail. It was often said the river was "too thick to drink and too thin to plow," but the land on each side made one of the world's great natural thoroughfares.

Fredrickson, the Thomas dealer in Omaha who drove a pilot car to Cheyenne, Wyoming, said the path through the prairie was in many ways an ideal road. "There is just enough sand in the soil to prevent mud and there is practically no grade for five hundred miles. The automobile that cannot make time over the Mormon Trail has no business in a race of any kind."[26]

He said under good conditions the trip from Omaha to Cheyenne would take about three days. Roberts promised to go fast enough to "set the prairie on fire," but the Thomas crossed Nebraska in the rain, which made the trail along the Platte River somewhat muddy. At least it was better than the Iowa gumbo. "We ran across the open prairie on the grass, following the railroad," Roberts said. "I had some good shooting on the way. Wild duck rose from the Platte thick as clouds and we got coyotes and prairie dogs often."[27]

They drove for long stretches at fifteen miles per hour without seeing any people. On one day they passed only ten houses in 105 miles. To relieve the boredom, Roberts raced a cowboy for a little while, but the horseman gave up after two miles when his horse tired. The car passed spindly windmills that creaked in the wind, pumping water to the isolated people on the prairie. When the Thomas Flyer entered a town, Fredrickson, driver of the pilot car, paid close attention to the reaction among farmers and ranchers. The Omaha auto dealer said the contest had done more to create public interest in cars than all the auto shows ever staged in the Midwest.

As the Thomas roared across Nebraska, its passage created a contest of a different sort on the streets of Denver. The cars never came within one hundred miles of Denver, but the race to Paris was big news in the region's major city. Denver's major publishers disliked each other so much that they turned any big news event, such as the race to Paris, into a game of one-upmanship. These publishers could also fight with more than words.

About two months before the Paris racers reached the Rockies, *Rocky Mountain News* publisher Thomas Patterson was walking to work when he heard someone say, "Good morning." A moment later, Patterson was greeted with a fist in the side of the head. The assailant was Fred Bonfils, one of the publishers of the *Denver Post*. Articles in Patterson's newspapers that alleged the *Post* worked to shelter vice and blackmail merchants had infuriated Bonfils. A judge later fined Bonfils fifty dollars for this bit of journalistic excess.[28]

Bonfils's *Post* was a loud and raucous journal building a reputation as the "most lunatic newspaper in America," as John Gunther once put it. The *Post* ran rabbit-hunting contests, dog shows, beauty shows, and horse races. It hired Houdini to escape from a straitjacket while

he was suspended upside down from the *Post*'s balcony. On another occasion, the newspaper had a vaudeville performer put a fork in his mouth and catch a turnip that was thrown from the twelfth floor of the building across the street. By promoting such adventures in big type and red ink, the *Post* carried sensationalism to an extreme.[29]

As on many other subjects, each newspaper boasted that its coverage of the race was superior to that offered by the competition. The *News* sent a Locomobile pilot car to lead the Thomas from western Nebraska to Cheyenne, Wyoming. "With its usual enterprise, the *Rocky Mountain News* has arranged to give its readers the first authentic reports and photographs of the New York-to-Paris automobile racers while they are in this part of the country," the *News* reported.[30]

The men on the Locomobile planned to open all the ranch gates along the road, order all the meals for the Thomas crew, and clear all bridges and narrow areas of farm wagons. The newspaper paid more attention to the performance of its pilot car than to the race. A typical headline said, "Thomas Car Carries American Flag Far Ahead of Foreigners, Guided by News Locomobile."[31]

The *Post*, meanwhile, said it had arranged to assign one of its men to what it said was the official *Denver Post* pilot car. The *Post* said the *News* car was a joke and that it had fallen far off the pace. The *News* responded that its car had always kept the lead and that the *Post* story was a fabrication.

In addition to the competing pilot cars, the two papers had competing interviews with the driver of the Thomas Flyer. Roberts supposedly told the *Post* that the *News* car was more of a hindrance than a help and that the stories in the *News* were fake. He supposedly told the *News* that the assistance of its car "will be one of the brightest memories of the whole trip."[32]

The newspapers agreed on one point: It took 3½ days for the Thomas Flyer to reach Cheyenne from Omaha. Now that the race had shifted west, Roberts started acting the way an easterner figured a westerner would behave. Outside of Cheyenne, a train slowed to the same speed as the Thomas Flyer and the engineer blew his whistle. Roberts drew his revolver, waved it in the air, and fired a couple of shots.

The stunt drew cheers from those in the long line of cars who gathered to escort the Thomas into Cheyenne. Cowboys shouted and twirled their lariats as they rode into and out of the procession. H. H. Buckwalter of Denver filmed the arrival. When the people of Cheyenne watched themselves on the silver screen two weeks later, the movie shared top billing at a vaudeville theater with a presentation by "the Devan Brothers and their acrobatic dog." Buckwalter's camera captured a "sea of heads swept away by a storm of waving hats," the *Cheyenne Daily Leader* reported. The newspaper added that it was a shame the camera could not capture the cheers. About eight thousand people, or half of the town, showed up to see the mud-covered men and car.[33]

The film opened with Charlie Irwin driving a team of galloping horses through the center of town, followed by cowboys and thirty-five cars, many of them from Denver. The Thomas Flyer rolled through the dust, with Captain Hansen snapping pictures for posterity. After the car pulled up to the garage, the men waded through the crowd for a half-hour shaking hands. At a banquet that night, Cheyenne demonstrated its position as the "most wide-awake city in the West," the Cheyenne newspaper said. The street outside the Cheyenne Industrial Club was lit by long strings of electric lights and torches of different colors. The seventy-five guests for the eight-course dinner wore everything from flannel shirts to business suits for the Sunday night affair.

The Cheyenne newspaper, which identified Hansen as the "discoverer of the magnetic pole and the Northwest Passage," said the Norwegian advised the banquet guests that any town with the enthusiasm of Cheyenne should change its name to "Shine-on."

Judge J. M. Carey addressed the gathering and said the automobile was bringing the earth closer to a single worldwide language by knocking down transportation barriers and drawing nations closer together. "You are traveling the same course blazed by the pioneer who crossed the plains behind a team of oxen," said Carey, a former United States Senator and future governor of the state. "You will receive a great welcome because you are in a great competition, because you travel in an American car, because it is guided by an American and because it carries the emblem 'Old Glory.' Tonight, the whole world is thinking of this automobile."[34]

W. D. Deming, editor of the *Wyoming Tribune*, gave the Thomas crew a letter for the president of France and delivered an address titled "Carry the Message." He said the world was watching Cheyenne that night. "It will be read around a million firesides that you have climbed from sea level to an altitude of six thousand feet; that you have left the rain and the fog of New York, the mud of Iowa and the snow of Nebraska and are today basking in the perennial sunshine of the capital of Wyoming," Deming said.

"And when you return to the effete but highly interesting East, will you carry the message that Cheyenne is no longer one thousand miles from nowhere, and beyond the frontier, but is merely a few days journey by automobile from New York; that you picked blackberries and bananas along the way; that you have had three square meals a day in modern hotels and that every obstacle encountered was soon

forgotten as you gazed into the wells of blue and caught smiles that radiate from the ruby lips of the wily western girls," he said.[35]

Deming wound up his address by warning the men how hard it would be to cross the Rocky Mountains. It reminded him of the story of the woman who got on a streetcar with twelve children. The conductor asked, "Madam, are all these your children or is it a picnic?" The woman replied, "They are all mine and I tell you it is no picnic."

When the other racers pulled through Cheyenne, the cowtown provided the same sort of noisy celebration with horses, gunfire, and flags. It was fitting somehow, in a railroad town that forty years earlier had been as wild as any of the movable camps known as Hell-on-Wheels. The days of frontier justice weren't long gone from Cheyenne. Five years before the race, gunman Tom Horn had been hanged at the courthouse.

The Cheyenne Industrial Club sponsored banquets for every race crew. The menus featured dishes from the guests' homes, and the decor was changed to highlight the national colors of the visitors. Judge J. M. Carey, ever in demand as a public speaker, lectured Scarfoglio and his companions on the triumphs of Rome, the classic poets, and the Italian masters of art, literature, and music. A week later he addressed St. Chaffray on the debt owed by the United States to France. The following day he told Koeppen that German immigrants to the United States blended into American culture more easily than other new arrivals. "Why the Germans hold office almost as soon after their arrival as the Irish," he said.[36]

The wild receptions bestowed by Cheyenne's residents on the racers, the cowboy greetings, and the impromptu salutes with gunfire reinforced preconceived notions the contestants held about the land, its people, and the use of firearms. Most of the racers made a point of mentioning

Emilio Sirtori, left, and Heinrich Haaga, display their weapons in the American West. (*ROUND THE WORLD IN A MOTOR-CAR*, 1909)

their shooting prowess in cables to New York. Sirtori, the Italian driver, posed for one photo wearing a big gunbelt with his hand on his revolver and a cigar clenched in his teeth. His other hand was on the shoulder of his German mechanic, Haaga, who carried a rifle. The racers fired at prairie dogs and rabbits, and the de Dion crew even shot an eagle and placed it on the hood of the car. Comments about the danger of wolves in the wilderness came up repeatedly as well.

On March 21, the front page of the *New York Times* carried a harrowing tale about the Italians that the newspaper described as the

"most exciting experience that has befallen any of the racing cars since leaving New York." One day in Wyoming, the men on the Zust heard cries that sounded like children, but as the sounds grew louder, the men realized that it was a large pack of timber wolves.

"At first the wolves kept at a safe distance, but gradually became bolder and when the car stopped for a moment at the foot of a steep hill they surrounded the crew," the *Times* said. "Running in a circle, the beasts drew nearer and nearer. There were not less than 50 wolves in the pack. The crew attempted to pull away from the beasts, but the heavy roads and steep climb made this impossible."

The sound of the horn and the glare of the searchlight did nothing to scare away the wolves, who kept getting closer. "Finally, Scarfoglio and his companions got out their rifles and opened fire. By this time the beasts were snapping at the trappings, mud guards and rear of the car. At the first fire, three wolves dropped in their tracks. For a time the rest did not know what to do. Some set at work to devour the dead and the balance circled the car. Shot after shot was fired and when the ammunition was all but exhausted the few remaining wolves dashed away into the timber," the *Times* reported.[37] Ranchmen went to the spot the next day and picked up twenty carcasses.

This tale of adventure, which sounded like a scene out of "The Three Little Pigs," was too dramatic even for Scarfoglio. Some days later, a Los Angeles reporter whom Scarfoglio described as an "illustrious but greasy personage" asked about the wolf attack. Scarfoglio called it a "stupid fable" invented by an imaginative newspaper stringer in Wyoming. The most ferocious animal he had seen on the trip was a jack rabbit, Scarfoglio said, and "the only victim of our guns was an innocent sparrow which was airing itself on a telegraph pole."[38]

FIVE

RIDING THE RAILS

A CROWD GATHERED early in Cheyenne to watch the Thomas Flyer resume the race around the world on March 9. When the car failed to make its scheduled 8:00 a.m. start from the Capitol Garage, officials announced that mechanical problems would cause a short delay. By 10:00 a.m. as many as one thousand people waited impatiently for some action. They did not know that the delay in sending the Thomas Flyer on its way stemmed from a far stickier mess than any Iowa mudhole: George Schuster was on strike.

As had been planned, Roberts left the car in Cheyenne to return to New York, where he had other races to run. The Thomas company balked at naming Schuster as his replacement. The car company wanted E. Linn Mathewson, the twenty-one-year-old Thomas distributor from Denver, to take the car through to Ogden, Utah. From Ogden to California, the Thomas would be under the command of another twenty-one-year-old Denver driver, Harold Brinker. Both men were well-known, and testimonials from them about the virtues of the Thomas in the Wild West would help to sell more cars.

Schuster, a practical and intensely competitive man, had no doubt that he deserved a chance to do the driving. At thirty-five, he had worked with bicycles and automobiles longer than Roberts, Mathewson, and Brinker combined. He was aggressive and not easily deterred

when he knew he was right. And he knew he could keep the Thomas Flyer in first place all the way to Paris. According to news reports, he got his point across to E. C. Morse, the sales manager for the Thomas company, in a highly effective fashion.

"AMERICAN CAR DELAYED BY A ONE-MAN STRIKE," said the headline in the *Cheyenne Daily Leader*. "Schuster, after a heated conference Sunday night, refused to continue with the car unless he was given the wheel here, and when the conference ended he and the management were at a deadlock," the newspaper said.

The standoff continued the next morning as Morse, the factory representative who had come from Buffalo to supervise the change of drivers, tried to make peace. No one underestimated Schuster's mechanical skill, but the company wasn't ready to let him take charge. Other reports said the company wanted Brinker or Mathewson to drive all the way to Paris.

While the stalemate continued, Hansen entertained the people in the street, "alternating between cracking jokes in broken English and paying elaborate court to Miss Katherine Mackenzie, the Cheyenne beauty," the newspaper said.[1]

Finally, Morse and Schuster reached a compromise. Morse assured Schuster he would take over as driver and captain after the car reached San Francisco. As a practical matter, Schuster was already in command of the car. He never hesitated to voice an opinion, and the younger men listened to what he had to say. Schuster was satisfied that the company had agreed to make the arrangement official in San Francisco.

Schuster rejoined Mathewson, Miller, and Hansen; the Thomas Flyer was back on the road before noon. The closest competitor was the Zust, five hundred miles behind in Omaha. St. Chaffray was seven

hundred miles away, while Koeppen and Godard trailed by nine hundred miles.

While in Cheyenne, Mathewson gave a short ride to a thirteen-year-old boy from Berthoud, Colorado, who was known as the Kid Agent. The son of a doctor, young Floyd Clymer had been a car dealer in his home town for two years, selling Reo, Maxwell, and Cadillac cars. After the race he began selling Thomas autos too. "It is a wonderful racer—better than all others, I think," Clymer said in a newspaper ad after his ride with Mathewson. Clymer, who became a publisher of automotive books in later years, did sell one Thomas Flyer to a farmer after the race.[2]

Beyond Cheyenne, the *Denver Post* continued its flamboyant treatment of the race, assigning Charles Van Loan to follow the contest through the Rockies. Van Loan, who later rose to fame in New York as a sportswriter for the Hearst newspaper chain and a short-story writer, was a close friend of another Denver reporter, Damon Runyon, then working for the *Rocky Mountain News*.

Runyon, who thought of himself as "the greatest newspaper stunt man of my time," would have been a natural to cover the race, but he was occupied elsewhere in March of 1908, writing about a controversy over the price of sugar beets in the Arkansas Valley. Runyon appreciated Van Loan's style and described him as the "master satirist of all the sportswriters of his period." Van Loan's freewheeling style did create some ill will back in New York, however.

The dispatches that appeared under Mathewson's name in the *New York Times* were mostly rewritten versions of articles Van Loan sent to the *Denver Post* in which Van Loan used various nicknames for the cars. He called the German car the "sauerkraut wagon" and referred to the Italian car variously as the "spaghetti special," the

"benzine barouche," the "cathedral on stilts," and the "macaroni fleet." The *Times* printed letters from three Italians objecting to the wisecracks about Scarfoglio's car. The Thomas company apologized by saying westerners often used nicknames as a joke and meant no harm.[3]

The thirty-one-year-old Van Loan rode into the Rockies in a two-cylinder Reo that served as the pilot car for the Thomas Flyer. He said the American racer looked more like a battleship than an automobile; the crew rode atop a mountain of luggage and extra equipment.

Before leaving Cheyenne, Schuster had spent part of the five hundred dollars he had received for expenses to buy a .38-caliber Colt with a six-inch barrel. It was wide-open country beyond Cheyenne, and Schuster might need a gun, Morse told him.[4] Charlie Duprez, the photographer, also bought a gun, a .38-caliber Iver Johnson.

Duprez, seventeen, described himself as "quite a student of dime novel literature." He had watched as Schuster took pot shots from the car at jack rabbits, and he wanted to do the same. Duprez, who rode in the pilot car with Van Loan, started firing at a rabbit, but in the excitement of the hunt, he neglected to notice Schuster in his line of fire. Duprez, who years later described Schuster as a "tough, cranky hombre," had his gun confiscated after the incident.

"I suppose it's lucky that I missed him for it would have been tough to be a murderer at seventeen," Duprez said, "But I've often wished I could have sliced off part of his ear. Anyway, almost hitting him was bad enough and from then on Schuster really made things tough." The photographer said that at the end of each day when Schuster "had his worst tantrums I always was his main target." Schuster cabled New York and demanded that Duprez be replaced; in San Francisco Duprez lost his position and headed home.[5]

From Wyoming to California, the racers passed through some of the most remote country in the United States. For transcontinental travelers, the change from the Great Plains to the Rockies was gradual; at first, the ascent was hardly noticeable, but soon the wheat fields gave way to compact reddish foothills and rising terrain. West of Cheyenne, the highest part of the Great Plains provided a natural ramp to the roof of the continent.

Not long after leaving Cheyenne, the motorists spotted a huge granite pyramid in the distance on Sherman Summit. After a steady climb of more than twenty miles, they arrived at the base of this monolith in the middle of nowhere, dedicated to two shovel makers from Massachusetts. The Union Pacific Railroad had built the salmon-pink pyramid twenty-six years earlier to honor Oliver and Oakes Ames, key figures in the history of the first transcontinental railroad. A likeness of Oliver appeared on the west side, while Oakes was featured on the east of the sixty-five-foot pyramid. Oliver had been president of the Union Pacific; his brother was a former congressman.[6]

Oakes, known to some headline writers as Hoax Ames, had helped push the 1864 Pacific Railway Act through the Congress. He greased the legislative machinery by passing out railroad stock. Later investigations revealed that several of the railroad promoters had earned huge profits by setting up a dummy construction company and contracting with it at inflated rates.

The Ames monument stood six hundred feet from the original roadbed of the railroad at one of the wildest and most dramatic spots on the entire transcontinental route, amid grass, sagebrush, rock outcroppings, and mountains. The crests of the Colorado Rockies are off to the south, the Medicine Bow Range and Elk Mountain stand to the west, and the vast open plains extend to the southeast.

When the trains ran on time, the conductors would stop briefly at Sherman Summit, allowing the passengers to walk about while the locomotives were inspected.

In 1901, the railroad realigned the tracks four miles to the south of Sherman Summit. The town disappeared, leaving the monument as its tombstone. The trains were now just a sound in the distance, but the monument was still a major milestone for the men on their way to Paris. At 8,275 feet, it was the highest spot reached on the trip across the continent. The pyramid can be reached today by a dirt road that cuts off Interstate 80, but few people bother. Leaving the Ames monument, the Thomas Flyer rolled into Laramie at about twenty miles per hour. The Thomas crew watched as a pair of runaway horses pulling a small wagon took off toward the railroad tracks. A cowboy roped one of the frightened animals, averting a collision with a freight train.[7]

Schuster overhauled the car in Laramie. Countershaft housings that helped support the front end of the rear springs needed to be replaced. Schuster and Miller worked through the night at Elmer Lovejoy's garage. Lovejoy had brought the first car into the state in 1898, but Wyoming saw so few tourists in automobiles that as late as 1913 the only map available of the route to Utah was a hand-drawn sketch by Lovejoy. He would loan it out to travelers with the understanding that they would mail it back to Laramie.

In addition to Lovejoy's car, the town of nine thousand had about sixty other automobiles by 1908. There was also a continuing debate over just how long the horse would remain a major means of conveyance. Real estate salesmen and doctors adopted the auto first. Ranchers were slow to make the switch, but "the prejudice which they once bore toward it has passed away, and several ranchmen now own their own machines," said writer J. Tidball, who analyzed the situation in

1908. He said ranchers who lived twenty or thirty miles from Laramie could now go to town and return home in a single day. "Not far from Laramie a wealthy sheep man makes use of a four-cylinder machine for the purpose of herding sheep, and his reports would seem to indicate that soon the art of herding sheep on foot will be a thing of the past," Tidball said.[8]

Tidball compared the cost of buying and keeping a team of horses for twelve years with the cost of buying and running a car. The total came to $5,896 for the car and $4,074 for the horses, but the car could be expected to cover one hundred thousand miles, he said, while the horses would be lucky to cover thirty-five thousand miles.

Economics and convenience were making the automobile a fact of life in the Wild West, but the image most Americans held of the region still revolved around gunfighters and cowboys. Novelist Owen Wister had helped create the cowboy mystique with his popular 1902 novel, *The Virginian*. Because of Wister's book, the town of Medicine Bow, Wyoming, where the Thomas crew stopped for lunch the day they left Laramie, was world famous for a shooting that had never happened.

Wister, who had taken fifteen trips through the West from 1885 to 1902 and had never seen a shootout, helped glamorize the gun-toting cowboy for all time. Van Loan said the town was trying to capitalize on the fictional events depicted in Wister's book. "One obliging young man offered to show us the exact spot in which Trampas would have died had there been 'any such a person,'" Van Loan reported.[9] After splitting a mince pie at the Cedar Street Hotel, Duprez, who was called the "kid photographer" by Van Loan, took a picture of the group.

Duprez neglected to warn the citizens of Medicine Bow that a loud pop and flash were part of the process, and several people jumped.

"Perhaps they thought the Virginian had returned," Van Loan said. "The fresh youth from Park Row laughed uproariously. If someone does not kill this brilliant suckling before he reaches San Francisco, he may be brought to see the error of his ways."[10]

The next day the Thomas Flyer and the pilot car crossed the frozen North Platte River at Fort Steele. Hansen walked out on the ice and, finding it was eight inches thick, he fired two shots with his revolver, the signal that everything was okay. The people in Rawlins cleared the roads for seven miles from their town and welcomed the racers to a late-morning banquet at the Union Pacific Hotel. The menu featured such dishes as "roast chicken, demi-glass Hansen," and "baby brook trout saute Mathewson." Five toy cars decorated the center table.

When the foreigners wrote of their experiences in Wyoming a little while later, they portrayed a wild and uncivilized country unsuited for auto travel. Scarfoglio's Zust picked up a guide in Rawlins, a sheepman who owned several large flocks. He invited the Italians to stop for lunch at Wamsutter with several of his men. Scarfoglio shared corned beef and canned fish with these men, who ate with their revolvers on the table, bridles wrapped around their arms and hats on their heads. "Thus they live," Scarfoglio said, "in a perpetual state of readiness for war."

The Italian thought they were the ideal Americans. "They know no police, no judges. Their whole life is lived in the wind and the storm and they despise the man who is always under a roof."[11] That night the guide "ate with dignity and got drunk with even more dignity. A policeman found him firing his revolver at the electric lamps and placed him in prison."

The people throughout Wyoming warned all the drivers in turn that their real trouble would begin at the Green River near the

southwest corner of the state. Mathewson's response: "Sufficient unto the day is the evil thereof and we are not going to cross gullies until we come to them."[12]

Mathewson and Schuster stripped the car of much of its baggage to reduce weight for the mountains. They shipped the extra gear ahead on the railroad with Hansen and Duprez. At the ghost town of Point of Rocks, which had been a supply point for the gold fields to the north, the Thomas raced with the westbound Overland Limited for about two miles. "We found a level stretch and Mathewson let the big car out to 40 miles an hour and Miller unfurled the big American flag and saluted the passengers, who responded with handkerchiefs from every window. Every train which we have seen has saluted the American racer and from the car windows the passengers motion us on always westward," Van Loan said.[13]

At Green River, the residents advised against trying to drive the Green River canyon. They said the men would be sleeping in the snow if they tried it, for no cars had been through there all winter. The Thomas went ahead anyway and made it to the top of the grade. "There did not seem to be enough air to go around up there on the top of the Rocky Mountains," Van Loan said.[14]

The next day was Friday the thirteenth, an unlucky one for the pilot car. It broke an axle when the car struck a railroad track, and the Thomas went on alone. Because the pilot car was out of commission, Van Loan rode the Los Angeles Limited to Ogden. The *Rocky Mountain News* accused him of being a coward and ridiculed him for riding the rails. "As a cure for 'frigidis pedis,' known to the people of the world as 'cold feet,' a snug, warm corner in a Pullman is much more to be desired than the wintry blasts and snowdrifts of Wyoming and Utah," the *News* said.

The *News* said the *Post* was "the laughing stock of those who were in the American party" because Van Loan couldn't stand the chill in his "tootsie wootsies." The *News* published a poem that it said had been written by the mechanic in the Thomas car, meaning either Miller or Schuster. But it's more likely that someone at the newspaper penned the following lines:

> He watched us dig for a minnit,
> To get 'local color,' he said;
> Then hoofed it back on the railroad track
> To where he could find a bed.

> Next day he wrote for his paper
> The thrillingest kind of a tale
> Of a bitter fight with the snow all night,
> In the teeth of a howlin' gale.

> He kept up the game to Ogden;
> He'd ride for a few miles each day,
> Then this newspaper man, whose name is Van,
> Took the train the rest of the way.[15]

The *Denver Post* saw to it that the "newspaper man, whose name is Van," received a proper defense. After Van Loan and Mathewson returned to Denver a few days later, a *Post* headline said: "MATHEWSON AND VAN LOAN GIVEN GRAND OVATION." "Never have two men, after accomplishing a difficult and dangerous feat, been accorded a warmer recognition than fell to the lot of E. Linn Mathewson and C. E. Van Loan at the Adams Hotel last evening," the *Post* reported.[16]

In his newspaper dispatches, Van Loan disclosed the breakdown of the pilot car, but failed to provide many details of his train trip. Instead, he found it more interesting to tell about the Thomas Flyer's trip on the railroad tracks. Concerned about heavy snow through southwest Wyoming, Mathewson had asked the Union Pacific office at Cheyenne if he could drive on the railroad. The company approved the request and assigned a brakeman and switchman to take seats in the car.

The Union Pacific issued orders for the "automobile extra" and gave it priority over everything except express passenger trains. Dispatcher L. L. Brown carried red lights and fuses as the Thomas bumped over the railroad ties. The car's right wheels ran outside the track on the edge of the railroad ties.

The Thomas failed miserably as a train. It couldn't keep to its posted schedule and Brown put out flares warning the westbound express to slow down. Three tires blew in short order and had to be replaced. The car bumped along through the mile-long Aspen tunnel with Schuster seated on the radiator.

In the glare of the spotlight the mechanic waved his arms to direct Mathewson, who couldn't see the ties in front. The Thomas traveled on the railroad tracks for about sixty miles in Wyoming and Utah. The Union Pacific's Brown said later the men on the Thomas had accomplished a "most remarkable feat" and the other racers would be hard-pressed to duplicate it.[17]

He had no idea how right he was. The Union Pacific refused to allow the other cars on the tracks. The railroad said the experience with the Thomas had proven it was dangerous to mix automobiles with trains in the mountains. The *Denver Post* said the action by the Union Pacific had "cast a blot on American sportsmanship."[18]

The railroad denied it was playing favorites. The Union Pacific said the Americans had asked first, so their request was approved. The railroad said it wasn't until the Thomas had driven on the tracks into Utah that everyone realized that the car was knocking gravel ballast away from the railroad ties. Section crews had to go over every mile to shovel the gravel back into place, the railroad said.[19] The foreigners raised new protests at the railroad's ruling. "The truth is that the Union Pacific is much pleased—American as it is—at being able to place obstacles in front of the wheels of a competing machine," Scarfoglio said.[20]

A. L. Ruland, the American automobile agent who accompanied the Zust across most of the continent, said when he wired the Union Pacific headquarters about use of the track through Wyoming, he was told that the division superintendent had violated orders in allowing the Thomas to run on the tracks. He said he saw the tracks that had been damaged by the Thomas and said the Union Pacific denial was "wholly justified from their viewpoint, though we felt they should not have extended the courtesy to one car and not to another."

Ruland added that the Union Pacific had been a big help to the Zust, allowing the Italians to use its shops at Omaha and Ogden, bringing spare parts by train, picking up the car twice, and taking it to Ogden for repairs.[21]

The Union Pacific's refusal to allow the other racers on its tracks made the trip somewhat more difficult than it had been for the American car, but the Thomas did not gain a significant advantage. On or off the tracks, the cars all took about the same amount of time to cross this part of the Rockies. "We made as good time over the mountain as the Thomas did through the (Aspen) tunnel, though it shook up the car badly, was dangerous to the car and the men, and

exhausted the crew badly," Ruland said. "Except Sirtori, all of us had to climb the mountain on foot, as we would not add our weight to the heavily laden car."[22]

Beyond Ogden, the cars kept fairly close to the old Golden Spike Route of the Southern Pacific that looped to the north of the Great Salt Lake. No one cared if they drove on these tracks because nearly all trains now crossed the lake on a forty-mile trestle. With a lead of three hundred miles and growing, the men on the Thomas battled through blowing sand and sagebrush and stopped for the night at Promontory, a lonely spot in the wilds of Utah.

On May 10, 1869, Leland Stanford, the president of the Central Pacific Railroad, had come to this sagebrush basin to swing at a golden spike. He missed, but it was the thought that counted. A telegraph operator at Promontory tapped out "Done" and a nationwide celebration marked the end of the race to finish the first transcontinental railroad. The Liberty Bell rang in Philadelphia, while crowds paraded in Omaha, listened to speeches in Boston's Faneuil Hall, and heard a one-hundred-gun salute in New York.

At the summit of the Promontory Range, two polished locomotives had rolled into facing positions at the junction of the two railroads. The Union Pacific had built to the west, while the Central Pacific worked toward the east. Workmen, soldiers, reporters, and railroad officials gathered for the symbolic act that closed the gap between east and west. Chief engineer Grenville Dodge spoke of Sen. Thomas Benton of Missouri, who had one day proposed that a Rocky Mountain peak be sculpted into a statue of Columbus in which the explorer would be pointing west across the continent and holding a tablet that said "There lies India."[23] "You have made that prophecy today a fact," said Dodge. "This is the way to India."

In 1942, with the United States desperate for steel during World War II, the railroad removed the tracks to Promontory and pulled the last spike. But a trip to Promontory was already a footnote to history in 1908. "After sleeping as best we could at this out-of-the-way place, which has not had even a telegraph station since the route of the Southern Pacific was changed, we rose in the darkness and at 5:15 were again on our way," said Brinker.[24]

When Scarfoglio came along this way, he said the old railway route was "like a corpse, the molecules of which are returning to the earth. It is rusting away and becoming part of the wilderness. The grass has invaded it, the sleepers are green with moss, the signal posts have fallen and the stations rotted away."[25]

The most direct route to San Francisco would have taken the racers from the high desert of Nevada through the Sierra Nevadas at Donner Pass southwest of Reno. Plans changed, however, when the motorists learned the Sierra passes had twenty-foot snowdrifts. More than half a century earlier, the members of the Donner party had learned the difficulty of crossing the Sierras in the snow. Thirty-five people died there, trapped by walls of granite and never-ending snow.

The Paris racers decided to avoid Donner Pass by taking a southern detour through the boom towns of Nevada.

SIX

THROUGH THE GOLD FIELDS

IN 1907, HARPER'S *Weekly* published an article headlined "The Gasoline Camel of the American Desert," in which it described the revolution created by the automobile in the sands of Nevada. A series of discoveries starting with a 1900 silver find in Tonopah produced a succession of boom towns, most of which briefly drew a crowd before disappearing into the sagebrush. A similar mass migration a generation earlier followed the discovery of the Comstock Lode at Virginia City, the most important silver find in the nineteenth century. One big difference was the speed with which the twentieth-century prospectors moved, Barton Currie wrote in Harper's.

"The modern gold-seekers could not wait for railroads and lost patience with the tedious stage route. So they have installed the Benzine Bus, as southern Nevada calls the big heavy-bodied touring car.

"Hundreds of cars are employed in this way. They have conquered the barren gold fields, annihilating distance, overcoming the hardships and tortures men and animals suffered in the earlier discoveries of the untimbered, unwatered treasure mountains. They are not the toys of leisure-loving millionaires down there; the hated juggernauts of over-peopled cities; the pests of the humble, conservative farmer—rather they are the tools of conquest."[1]

The lack of bridges and railroad crossings forced the drivers to cross railroad tracks the hard way in many areas. Here, the Thomas crew wrestles with the car west of Cobre, Nevada. (*MOTOR*)

There was great debate in the mining towns about who had brought the first car to Nevada. People in Tonopah, Goldfield, Bullfrog, Beatty, and Rhyolite all claimed the honor. Experienced drivers in these towns could earn more than many bank presidents, ferrying prospectors across the desert. The cars ran on seventy-five-cent-a-gallon gas along sun-baked stretches of sand that made excellent highways, except when it rained.

But stream crossings could always create the conditions for hard driving in Nevada, as the men on the Thomas Flyer discovered southwest of Ely. A rancher had warned them of a rocky streambed where quicksand had been marked with large boulders. "Vile came to grief at the bad crossing," Schuster said. "The car had gotten partly across, but while it was going up the steep bank, the footing for the wheels was so uneven that it caused a terrific strain, with the result that when we reached the top of the bank, six teeth had been broken from the drive pinion."[2]

The transmission case cracked across the bottom and the car stopped dead. After surveying the damage, Schuster hiked back to the Twin Springs Ranch. He hired an old horse for twenty dollars and set off on a seventy-five-mile ride to Tonopah, where he hoped to find the parts he needed for repairs.

People in Tonopah became worried when the car failed to show up that night. At about midnight, four men left in Shorty Kutzkau's Simplex car to search for the Thomas Flyer. Newspaper reports said that the men found Schuster fifty miles out, near Stone Cabin. Schuster said he had stopped for the night at a ranch, where he stayed in a lean-to near a stable. He awoke at the sound of someone moving in the darkness and reached for his gun, wondering if he was about to be robbed. The intruder turned out to be a member of the rescue party from Tonopah.[3] Early the next morning, Schuster borrowed the parts he needed from a doctor's Thomas Flyer and returned to fix the race car.

The repaired car and its tired crew arrived in Tonopah at 11:00 on March 20. Sentries at the Rescue Mine sent up rockets to signal the arrival of the car, while a long blast on the Tonopah Extension whistle helped draw a large crowd to Crumley's Nevada Club. A band played, youngsters set off fireworks, and souvenir hunters cut bits off of the American flag that hung from the rear of the car.

Tonopah, a treeless mining camp of one-story wood cottages and cactus window gardens, had a brief, but rich history. Eight years earlier a rancher had camped for the night with his burros near here. According to one story, when Jim Butler awoke the next morning he found his burros at an outcropping that attracted his interest. He knocked off a few pieces of what would become one of the richest silver strikes in history.

The town quickly became the major outfitting point in south-western Nevada for thousands of prospectors looking for a lucky break. The boom triggered by Butler's burros and the discoveries that followed quickly at Goldfield, Bullfrog, Rawhide, Manhattan, and Rhyolite put a new stamp on mining in Nevada and energized the state, which had been losing population since the decline of the Comstock Lode.

The foreign racers found this string of short-lived towns exciting and puzzling. "We drink everywhere champagne offered by these gold cities," St. Chaffray said. "It is, I suppose, because the people want us to know that labor can make of a desert a paradise and that sand and snowstorms are nothing if men are willing."[4]

Across the California border in Greenwater, Scarfoglio discovered what a mining camp looked like when the good times were gone. Greenwater had boomed in 1906 and 1907 on the strength of a copper find. The town prospered until the shallow deposit of ore gave out and the inhabitants gave up. At its peak, the town had a population of five thousand, a post office, a bank, two grocery stores, and eight saloons. Scarfoglio said the town's buildings were still intact, as if everyone had left in the morning and intended to return that night.

"The doors and the windows are closed, but through the panes one can see the beds ready, kitchens shining with brass utensils, clothes still hanging on their pegs," he said. "A printing office displays behind its windows a row of linotypes and on the walls are still affixed the announcements of a production at a local theatre—Madame Butterfly—sung by an Italian tenor."

He said only seven people remained in Greenwater and they lived in separate houses, but met each night at the home of the oldest for dinner. "Thus they live, like shipwrecked mariners in a desert island, recalling the glories of the mummified town around them, and re-reading the old numbers of the newspapers," the journalist said.

"Greenwater concludes the analysis of the American town. We have seen the germination at Ely; the flowering at Goldfield; the rotting away at Greenwater. Thus, depicted on the desert in three great strokes, is the whole of American psychology."[5]

Earlier, the crew of the Zust stopped in the Nevada desert at the home of an abandoned soul who, in Scarfoglio's mind, typified the rootless quality of American life. Not wanting to spend the night in the desert with the coyotes, the crew of the Zust had approached an isolated house where they saw a single kerosene light shining in a window. An old Frenchman with a flowing white beard invited Scarfoglio, Sirtori, and Haaga into a large room with walls decorated with red, blue, and violet paper flowers that defied the dry climate outdoors. An iron bedstead stood in the corner, and the room was packed with books, the works of Plutarch, Schiller, Homer, and Shelley among them. Tennyson's "Idylls of the King" was open on the table.

They consumed canned oysters, peas, bananas, and a cup of wine, while their host spoke softly about why he was spending his old age tending a poor-paying mine in the desert. He motioned to an old photograph of a woman with two children and said that he had left France as a young man, intending to find his fortune and return. He had been away 37 years, prospecting from Australia to Alaska. "Now he is alone in the desert, and has lost all trying to rebuild what he has himself destroyed," Scarfoglio wrote. "For 37 years he has worn his fingers to the bone digging in the sand trying to realize his shining dream, but in the 37 years he has not proceeded one step, so that he could regain what he had lost, and he is just as lonely now as the day he left his country with a pack on his shoulder, and took the main road."[6]

Leaving Nevada, the racers confronted the last major geographic obstacle before reaching the Pacific Coast—Death Valley. The Thomas tackled it on March 21, crossing Daylight Pass and going down a steep canyon to Hell's Gate. The spot earned that nickname when mule teams leaving the walls of the canyon would supposedly shake their heads as soon as the scorching summer heat touched their noses. "They thought they had stuck their nose through the gates of hell," one teamster said.

The Thomas edged its way down the old trail to the Stovepipe Wells, at 4.9 feet below sea level. Brinker stopped at a tent and rusty pipe, where the crew bought water at ten cents a pail. Automobiles rated a place on the "free" list in most parts of the West, but not at Stovepipe Wells. The latest government maps showed a blank space in Death Valley, and cars were as rare as blizzards. Summer temperatures could hit 130 degrees and the most common vehicles were borax wagons pulled by one-hundred-foot-long teams of mules.

It took the Thomas several hours to cross Death Valley and everyone except Brinker had to help push the car through the sand. After midnight they began to climb through Emigrant Canyon in the moonlight. The men stopped for a few hours at Ballarat, a small mining camp.

Meanwhile, interest in the race was building in Los Angeles. Eddie Thomas, the son of the company owner, was waiting to show off the car to legions of potential car buyers in southern California. There was one problem, however. Schuster was more interested in winning the race than selling cars. He was trying to get to San Francisco as fast as he could and he knew he could save a few hundred miles by skipping

Los Angeles. The next day the Thomas Flyer went to Mojave and then turned northwest to Bakersfield, taking an inland route to San Francisco, via Fresno.

Los Angeles, the city that would become synonymous with cars and highways, was left in the dust, off the beaten track. The Thomas company sent telegrams to Schuster asking him to turn back at Bakersfield, but to no avail.

"A big body of automobilists from Los Angeles, with a press car, waited at San Bernardino all day for the coming of the Thomas car," the *New York Times* reported.[7] The paper said the failure of the car to go to Los Angeles was a "keen disappointment to the inhabitants of the whole surrounding country, who are thoroughly wrought up over the race."

The *Denver Post* reported that thousands of "automobilists and auto bugs" also lined the road from San Fernando to Los Angeles, waiting for the car that never came. At Duarte, 110 cars lined up, while the mayor of Los Angeles and members of the Good Roads Commission waited in San Bernardino.[8] A few days earlier the mayor and other community leaders had written the *New York Times*, asking that Los Angeles be added to the race route. "We will make all gasoline arrangements if you sanction the change. This will give a half-million more people a chance to see the cars," Mayor A. C. Harper said.[9] The *Times* replied that as long as the cars reached San Francisco, the exact route was up to the driver.

Schuster, Brinker, and Hansen reached Bakersfield at 1:00 a.m. and had a late-night banquet at which Captain Hansen broke open a bottle of wine in honor of his daughter Lydia's birthday. Everyone drank a toast to the girl before turning in, without giving Los Angeles another thought.

The Americans completed the cross-country run on March 24, arriving in San Francisco forty-one days, eight hours, and sixteen minutes after leaving Times Square. The car had traveled 3,832 miles. A half-mile procession of cars had formed as an escort at San Jose and a big crowd waited at the ferry terminal in Oakland. The Thomas Flyer reached the other side of San Francisco Bay as the sounds of a brass band filled the air.

Crowds had jammed the streets long before the car's 4:30 p.m. arrival. Factory whistles sounded and automobile drivers blew their horns on Market Street. A reporter for the *San Francisco Chronicle* said it was "the greatest automobile demonstration ever seen in San Francisco."[10] Flags and bunting covered the buildings along the way. Brinker drove to the showroom of the Pioneer Automobile Company, where the car would be exhibited before resuming the chase.[11]

"The record of the Thomas car from New York to San Francisco was a remarkable feat," the *New York Times* concluded. "Many skeptics declared when the New York to Paris racers started out from New York in the dead of winter that none of them would get across Wyoming until summer, some that they would not reach Chicago and a few that they could not cross New York state."[12]

The Thomas Flyer arrived in San Francisco three weeks short of the second anniversary of the greatest catastrophe ever to strike an American city. The city had rebounded from the disaster, but the aftereffects of the 1906 earthquake and fire remained. City officials were killing two thousand rats a day to prevent a reappearance of bubonic plague.

The fire had destroyed the financial and retail districts, Chinatown, and the heart of the city, wiping out twenty-eight thousand buildings. But rebuilding began as soon as the ashes cooled. In the twenty months

since reconstruction had started, new buildings had appeared at the rate of one per hour. "Stand on the hills and the observer could not tell that he was looking at a city that two years ago was destroyed," the *San Francisco Examiner* said. Most of the burned area appeared to be covered, but thousands of property owners had yet to raise the money to build again.[13]

"The capital of the west is like that of ancient Rome," St. Chaffray said later, "as the greater part of the streets are glorious ruins. The golden sunset is undulating, warm and voluptuous. The rays light up again the ruined walls with a red glow."[14]

It was a matter of some controversy that a new street plan was not instituted after the fire to correct the mistakes of the past. A report in the *Examiner* said that while the debris from the fire was cleared in half the time the experts said it would take, the modern street plan got lost in the crush. "San Francisco is being rebuilt on exactly the same lines that proved so inconvenient in the past," Earle Ashley Walcott wrote. "The city's street plan was laid out by surveyors whose highest abilities were adapted to laying out town lots on a flat prairie. So when they came to plat the streets of San Francisco, little eccentricities like hills were ignored, and lines were run straight over 40 percent grades, as though climbing cliffs was as easy as running on level ground."[15] In both old and new San Francisco, Walcott said, the "first principle of courtship" applied to the street design. That is "the longest way around is the shortest way home."

Three hours after the Thomas made its triumphant entrance into the city by the bay, a second competitor arrived in San Francisco. This was something of a shock, for the Thomas racers thought they had a lead of eight hundred miles and more on the rest of the pack: Scarfoglio was in Utah, while St. Chaffray and Koeppen were in Wyoming. The

man who had spent most of the race in last place, however, had jumped ahead of the others by taking the train to San Francisco. Baron Godard's car would soon follow on a westbound freight.

Beset by numerous accidents and mechanical problems, the Baron had turned to the steel rail in desperation. He claimed that the race rules allowed him to ship the car west if he desired. As he disembarked from the train in San Francisco, the Baron talked of the blizzard in Indiana, the theft of his possessions, and his hopes for the future. "I will win yet," he said. "The Motobloc will lead the procession into Paris."[16]

The Baron promised to get his car repaired on the West Coast and be ready to sail for Alaska in a few days. "This race across America is merely a trifle compared to the journey through Alaska and Asia. I have some experience there and the advantages which the Thomas car enjoyed in this country will be mine when we get into Siberia. In the Peking to Paris race I learned many things and hope that my knowledge will stand me in good stead, as my competitors will have to find out many of these things for themselves."[17]

As the Baron had made his way west on the train, he leveled various charges at the American entry: he said the Thomas had gone through three new engines since it left New York and that the race across the United States was trumped up for advertising purposes. These comments failed to win many friends for the Baron on American soil.

In Omaha, the *Evening World-Herald* said the Baron had made his part of the race into a farce. The newspaper claimed Godard and his crew had told one man they planned to sit in the car while it was on the train, take their meals in it, and pretend it was under its own power. There was a suggestion that they would cross Siberia in a similar fashion.[18] When Godard reached Denver, his charges about the Thomas drew denials from Linn Mathewson, who had driven the Thomas

from Cheyenne to Ogden. "If the Motobloc crew wins anything in this race, it will be the booby prize," Mathewson said. The Denver car dealer placed two bets of one thousand dollars that the Thomas would go as far in the race as any of the foreign cars. He also offered to give two thousand dollars as "a little present for Mr. Godard or anybody else who can prove that the engine which is now in the Thomas is not the same one which carried her out of New York and has been in continuous service ever since," the *Denver Post* said.

The *Post* said that Godard was welcome to come by to collect Mathewson's money if he could prove the truth of his allegations. "Otherwise it might be well for him to pack up his unmanly squeal and ship it by freight along with his disabled automobile. Colorado does not love a quitter," the *Post* said.[19]

The *Post* said that while Godard deserved to be kicked out of the race for taking the train, he was not the only one who deserved rebuke. "It seems a pity that the men who promoted this race did not have judgment enough to acquaint themselves with conditions before the cars left New York City, and thus would have saved about a thousand misunderstandings, and the contestants would have had some idea of what they were setting out to do."

"As a race, the New York-to-Paris proposition has been a hodge-podge of bad judgment, ignorance and obstinancy from beginning to end and that the American car was able to secure a lead of 900 miles in a contest of this kind is really a remarkable performance. In a race where every driver seemed to be a law unto himself it was the American spirit of hustle and get there that left the nearest competitor nearly 1,000 miles behind."[20]

Godard and the others had been told they would be disqualified if they took the train, and the race organizers were true to their word.

The Baron was eliminated. He received a cable from the owners of his car: "Quit race, sell car and come home."[21]

The Baron stayed in the city for a few weeks, but he couldn't keep out of trouble. He was arrested and charged with going fifty miles per hour along the ocean boulevard. He was released on twenty dollars bail. The Baron got out of town just as custom officials began looking for him. They wanted to know why he had sold the Motobloc without paying the 45 percent import duty on the car. The car was worth about $10,000 new, which means the government wanted a duty of $4,500. Godard's car was sold at auction to a Nevada mining man who picked it up for $1,650, believing the import duty had been paid.[22]

During the sale, an attorney rushed up to the auctioneer, waving a bill for $600 over his head. An Iowa farmer who said he had towed the Baron's car had hired the attorney to collect the money. "Godard submitted to the payment of the bill out of the proceeds of the sale and departed with the other $1,000 or more," the *San Francisco Chronicle* reported. "He is now said to be on his way to Paris, while several irate persons are wishing that he was still here. Among these are the man who bought the machine, which the government now threatens to seize, and the New York bondsmen."[23]

From beginning to end, nothing went right for Baron Godard on the race to Paris. Returning to France later that spring, he had no shortage of stories about the United States. "Stripped of their verbosity," the Automobile said of Godard's complaints, "they amount to 'bad roads, bad food, scant hospitality.' "[24]

Godard was not the only one to suffer. All of the drivers had their share of blown tires, broken axles, and miscellaneous engine troubles. *Motor* magazine said that had the foreign cars been driven as well as the Thomas, the race might have been closer, but "careful driving was

not a characteristic of any of the other competitors."[25] *Motor* said the "stupidity and obstinacy" of the Italians led to breakdowns of the Zust, while the de Dion had a dozen breakdowns that would have been avoided with proper handling.

Even the Thomas car had numerous mechanical problems on the trip across the country, but the company always insisted that "repairs were insignificant." That the car performed so well on the trip across the continent was testimony primarily to the abilities of Schuster and Miller as mechanics, but the company wanted to advertise the car as trouble-free. A telegram Schuster received in Wyoming reflected the company line on the content of the news reports they wanted relayed to Buffalo: "Never mind what men did, send what car did."[26]

When other United States car makers alleged that the Thomas Flyer was not an ordinary car off the showroom floor or that it had undergone major repairs, the Buffalo company threatened court action. "We hereby notify them that their statements are false and malicious and must cease, or they will be prosecuted to the fullest extent of the law," E. R. Thomas said.[27]

In San Francisco, Schuster, who was now officially in charge of the car, worked with Miller and Hansen for two days to get ready for Alaska and Siberia. The company would never admit it, but the car did require some work. Schuster replaced the countershaft housings for the fourth time since leaving New York and installed new springs, a new transmission, new wheels, and new driving chains. The company wanted to add a one-thousand-pound enclosed car body so that the men would be protected from the arctic cold, but Schuster knew the extra weight would be disastrous, so he refused.[28] The Thomas had gone through six tires on the trip across America, and Schuster figured he would need thirty more to finish the race.

About ten thousand people stopped by the Pioneer Garage to get a look at the car. The president of the Pioneer Automobile Company, E. P. Brinegar, said he would keep the car near the corner showroom window so that the public could watch the repairs.

Among those who helped to get the Thomas ready for the next stage of the contest was Eddie Thomas, the son of owner E. R. Thomas. There was strong sentiment among some people that the Alaska leg of the trip should be eliminated. Eddie Thomas agreed. He announced that Alaska had been scratched from the itinerary. He told newsmen the car was to be loaded aboard the ship *Manchuria* and taken straight to the Orient. Orders from Buffalo overruled Eddie, however, and plans were completed to ship the car to Alaska by way of Seattle.[29]

Government officials announced, meanwhile, that a letter was on its way from Secretary of War William Howard Taft. Schuster was asked to deliver the letter to the French Minister of War in Paris.

"The American public have watched with great interest the progress of the cars in the attempt to open up a new transcontinental route by means of locomotion," Taft wrote to his French counterpart. "The automobile, the manufacture of which has become one of our leading industries, is destined to assume a very important part in the economic welfare of the world. The perseverance and pluck of the contestants entitles them to the congratulations of all well-wishers of the development of mechanical ingenuity."[30]

Big Bill Taft's interest in the race was in keeping with his reputation as a friend of the auto industry. When he rode in a car to Jersey City during his presidential campaign that year instead of taking a train, the trip merited an article in a major car magazine.[31] "These buzz wagons are the finest things in existence for the enjoyment of the open air," the three-hundred-pound Taft once said.

The Italian Zust arrives in San Francisco in second place, nine days behind the Thomas Flyer. (FROM *MOTOR* MAGAZINE)

Taft's name came up in connection with the Paris race in another way that year. *Life*, a popular humor magazine, published a series of stories spoofing the race to Paris. *Life* said it was running a contest of its own in which a car called the Zip left New York with James Metcalfe, William Taft, and Anthony Comstock on board. At Forty-second Street and Broadway, Taft rose to make a speech: "Boys, don't forget that Teddy is a great man. When, after reading your morning paper, you get down on your knees and pray, 'Give us this day our daily dread,' remember that the greatest man in the world reigns over you and that he never reigns but he pours. In the meantime, if you want any more speeches supplementing the White House policy, call me up in Siberia."

While the Thomas sailed to Seattle and points north, Los Angeles finally earned a spot on the race route. The Zust crew was pelted with

flowers and oranges as the car made a triumphant passage to the *Los Angeles Times* office and the White Garage. "It matters not that the Thomas car is several days ahead of us," driver Emilio Sirtori said. "You will find that when Paris is reached the Zust car will be first into the city."[32] The Zust reached San Francisco April 4, nine days behind the leader. St. Chaffray was four days behind the Zust.

Sirtori said that southern California reminded him of Italy and that California's roads were the best he had seen. The worst part of the trip was through Wyoming, he said, where the steep trails and rough going created many problems. The worst snow was in Indiana and the worst mud in Iowa.

Wyoming also proved to be difficult territory for the Commissionaire General and his crew. First, the de Dion overturned in Wyoming and it took eight hours to get it upright. The next day the car was stuck in the mud and after the crew pulled on ropes unsuccessfully for ninety minutes, the Commissionaire General sought outside assistance.

Two men St. Chaffray described as "robbers" and "Hungarian tramps" walked up to the car, but refused to help move it. "Lascaris, our companion since Chicago, is acute," the Commissionaire General said of the incident. "He had a clear view of the situation and saw the movement of the tramps. He took out his revolver and gently told the robbers to help us for the sake of their lives. The Hungarians proved to be clever workmen under the show of well-armed Lascaris and Autran. They helped strongly and, thanks to them, the big car got out of the mud and we came to Ogden."[33]

In Death Valley, Lascaris was temporarily blinded by the sand, and St. Chaffray and Autran went to get help. They found a man with a burro who set off to get aid, while St. Chaffray purchased the man's

tent and brought it back to the car to put it under the wheels for traction. "We had to use the canvas often to rescue the car from the sand. But the tent was old and had been burned by the sun and gave way. We saw our efforts would be vain. We are exhausted again and decided to sleep under the car," St. Chaffray wrote.[34]

While climbing out of Death Valley, they came across a borax wagon pulled by twenty-four mules. The noise of the car spooked the animals, and the mule drivers jumped out and ran toward the de Dion with their revolvers drawn, making threatening gestures. The guide, a former wagon driver, calmed the mule drivers down before any shots were fired.

It took the Frenchmen twenty-two hours to cross the valley, but soon they were in California. "We are traveling again on flat roads and we see bridges conducting to San Francisco," St. Chaffray said. "People drive horses no more by preference. The motor is king."[35]

A. L. Ruland, who rode in the Zust most of the way across the country, said he would not make the trip again if he were paid fifty thousand dollars for the privilege. "I have no desire to put my life in jeopardy and without exaggeration I say I was in imminent danger of death with all four occupants of the car four distinct times between New York and Ogden. In retrospect, the experience is all right and I'm glad I had it, but I will know better than to attempt to cross the United States again in winter," Ruland said.[36]

He said the car nearly went over a cliff once before it was stopped by the front axle, which caught on the ground. Putting aside his personal travail, Ruland said he was impressed that the race had captured the nation's attention in a unique way. In the most isolated settlements across the country, people knew all about the race and the contestants. "We would come to a lonely house without telephone

communications, miles from anywhere and find the solitary occupant out looking for us. He knew the Thomas had gone by and that we were second and knew the French and German cars were coming. He knew our names and all about us apparently, and was as much interested in the outcome of the race as the hundreds who stand each day in front of the *Times*'s bulletin boards to watch the progress of the cars."

SEVEN

NORTH TO ALASKA

THE THOMAS FLYER picked up five extra passengers in San Francisco—carrier pigeons that were to be released in the Alaska wilderness. As Captain Hansen explained, the winged messengers would keep the outside world informed of the car's progress through the tundra when the Thomas was beyond the reach of the telegraph. Schuster thought the idea was nonsense and said there was no place to put the pigeons, but Hansen insisted.

The captain's inspiration may have come from Salomon August Andrée, the lost Norwegian explorer Hansen had helped look for a decade earlier. Andrée had carried thirty-two carrier pigeons with him when he tried to go to the North Pole by balloon. He intended to send back messages by pigeon on how his flight was going. Unfortunately, the pigeons failed to carry back the most important news about the expedition: the balloon went down on the pack ice three days after launch, and the men perished on an arctic island three months later.[1]

Hansen held forth on the power of pigeons and other aspects of arctic exploration during the two-day trip from San Francisco to Seattle aboard the *City of Pueblo*. He puffed on his pipe and described the hardships ahead. Schuster slept most of the way, trying to build up his strength after six weeks of long days and short nights.

The snow-capped peak of Mount Rainier came into view as the steamship arrived on the bright blue waters of Seattle's Elliott Bay. Miller and Schuster had their pictures taken before dodging the newspapermen at the dock. But Hansen, described by the *Seattle Post-Intelligencer* as a "debonair rover," had all the time in the world for interviews.

Word that the Thomas Flyer had arrived spread quickly through the hills of Seattle. Seventy automobiles had lined up on the waterfront and three thousand people gathered behind police barricades. "Ringling's circus in its palmiest days never drew anywhere near the crowd that followed the 'Flying Tommy' from the pier along First Avenue," a *Post-Intelligencer* reporter said. When a hoist deposited the car on the pier, a crowd rushed ahead, "possessed of an uncontrollable desire to affix their autographs to the top and sides of the rakish machine," another reporter said.[2] A bystander said it seemed as if the people in Seattle had never seen a car before.

Schuster, Hansen, and Miller made their way to the Butler Hotel along with a fourth man who introduced himself on the dock. He was thirty-one-year-old George MacAdam, the *New York Times* reporter assigned to ride with the Thomas Flyer the rest of the way to Paris. A thin, short man who looked a little frail, MacAdam was willing to try anything once. Although he was not as flashy as Skipper Williams, MacAdam was a solid reporter with a literary flair. He had received his first newspaper training at the *New York Sun*.

On the way to Seattle, MacAdam had stopped in Buffalo to meet E. R. Thomas and others in the auto company, "Mr. Thomas, the high muck-a-muck of the company, gave me two volumes on Asiatic Russia," MacAdam later wrote to his mother.[3] "He inscribed in the flyleaf good wishes, bon voyage a la auto, and signed it... He wants me to have

all Alaskan sheriffs, Chinese Mandarins, Kalruuck Nabobs and other distinguished personages that we meet by the wayside, add their signatures to the list. The books, after completing their autographic tour of the world are to be returned to him."

The auto company agreed to pay all of MacAdam's expenses. In return, it wanted him to send a daily five-hundred-word telegraph report on the progress of the race to headquarters in Buffalo. He was also to take at least five photographs a day showing the car conquering one obstacle or another.

"Special attention must be paid to the matter of photographs, as we depend as much if not more on the photographs for the publicity which we will get out of this race, as we do on the reports," Commercial Manager E. C. Morse wrote MacAdam.[4] Morse asked for as many side views of the car as possible and advised MacAdam that "we want the car to be the prominent object in the photograph."

MacAdam would also telegraph news reports on the race to the *New York Times* and, after reaching Siberia, *Le Matin*. Morse wanted MacAdam's reports to emphasize the superiority of the Thomas car over anything else: "It is especially requested that you do not dwell upon any work done on the car, but dwell fully upon the difficulties which the car and the crew met and successfully overcame," Morse said. "The idea is that your articles and dispatches should be along the lines of reading matter, as we do not want any reports to appear in the nature of an advertisement. Of course, the Thomas car is to be spoken of favorably at all times. Mention names in mail reports of prominent people met enroute."[5]

MacAdam had been acquainted with the car company's managers for only a few days, but he was flattered by the tone of a letter of introduction written by Morse to Schuster: "This will introduce to

you Mr. George MacAdam, our special news and photo representative. He is a good fellow, strictly on the square and in no sense a dead one."[6]

The trip across the country by rail was a first for MacAdam, and he was exhilarated with his closeup look at the continent. "You have no conception of the space between here and New York," he wrote his father. MacAdam raved about the Great Plains, the land boom in Spokane, the apples from Wenatchee, and the scenery in the Cascades.[7]

MacAdam said he wasn't homesick, but he did send a suitcase of dirty clothes back to New York because they were too good to throw away and there was no room in the car. His father wrote to him several times in the months ahead, warning him each time of the dangers of drinking the water on foreign soil.

Despite the demands by the Thomas company to focus on the hardships overcome by the car, MacAdam's dispatches to the *Times* pointed out problems with the machine when they occurred. MacAdam told his parents not to take the dangers as seriously as he was to recount them in the newspaper, however. "My last word of instruction from Mr. Thomas was: 'What I want the Thomas car to do is to get to Paris. Don't take any risks.' And we're not going to."[8]

With MacAdam now on the crew, there were three Georges on the car. To hold confusion to a minimum they addressed each other by their last name or a nickname. Schuster went by "Schus," while MacAdam was dubbed the "hot air artist." The correspondent took a liking to Hansen right away. MacAdam said that when Hansen wore his foreign uniform with gold braid and various insignia, "He was the glinting synosure of all eyes" when he appeared in hotel lobbies or on the street.[9]

Like Hansen, MacAdam enjoyed the spotlight. "It's a very enjoyable thing to be a Personage, to be introduced as 'Mr. So-and-so, going

on the New York to Paris race' and to be pointed out in hotel lobbies and on the street. We may be in a fairly small puddle, but just now we feel puffed out to fair-sized frogs. Verily, vanity of vanities, etc., etc., etc.," he wrote his mother.[10]

Everywhere he went in Seattle, MacAdam met people who said the racers would have no chance in Alaska. Many miners who spent summers working the creeks in Alaska, spent winters working the hotel lobbies in Seattle. People who had been to Alaska were as common in Seattle as "huckleberries in Pike County, Pennsylvania," MacAdam said. Ever since the Klondike gold boom in the Yukon eleven years earlier, Seattle had been the main point of departure for travelers to the north.

The city's population had nearly tripled since the Klondike strike. The initial attack of gold fever had long since subsided, but Seattle remained the biggest winner of the gold rushes to Dawson, Nome, Fairbanks, Ruby, and Iditarod. The secret to cashing in on gold discoveries two thousand miles away was to sell equipment and supplies to the northbound prospectors.

A decade earlier inventors and crackpots in Seattle tried to make their fortunes from a dazzling assortment of mechanical contraptions designed to make traveling easier in the ice and snow. One idea was for a "snow and ice propellor," a machine that resembled a huge mechanical caterpillar wearing ice skates. The design called for a sixteen-foot sled with three cylindrical cranks, connected to several arms and ten legs. At the foot of each leg was an adjustable ice skate. The propellor was to have a gasoline engine that would enable it to carry nine men at speeds of up to sixty miles per hour.[11]

Another inventor had proposed an enclosed vehicle that would rest atop huge tubes that looked like screws. "The principle is the old

one on which the screw is worked," the *Seattle Post-Intelligencer* explained. "The tubes revolve and the spirals catching in the snow or ice propel the entire structure." Had this machine been built, it might have done nothing more than screw itself tightly into the ground, but the designer believed his vehicle could cross rough ice and dig through sand bars on the rivers.

Limited knowledge of the north, combined with unlimited enthusiasm, created a dangerous mixture. As one student of these gadget plans put it; "the hopeful and the gullible, the innocent and the con-artist all came into full flower in the Klondike transportation business."[12] In the years that followed, those who had been to the Yukon and Alaska learned that no miracle machine could handle the terrain. They put their faith in dogs, horses, and strong backs.

Many of the Alaskans MacAdam met in Seattle placed the automobile racers in the same category as the crackpots who had generated so much newspaper coverage during the gold rush. Several people told MacAdam that the cars might make it about a mile out of Valdez. Charles Hamilton, who had come over the trail from Fairbanks to Valdez the preceding month, told a story about a man he met driving a sleigh on the trail. When asked what he was hauling, the sleigh driver said: "Gasoline for some fools that are coming up here in automobiles. Hope they have an easier trip than I've had with this sleigh." Hamilton warned MacAdam that the people in Alaska expected the cars to disappear in the snowdrifts. "You are sailing for Alaska on April 1," he said. "You know what date that is."[13]

In preparing for the frigid weather in the north, Schuster and his crew purchased new ankle-length coonskin coats along with walrus-hide boots. Schuster got a rifle and shotgun sent by his wife and a message from his young son asking that he bring a monkey back with him to

Buffalo. He bought six spare tires from local stores and strapped them to the rear of the car. Schuster also received a letter of credit for forty-eight hundred dollars from Eddie Thomas.[14]

Despite all the negative talk about the race through Alaska, Schuster refused to give up. He said many people had claimed it was impossible to cross the continent in winter, and they had been proven wrong. After conquering the snow in Indiana and the mud in Iowa, he said he would not accept anyone else's verdict about what was impossible until trying it himself.[15]

On April Fool's Day, the steamer *Santa Clara* set sail from Seattle, carrying the Thomas Flyer and its four-man crew, one hundred railroad construction workers, forty-five other passengers, and a load of steel rail. The steel rail and the construction workers were bound for Cordova, Alaska, where a 196-mile railroad was being built to Kennecott.

Wearing his gold braid uniform, Captain Hansen wasted no time in finding the most prominent man aboard: a man named Robinson, an assistant to railroad builder Mike Heney. Heney was working for the Guggenheim interests on a railroad that would connect the coastal town of Cordova with the huge copper deposits inland at Kennecott. Robinson knew the crew on the ship and introduced Hansen, MacAdam, Miller, and Schuster to the officers. The racers ate with Robinson at the captain's table.[16]

MacAdam was stunned to learn that a woman who was also invited to dine at the captain's table lived out of wedlock with a saloonkeeper in Alaska. The chief engineer on the vessel set the correspondent straight on the social graces of the far north. "Wait until you get up to Alaska and you won't be surprised any longer. They don't ask the business of anyone, man or woman, up there. Let me tell you this

about Alaska: it's a hard, cruel country—a place where no one stays because he wants to. They may tell you different, but they're all sticking it out in the hopes of making a 'strike' and then it's back to the states for them. Women are scarce, real wives scarcer. It's a place where life is too hard to bother about social niceties. Anything goes."[17]

The ship's captain plotted a course off the coast of British Columbia, along the east side of Vancouver Island. At noon the second day, Captain Hansen released two of the carrier pigeons. The message read: "On board S.S. *Santa Clara*. One day out from Seattle. Greetings from the Thomas Flyer in the New York to Paris race." He released the messengers and waited for them to soar over the ship, gain their bearings, and beat it back to Seattle.

Leaving their cages, the birds flew up and took a position on one of the ship's cargo cranes, where they stopped. Hansen and other passengers coaxed and yelled, but the pigeons wouldn't budge. Finally one flew off a little way before it was attacked and killed by three or four gulls, MacAdam said. A crestfallen Hansen agreed that the other pigeons should stay in their cages.

For long-distance communications, the Thomas crew would have to be content with the less romantic government telegraph system in Alaska. A decade earlier it had taken six months to get a message delivered from the Yukon River to Washington, D.C. The influx of people to Nome and other boom towns had created an urgent need for better communications. To speed messages to and from the north-land, by 1904 the U.S. Army installed an extensive system of overland telegraph lines and undersea cable. The Washington-Alaska Military Cable and Telegraph system would allow the racers to send telegraph messages to New York from nine points between Valdez and Nome.[18]

Like the pigeons, however, the telegraph system was not completely reliable. An earthquake had damaged the undersea cable off the Alaska coast, and heavy snow had knocked out the land lines through Canada. Telegraph communications ceased while crews set out to repair the downed lines in Canada.

As the *Santa Clara* headed through the open waters of the North Pacific, heavy winds and high seas battered the ship. MacAdam and most of the other passengers stayed in their beds. He said it was like being turned over and over inside a barrel on a lopsided merry-go-round. On his first day of seasickness, MacAdam forgot to wind a watch he was carrying that was set to New York time. It was a cheap watch and he was unable to change the time, but he kept it so that "a glance at this watch and I can tell just what the boys are doing back in Times Square." When he left his bed long enough to see that the watch had stopped, he tossed it into the Pacific.

MacAdam was flat on his back most of the way to Alaska. All he saw outside his porthole was snow, hail, and seawater. "It was during these days of seasickness that Chief Engineer Hare showed his kindness. Every day—sometimes two and three times a day—he would drop first into one, then into the other staterooms occupied by the Thomas crew," MacAdam wrote. "To a man lying hour after hour in his bunk, nothing to do but watch his clothes on the hook-racks swinging with each roll of the ship, like too many pendulums, or watch the sea and the sky alternate in filling the square of his stateroom window, the Chief's visits were welcome oases in an otherwise desolate stretch of time. The Chief has not only the gift of the storyteller, but also a remarkably rare collection of stories—mostly of the smoking room variety."[19]

Schuster had been given a copy of *From Peking to Paris in a Motorcar* by Luigi Barzini. He read a little of it on the way to Alaska and noted that he and Prince Borghese were both thirty-five when they took their epic drives. Schuster had other reading material as well—a 20-page letter prepared by E. M. West of the *New York Times* sports staff. West did not know how to drive a car, but his report outlined why it was feasible to pilot one across Alaska. West, who went into advertising in later years, helped coordinate the race coverage.

West relied heavily in his report upon the statements of various experts and upon field research conducted by John Klein, the *Times* man who had gone to Alaska in January. Klein, a journeyman who had covered the Boer War and worked for various New York newspapers in his career, had made the arrangements to ship gasoline to roadhouses between Valdez and Fairbanks. Based on his report to New York, the *Times* said that when the race reached western Alaska, one hundred Indians would probably have to be hired to pack down the snow with snowshoes on a ninety-mile stretch.[20]

Klein said the cars should be stripped down to the essentials and that the motorists should carry as much gas as they could manage. In roadhouses spaced about twenty miles apart on the trail to Fairbanks, meals and sleeping accommodations could be had for about four dollars a day. Klein, who said he traveled part of the way to Fairbanks, interviewed more than fifty freighters, miners, businessmen, and others about trail conditions. He said the racers could expect a solid trail out of Valdez if they reached Alaska by late March.[21] With the Thomas now set to arrive in the second week of April, the motorists wondered if they were too late.

The ship made its first stop at Cordova, southeast of Valdez, to deliver the railroad steel. The construction of the Copper River and

Northwestern Railway had attracted thousands of workers to the town and made Cordova the hub of south-central Alaska early in the century. The Thomas crew hurried ashore, glad to be back on solid ground. Chief Hare, who had entertained the men aboard ship, did the same on land. He led them on a mile-and-a-half walk to the heart of Cordova. MacAdam said the town had nine dance halls, two general supply stores, and a shoemaker. "Chief Hare led the way around a huge heap of beer kegs that lay tumbled in the street, symbol of the city's chief activity," MacAdam wrote.

The Thomas crew dropped in on a dance where a three-piece orchestra provided the entertainment and the roughly dressed men paid a dollar to dance with one of the ladies. MacAdam and Hansen were soon gliding over the dance floor.

At 1:00 a.m. the Thomas crew headed back to the ship, accompanied by several leading citizens of Cordova. George Miller answered what MacAdam called the "three inevitable questions. How fast can she go? How many horsepower has she? How much does she weigh?" After the Cordovans left and the ship set sail, MacAdam looked over copies of newspaper articles he had received from the editor of the Cordova paper. The articles about the trail to Fairbanks told of fatal and near-fatal accidents and mentioned that the trail was breaking up early.

At 3:00 p.m. the following day the ship arrived in Valdez. MacAdam said the entire population turned out to welcome the first car ever seen in this part of Alaska and its four crewmen. The shopkeepers, laborers, and dance hall musicians in the city's brass band could be heard from aboard ship as the *Santa Clara* neared the port. A whistle from the town's steam laundry heralded the occasion.

As soon as the ship tied up at the dock, a mad scramble began. Men and boys climbed over the side, while women went up the

The crew of the Thomas Flyer arrives in Valdez, Alaska, on April 8, 1908. Seated at the wheel is driver George Schuster. To his left is mechanic George Miller. Standing in the rear of the car, wearing a fur coat, is Captain Hans Hansen. The man seated to his right is George MacAdam of the *New York Times*. (COURTESY OF GEORGE T. MACADAM)

gangway. One of the hundreds of people at the dock was a boy named Norman Brown, who as an adult became publisher of the *Anchorage Daily News*. "I was only 6, but the arrival of the car was the biggest thing that had ever happened," he said.[22] One of the notables meeting the ship was a man called Red Bill, who had a thick mass of red hair that reached below his shoulders. A supporter of William Jennings Bryan, Red Bill had vowed in 1896 that he would not cut his hair until Bryan was elected president. Twelve

years later Bryan was still running for president and Red Bill was still waiting for a haircut.

After leaving the ship, the Thomas Flyer traveled two hundred feet under its own power to a warehouse, where it would stay while the crew investigated Valdez. The men walked along a street where a narrow sleigh track cut through long snowdrifts that varied from three to twelve feet in height. "The houses almost without exception are one-story frame buildings without exterior grace or ornament," MacAdam said later. "They bear most impressive testimony to the fact that Alaska is not a land of permanent homes, but a place to tolerate until the lucky 'strike' has been made."[23]

The town of about two thousand had two banks, an express office, three good hotels, a daily and a weekly newspaper, telephones, an electric light system, and more snow than any of the men had ever seen. Hemmed in by mountains and glaciers, Valdez measures its winter snowfall in dozens of feet. As warm moist ocean air flows north out of the Pacific, it collides with the Chugach Mountains, making heavy snow almost as predictable as the sunrise.

MacAdam said the snow was so deep that house numbers were of no use. The people in sleighs rode on a level with the rooftops. "Everyone must know his own chimney-top," MacAdam said.[24] More snow was falling as Schuster made arrangements to check on road conditions in a horse-drawn sleigh. The proposed race route followed the 376-mile winter trail to Fairbanks, crossing two mountain ranges, rolling hills, and the broad expanse of the Tanana Valley.

Valdez had been founded on the strength of rumors that it was an "all-American" gateway to the gold fields, and that stampeders could avoid paying Canadian taxes on their belongings. Thousands who tried to cross the Valdez Glacier learned to their sorrow that the rumors were

false. "To the men from the industrial cities it must have seemed like a nightmare," historian Pierre Berton wrote of this episode. The trail to the summit was twenty miles long and so steep in many spots that a block and tackle had to be used. Tortured by snow blindness, exhaustion, scurvy, and poor food, all but a few who tried to cross the glacier gave up and went home. Later, the United States Army bypassed the glacier and cut a trail through Keystone Canyon and over Thompson Pass, creating what became the principal winter route to the center of Alaska.

Dog teams had been used on the trail as early as 1902, when a gold discovery led to the founding of Fairbanks. Completion of the telegraph line and the creation of the Alaska Board of Road Commissioners focused new attention on the need to improve the trail. The president of the board was Major Wilds Preston Richardson, Alaska's most important early road builder and a man with a sense of humor.

A few months before the race, the three-hundred-pound Richardson climbed aboard a horse at a Washington army post to take the fifteen-mile horsemanship test ride that President Roosevelt required of all officers to see that they were in shape: "Just remember, this is a bigger joke on the horse than it is on me," Richardson said.[25]

Richardson supervised construction work on the Valdez-Fairbanks Trail, gradually turning the narrow path for pack animals into a narrow trail for horse-drawn sleighs. Years later, the road to Fairbanks was named in his honor. The Alaska road builder often traveled to Washington, D.C., during the winter months, meeting with congressional committees and military officials.

In late 1907, he returned to the East Coast in time to attend the Army-Navy football game in Philadelphia. Asked about the condition of the trail to Fairbanks, he told the *New York Times* that the cars would face a severe test in Alaska, but not an impossible one.

"It is feasible enough for automobiles to get through Alaska, but it will not be easy," he said. "I am convinced that automobiles can pass over this road without trouble. The stage makes a trip twice each week between Valdez and Tanana, carrying the United States mail and also passengers, while there are freight teams on sleigh runners going over the road at frequent intervals. The snow becomes packed hard and will hold up an automobile."[26]

Aman who worked with Richardson on the road commission, Captain George Pillsbury, disagreed. He said the racers would not get 150 miles beyond Valdez, and that they'd be stopped by the narrow trail, deep snow, and huge chuckholes.[27]

Regular automobile traffic on the trail to Fairbanks was still a decade away, and even then the road commission admitted that much more work remained to be done before "these and other roads throughout the territory can he claimed as automobile roads."[28]

The conflicting views of Richardson and Pillsbury reflected a similar split among the rest of the people of Alaska. Some desperately wanted to believe it was possible for a car to cross the wilderness, because that would help bring progress to the backward territory. Others said the scheme was the work of fools. Attempting to find out if the Bering Strait could be crossed by cars, the *New York Times* wired the editor of the *Nome Nugget* for information. The editor from the gold rush town responded: "Possible to cross. Nome will give every assistance to autos across strait. Gasoline plentiful."[29] The Standard Oil Company said it had sixty-three hundred gallons of gas at Nome and would reserve whatever was needed to keep the cars supplied for the first nine hundred miles through Siberia.

W. H. Maupin, who had carried the mail between Fairbanks and Valdez, said a positive mental attitude would help. "In Alaska it is very

much the same as in other parts of the world. If a man thinks he cannot do a thing and sets out with that belief the chances are that he will fail to accomplish the object," Maupin had told a reporter. "It is not claimed that it will not take work to get through over the Valdez road, but it is absurd to say that autos cannot pass over it."[30]

Meanwhile, representatives of the Thomas, Zust, and de Dion had contacted the manager of the steamship *Corwin*, the first ship to arrive in Nome each year since 1902. Manager L. H. Gray approved a charter to take the cars from Nome to Siberia in early June.

Some newspapers in Alaska and the Yukon derived great amusement from the plan to drive to Nome. The *Weekly Star* in Whitehorse, Yukon Territory, headlined one story about the race: "Foolish Venture, Automobile Cranks Against Hard Proposition." The *Nome Nugget*, on the other hand, acknowledged that there were many skeptics in Nome and elsewhere, but that the city should remember it could get no better advertising than that associated with the race.[31] Nome had at least two cars at that time, one of them a Thomas Flyer that carried people along the beaches in summer.

Even the most optimistic people realized it would be difficult to get to Nome on four wheels, however. Reindeer Bill Huber, an experienced mail driver, said the cars could probably follow the dog teams that pulled loads of four hundred to eight hundred pounds down the Yukon River. Casey Moran, former editor of the *Fairbanks News*, said the hard-packed snow trails were as solid as asphalt. "An auto race through Alaska seems at first absurd, but when I think of it carefully, I believe it is one of those impossible possibilities," Moran said. "To be sure, it would not be a pleasure jaunt, but with the aid of block and tackle to help a car up the steep pitches in the roadbed, it could be done."[32]

As the spring days grew longer, proponents and opponents of the race agreed that time was as much an enemy as the snow and the mountains. Most of the trails in Alaska were usable only in the winter, when the snow was compacted into a hard surface. In the summer, almost nothing moved through the mud and those who traveled did so along the rivers.

In the winter of 1908, more traffic than ever had traveled the trail to Fairbanks. About twelve hundred people made the trip by stage, on foot, or by dog team. Two herds of cattle walked to Fairbanks, giving the miners a supply of fresh beef. Some men pulled their own sleds loaded with one hundred pounds of gear, while four-horse teams hauled sleds piled with two or three tons of everything from nails to eggs.

For many people, the standard means of travel was a horse-drawn sleigh. The sleighs made the run to Fairbanks in about eight days, at a cost of $150 per person. The Ed Orr stage line had 180 horses posted at thirty-nine stations between Fairbanks and Valdez. Occasionally, the sleighs passed a man on a bicycle. Most of the steamers ferrying stampeders during the gold rush days carried bicycles owned by hardy souls who pedaled on the packed snow and frozen rivers.

No one had to remind the men on the Thomas Flyer that unlike a bicycle, it was impossible to pick up a two-ton car and carry it over the rough spots. After what they had seen and heard during their first few hours in Valdez, Schuster, Miller, MacAdam, and Hansen had reason to be glum when they attended an evening reception in the federal courtroom. Songs by the Valdez mandolin club and a piano duet by the Schneider girls did not cheer them up.

Earlier, Schuster and Miller had taken a short trip in Dan Kennedy's horse-drawn sleigh. They realized the snows of Indiana could not

compete with Valdez. "On our little trip on the trail this afternoon we were told that the snow was about six feet over a man's head. It is useless to start a car on that kind of a road. We might get through the streets of Valdez, but not much farther," Schuster said at the reception.[33]

After Schuster revealed his worries, the editor of the *Valdez Prospector* announced that a cable from San Francisco had just arrived: St. Chaffray was ready to ship his car to Valdez. Schuster pledged that the Thomas Flyer would not turn back to Seattle until he was certain that the Alaska journey was impossible.

At 2:00 a.m., he and the others went out to see if dropping night-time temperatures would make the trails hard enough to drive on. The sleigh driver said he would show them a good sample of what the first fifty miles would be like. The worst part of the entire trip would be twenty-five miles outside of Valdez at Thompson Pass, where up to eighty feet of snow has fallen in one winter. The narrow trail was so steep that dog teams and sleighs careened down it at top speed. People on foot did all right only if they stayed on the hard-packed trail. Stepping off into the loose snow was like "falling into an ocean of feathers," as one weary traveler said. The racers had been warned even before they left New York that they would have to take the cars apart to get over the first mountain pass, but the difficulty of that chore didn't sink in until they faced it head-on.

Kennedy took them through the heavy snow to Camp Comfort, a log roadhouse nestled in the woods about ten miles outside of Valdez. Schuster made many measurements of the snow with a stick and checked the width of the trail. The Thomas required at least fifty-six inches to keep from sinking out of sight, but at many points the trail was forty-five inches wide or less. On seven occasions, the men had

to duck to keep their heads from hitting telegraph wires. Off the trail the snow was from five to fifteen feet deep.

The men ate ham and eggs at Camp Comfort and reboarded the sleigh to turn back toward the coast. There was no longer any need to talk about driving through Alaska: Schuster was convinced it was impossible.

"As the weary crew, spent with its exertions, returned to the town at 10 o'clock in the morning, a raven flashed across the trail and perched on a bare tree nearby," MacAdam said. "It might have croaked 'Nevermore,' and echoed the thoughts of the motorists."[34]

In his dispatch to the *New York Times*, MacAdam suggested that had the Thomas arrived in Alaska a few weeks earlier, it would have had a slim chance of success. An early thaw had weakened the crust of the snow, and the car couldn't have gone more than a mile in the drifts that were melting each day in the sun, he said. Schuster figured the only way to travel would be to take the car apart in small pieces and ship it by dog team. The cost to Fairbanks alone would have been about ten thousand dollars.

Back in Valdez, Schuster booked car and crew on the S.S. *Bertha*, which was preparing to sail to Seattle. Before leaving, he tried to drive the Thomas off the wharf and into Valdez, to be able to say that he had at least driven through the town. But the slippery, snow-covered pier was so narrow and dangerous that even this proved impossible. The Thomas crew had to be content to drive two hundred feet back to the ship, ending the shortest car trip ever taken to Alaska.

With Alaska now out of the picture, the sponsors of the contest had a choice: they could call off the rest of the race or change the route once more. They settled on the latter course and permitted the cars to sail across the Pacific and begin the race again in Vladivostok, on

the east coast of Siberia. The *New York Times* editorialized that the experience in Alaska was a "grievous disappointment" and that had the cars reached Alaska earlier in the year, they would have made it to Siberia. The *Times* hastened to say there "is still as good reason as ever for believing that the plan of the New York–Paris race was a practicable one in the sense that it was not doomed to inevitable failure."

According to this view, it was not the snow and ice in Alaska that stopped the Thomas, but the snow in Indiana and the mud in Iowa that delayed the trip to Alaska. The *Times* said there were plenty of valid reasons to keep going, despite the elimination of Alaska. "Nobody should make the mistake of supposing that the importance of the race has been seriously decreased by the enforced crossing of the Pacific from Seattle to Vladivostok instead of from one Bering Strait cape to the other. That this had to be done is a pity, but even now the racers are confronted by many a hundred miles of wild country where an automobile was never yet seen, and if they get to Paris, while they will have accomplished less than they hoped to accomplish, they still will have surpassed all previous achievements."[35]

No one was more disappointed with the change in plans than those in Alaska who had dreamed, in the words of the *Nome Nugget*, that the trip "would have meant that winter traffic throughout interior Alaska would have been revolutionized."[36] "No doubt the original plans would have been carried out but for the fact that so late a start was made from New York," the Nome paper said.

Five years after the race to Paris, the first motorist drove from Valdez to Fairbanks. It soon became a routine journey. Driving to Nome, however, has always been a different matter. Despite decades of discussion, a road to Nome has never been built. Political, financial,

and environmental roadblocks have combined to stop any attempt to complete the automobile trip across Alaska that began on the Valdez dock in 1908.

It seems clear that even if the weather had been colder and the season earlier, the New York–Paris racers would have never made it to the Bering Strait under their own power. And the difficulties in Siberia, where they would have had to travel upwards of one thousand miles between supply points, would have been much greater.

Even without melting trails, driving in Alaska and Siberia would have been far tougher than Indiana, where at least there were railroad lines and where the nearest town was rarely more than a few hours away. Commenting on the failure of the trip to Alaska, the *Alaska-Yukon Magazine* said that the far north was not ready for automobile travel. "Whenever an automobile enthusiast gets to talking about exploring Alaska in a sixty horsepower touring car, or crossing Siberia in a runabout, he is making a gasbag of himself, by which he can much more easily cross these countries as an aeronaut."[37]

At the time the Thomas was in Alaska, the *New York Times* reported somewhat facetiously on the first meeting of the Reed Hollow Earth Exploring Club. "North Pole a Hole; Likewise the South," the headline said. The founder of the club, William Reed, spoke on his theory that the earth was hollow and that the North Pole didn't exist. He believed it was a one-thousand-mile-wide hole that could lead explorers to the center of the earth, where the climate was warm and valuable minerals were waiting to be discovered.[38] Reed's ridiculous theory of "the hole in the pole" and the race to Paris both testified to the state of geographic knowledge in 1908. The technological revolution heralded by the airplane had yet to achieve full speed. When it did, people gained an increased

understanding of the outer reaches of the world and a more realistic view of the planet.

During the depths of winter in Alaska, even today's cars are subject to frequent mechanical breakdowns, and it is almost impossible to start them without electrically heating the engine when the temperature falls to twenty below zero. The weather is unpredictable and severe. During March in the interior of Alaska, no one goes anywhere in an open car. With all the advances in technology, however, a popular winter race across Alaska has become a highlight of the year for many people: the eleven-hundred-mile Iditarod Trail Sled Dog Race from Anchorage to Nome relies on what the decades have shown to be the ideal method of cross-country winter travel.

EIGHT

AN ACT OF SPLENDID FOLLY

WORD THAT THE Thomas Flyer had been coldly rejected by the snow in Alaska didn't faze the Commissionaire General, who told reporters in Seattle that he would head north anyway. "I have said there is no French word like 'impossible' and I meant it as far as trying to cross Alaska is concerned," he said.[1]

St. Chaffray talked of shipping his car to Skagway and sending it north over the White Pass Railroad to the Yukon River. The drive from there to the Bering Sea would have been one thousand miles longer than the Valdez route and far more difficult, but he wasn't worried. "The honor is not alone in getting to Paris first," he said. "It is in trying to pass places where others have failed and if you succeed your glory and honor is all the greater."

About an hour later, St. Chaffray decided that *impossible* was a French word after all. It turned out to be an Italian and German word, too.

St. Chaffray and the crew of the Zust booked their cars for Japan, where they would make connections for Vladivostok.

"We have cold feet. Our feet are cold because there is no more ice nor snow at the end of April in Alaska. We wanted ice, expected

snow, and all is over," the Commissionaire General said after boarding the steamship *Aki-Maru*.[2]

Scarfoglio said he was disappointed about bypassing Alaska and would have waited until the next winter in Valdez if the decision were his. "We are told that we should not have got beyond the Bering Strait and that we should hardly have been the narrators of our adventure. That would matter little. We had set out to perpetuate an act of splendid folly, not to open up a new way for men. We wished to be madmen, not pioneers."[3]

As St. Chaffray and Scarfoglio headed to Japan and the Thomas Flyer sailed back to Seattle, Lieutenant Koeppen gave up on driving across the United States. Of all the racers, Godard included, Koeppen had the most trouble keeping his car on the road.

On two occasions the Protos had to be taken by train from western Utah back to Ogden for repairs. Koeppen then decided to change directions and head northwest through Idaho. When the car broke down again, Koeppen shipped the Protos from Pocatello to Seattle by train.[4] To make matters worse for Koeppen, his driver was ill and had to return home to Chicago. Koeppen wired Berlin and asked that two mechanics meet him in Vladivostok and that they bring spare tires and extra parts.

Koeppen said he had no regrets about the money or time spent on the race. "It was not that the French proposed the New York–Paris auto trip that led me to engage in it," he said in his Seattle hotel. "It was the love of the sport and when I am finished my fortune is finished also. Yet I have my salary as an officer in the German army and I am content."[5]

The Americans believed that Koeppen should have been disqualified for taking the train, just as Baron Godard was. Koeppen said St.

Chaffray had told him it was all right, and cables from Paris confirmed that ruling. "It appears that this is a race in which everyone makes his own rules," the *Seattle Times* commented.

According to newspaper reports, Koeppen said he would continue in the race, but would not compete for any prize because of his railroad journey. Either those reports were inaccurate or Koeppen later changed his mind because when the race resumed in Vladivostok, the Protos was back in the running as a full-fledged contestant.[6]

The Americans, meanwhile, had left Valdez on April 9 on the steamship *Bertha*, hoping to reach Seattle before they fell too far off the pace. The ship's captain caught the spirit of the contest and made a record trip across the Gulf of Alaska to Juneau. The ship steamed through the protected waters of the Inside Passage toward Seattle. There were few lighthouses, beacons, or buoys, which meant that seamen navigated by dead reckoning through narrow channels where land was usually in sight. Sudden storms and low clouds could blot out familiar landmarks in an instant, however, creating extreme hazards to navigation.

While traveling through the Wrangell Narrows, a particularly dangerous stretch that had to be taken at high tide, Captain Olsen of the *Bertha* had to drop anchor twice to wait for snow squalls to end. While trying to steam through the tail end of the second squall, he nearly ended the race for himself and the Thomas Flyer. "The Captain, who was on the bridge, rang for full speed astern. He just saved jamming the *Bertha*'s nose hard on the rocks and adding her name to the long nautical obituary list of these waters. The *Bertha* passed the hulls of three vessels wrecked during the past two years, gaunt reminders of the dangers of navigation in these waters. Almost every point and reef has its story of shipwreck," MacAdam wrote.[7]

The ship's wireless operator tried repeatedly to contact a West Coast port to obtain news of the race. Schuster and his crew had heard nothing about their competitors and the anxiety was nerve-wracking. The operator finally raised Victoria, British Columbia, and learned that the French and Italians had left for Japan.

The Thomas company had acted to salvage what it could of the trip to Alaska by declaring victory. The company said it deserved the cup that *Le Matin* had promised the winner. E. R. Thomas said the original rules specified that the car that went the farthest north would be the winner if the excursion to Alaska and Siberia had to be called off. Thomas asked that his car be given a fourteen-day allowance over the others because it made the trip to Alaska and lost the nearly one-thousand-mile lead it had built on the run across the United States.[8]

Thomas said the Italians and French had violated the race rules by shipping across the Pacific without trying to go to Alaska. He added that the Germans had violated the race rules by taking the train to Seattle. That meant the world cup belonged in Buffalo, according to Thomas. One compelling reason to claim victory was that the stakes in the contest were rising every day. Eddie Thomas said it now appeared the race would cost the company $100,000. "It cost us $1,200 alone to find out the width of the snow trails in Alaska," Eddie said. "We are out to win."[9]

The time lost on the trip to Alaska made the foreign racers more competitive with the Thomas Flyer—and more suspect in the eyes of the E. R. Thomas Motor Company. The backers of the American car believed in the sentiment expressed by the "America against the World" banner at the firm's New York City dealership. A company official wrote to MacAdam that the French, Italians, and Germans "will not hesitate to resort to any means to cripple you." He warned MacAdam

to purchase padlocks and other necessary parts to lock the hood of the car at night. That would stop anyone from tampering with the engine. The company also requested that someone sleep in the car to prevent sabotage.[10]

"Above all, do not forget what I said about trusting foreigners," Commercial Manager E. C. Morse reminded MacAdam. "Of course, we do not look upon Captain Hansen as a foreigner, and personally I believe he will be absolutely square with you."[11]

Schuster, Miller, and MacAdam were getting along well, but relations between Schuster and Hansen were strained. Schuster didn't like Hansen because the Norwegian was interested in being a celebrity. MacAdam was called on to keep the peace. Morse said there may have been some "feeling" against the captain, "but in the main I think you will agree that it would have been a mistake not to have accepted his proposition" and include him in the crew.[12]

Another reason for the friction was that Hansen, who always wanted more money, could never extract any extra dollars or sympathy from Schuster or the company.

"Please explain to Mr. Schuster that the advance of $100 per month to Captain Hansen was also to cover his living expense. If he (Hansen) is not satisfied with this, then we will go back to the original agreement, which was to pay his expenses. I think with a little diplomacy you can arrange this satisfactorily," Morse told MacAdam.

In addition to his diplomatic duties, MacAdam wrote a daily story for the *New York Times*, served as press agent for the crew, and took pictures. The hot air artist had purchased a new camera for $218 and spent every spare minute learning how to work it. The publicity-conscious company wanted photographs showing the Thomas Flyer in action. The race photographs taken earlier in the race did not

measure up to what the people in Buffalo wanted. "The artist in most all cases seems to have failed to grasp the idea that what we wanted to do was to show the terrible and unusual conditions which the car had to encounter," a company official wrote to MacAdam just after the return from Alaska.[13]

Schuster wanted to leave Seattle on the same ship with Koeppen for Vladivostok, but the Russian bureaucracy intervened. The Americans picked up their passports at the Seattle Post Office. The large single sheets of heavy paper did not require a photograph, but had blanks for information about "age, stature, forehead, eyes, nose, mouth, chin, hair, complexion and face," as well as a request from the United States State Department that the bearer be given safe and free passage. The Russians required a visa with this document, but the nearest Russian consul was in San Francisco.

The consul refused to travel to Seattle despite an offer from the Thomas company to pay whatever he asked. The only alternative was to sail to Yokohama, get the visas, drive through Japan, and catch a steamer to Vladivostok.[14]

The Americans had led the way across the United States, but when the S.S. *Shawmut* hoisted its anchor, the crew of the Thomas Flyer found themselves in last place, trailing the Italians, French, and Germans. Schuster figured he would have to make up eleven days to take the lead in Siberia. But he believed the other cars were so heavily loaded that he would be able to surpass them. Captain Hansen, as usual, was confident: "We will reach Paris first," the captain said. "And when we do there will be a popping of corks that will be heard clear to Seattle."[15]

By this time the Zust and the de Dion were far out to sea on a small Japanese steamer that battled fog and then high winds on its

The American crew aboard the S.S. *Shawmut* on their way to Japan. From left are: Captain Hans Hansen, George Miller, George MacAdam, and George Schuster. (COURTESY OF GEORGE T. MACADAM)

way across the Pacific. Every night an old German woman, one of about twenty passengers on the *Aki-Maru*, played the ship's piano for entertainment, "destroying all the pleasure of the day," as Scarfoglio put it.[16]

She stayed away from the keys the fourth night out from Seattle, however, for one of the dozen Japanese passengers was near death from consumption. He had come to the United States in 1900 to seek his fortune, but he wanted to go home to die. Scarfoglio said the man died slowly, "like a lamp in which the oil had run low." After twelve days at sea, he perished. The ship's crew wrapped his body in a large Japanese flag and placed his revolver and knife in his violet silk belt.

The ship arrived in Yokohama three days later. At midnight a small boat approached the vessel, and an old woman boarded. She was looking for her son, who was booked on the steamer. A Japanese

officer told the woman her son had been buried at sea at 43 degrees, 53 minutes north latitude and 155 degrees, 39 minutes east longitude. The woman took the slip of paper containing the burial site coordinates and departed.[17]

Yokohama was a fishing village that had become Japan's principal port for foreign trade in the latter part of the nineteenth century. Scarfoglio said the city was beautiful by night, but by day it was as horrible as any settlement he had seen in America. "It is an ugly, wretched, European provincial town, with narrow streets, peripatetic sellers of matches and obscene photographs, policemen and mendicants; a vulgar, banal city, without electric light, without tramways, without elegant women; a town which fills the soul with disgust immediately," he said.

The Italian also concluded that the Japanese were not creative or imaginative because they were an island people. He said the influence of Europe "has passed over their minds like the water of a brook over a polished stone, without leaving any trace."[18]

Foreign analysts with more knowledge of Japan realized that Scarfoglio had it wrong. Japan's military victories against China in 1895 and against Russia a decade later had shown it was a nation to reckon with. But the Italian was not one to recognize the subtle points of foreign affairs. He was exasperated with the great effort it took to secure a permit to drive through Japan. The precious document required "one hundred different signatures, twenty schemes, thirty journeys, numerous yen and eight days' time." He finally found something to be cheerful about when the journalists at the Hotel de Paris said farewell in English. They spared him the "rhetorical banalities on the theme of Amerigo Vespucci and Christopher Columbus to which we were invariably treated at the end of every banquet in America."[19]

St. Chaffray and his two crew members were also in Yokohama with the Italians. The Commissionaire General was depressed and gloomy. He had learned that the Marquis de Dion, owner of the French car, wanted nothing more to do with the contest. St. Chaffray had few options, but he wanted to find a way to stay in the race. "Hence the three brave Frenchmen were wandering through Yokohama, worried, hungry, but steadfast. They will go on living by selling postcards, fortune telling or anything, but will drive on to Paris or die in the attempt," Scarfoglio said.[20]

The Marquis de Dion reportedly said that with the change in route, there was no point in going through the expense of continuing the race. De Dion, nearly as important a figure in France as Henry Ford was to become in the United States, now maintained that there was little to be gained by repeating much of a route that had already been traversed by ten-horsepower de Dion cars the year before in the Peking-to-Paris trip.[21]

He didn't mention that the de Dion's poor showing in the United States had embarrassed the French auto industry. As the editor of *Les Sports* put it, one of the best French cars had been beaten by "second rank" cars from the United States, Italy, and Germany. He said it was "deplorable to the name of France," even though the fault did not lie with the machinery. "The American car has triumphed because its ignorant, ill-equipped and unskilled rivals have had breakdown after breakdown," said Georges Prade.[22]

Despite the bad news from Paris, St. Chaffray set off through Japan, a three hundred-mile journey along narrow farm roads, compact villages, and steep mountain trails. It was a sharp departure from the wide-open spaces of America. Japan was a nation of ox-carts and rickshaws, with bamboo bridges built for pedestrians or small carts.

Scarfoglio described how the cars crossed one bridge that was so flimsy it shook when a child ran over it. The bridge tender was anxious when he heard the news that St. Chaffray and Scarfoglio were going to drive huge cars across his bridge. He demanded twenty yen in advance. "They will, at least, buy some flowers to cast upon the tomb of his poor bridge," Scarfoglio said.[23]

The crews stripped down the cars to the essentials, removing spare tires, extra gas tanks, supplies, and rear seats. The bridge heaved and bent mightily under the weight and seemed on the verge of collapse. Both cars made it over, but the supports for the last arch fell apart as the Zust pulled onto solid ground. The bridge tender and a small crowd watched the supports wash away in the three-foot-deep stream.

The racers stopped to calm their nerves and eat. Scarfoglio said that for the first time he was able to swallow raw fish "without experiencing an excessive amount of disgust." He said it tasted like soap. St. Chaffray remained disgusted.

The trip to Tsuruga concluded with a mountainous passage and an all-night drive by the two crews. The Zust followed the de Dion through the darkness, Scarfoglio occasionally searching at intersections to find the tracks of St. Chaffray's car. Scarfoglio said there was a sharp drop on one side of the road down to the ocean and a steep cliff on the other side. At daybreak the motorists spotted the port and put the two cars in a temple courtyard. They boarded a ship for Vladivostok and arrived in the Siberian port May 15.

Chasing after them was George Schuster and crew on the Thomas Flyer. The eighteen-day Pacific voyage for the Thomas crew had been calm, except for a two-day storm. Schuster, who was skeptical of Hansen and everything the Norwegian said, was not convinced that the captain would be of any use in Siberia. In a covert test of Hansen's

navigational abilities, Schuster asked the ship's first officer to invite Hansen to take the sextant readings on the voyage, as a professional courtesy from one mariner to another. "He reported to me later that Hansen was OK. He knew his stuff," Schuster wrote.[24]

The men walked the deck for exercise on the cold voyage and played catch with a twenty-pound bag of sand to stay in shape for Siberia. There were only four other passengers in addition to the Thomas crew on the *Shawmut*. Schuster checked on the car down in the hold and discovered that some of the Chinese crewmen had cut away the leather aprons that had replaced the metal fenders. They used the material to create new soles for their sandals. The ship's carpenter made new aprons from canvas.

Good news awaited the Thomas upon its arrival in Japan. The other cars had been ordered to wait for the American car to reach Vladivostok. In addition, the French race committee in charge of the contest had granted the Thomas a fifteen-day lead because of its trip to Alaska. The German Protos was penalized a like amount for the train trip from Idaho to Seattle. That meant the Thomas could be a month behind the Germans and two weeks behind the other cars, but still win the race.

Another announcement from Paris said that with the cancellation of the trip through Alaska and northern Siberia, the *Matin-Times* cup that had been promised to the winner was officially withdrawn. The scaled-down race evidently did not merit the Coupe du Monde. The race sponsors offered three new cash prizes of 240 pounds, 120 pounds, and 40 pounds for the first three cars to reach Paris.[25]

At Yokohama, the arrival of the racers had touched off a betting spree among European and American residents, much like the one that had marked the start of the race in New York. MacAdam heard of bets of up to one thousand dollars on the Thomas. He said that

American residents of Yokohama knew all about the race and that old copies of the *New York Times* were much in demand at the foreigners' clubs.

A lengthy report sent by MacAdam to the *Times* and comments by Schuster reflected some of the same racial prejudice displayed by Scarfoglio. MacAdam said that the crew of the Thomas entered Japan believing that the anti-Japanese talk they had heard on the Pacific Coast was justified. The officers on the *Shawmut* had told them the Japanese were "cocky, insolent, dishonest and American-haters."[26]

The United States and Japan had come close to war in 1906 because of the segregation of Japanese children in a San Francisco school. Relations between the two nations remained strained. While the race was in progress, an agreement was approved to restrict Japanese immigration to the United States. And a fleet of sixteen United States Navy ships was on a world tour because President Roosevelt wanted to show the Japanese that he wanted the status quo maintained in the Pacific. "I do not believe there will be war with Japan, but I do believe there is enough chance of war to make it eminently wise to insure against it by building such a navy as to forbid Japan's hoping for success," Roosevelt said.[27]

In one generation, Japan had catapulted from a feudal state to an industrial nation, but the world remained uneasy about the new power in the Pacific. MacAdam said the Japanese in the big seaports of Yokohama and Kobe did not behave in a friendly manner.

"These Japs seem afraid to yield even an inch on the sidewalk lest they be not properly asserting their new-found national importance," he said. However, when the racers arrived in what MacAdam called the "real Japan—the Japan that is as yet untainted by foreign influence," they were treated with unfailing courtesy and kindness.

Schuster said that aside from the bamboo bridges and steep mountain passes, he had no complaints about Japan. "The kindly hospitality of the natives caused forgetfulness of all the difficulties, leaving only the memory of the good time spent in crossing the land of the little brown man."[28]

After arriving in Kobe, the crew of the Thomas went to the Oriental Hotel, where they looked like "tourists given over to the eccentricity of patronizing first-class hotels dressed in third-class clothes," MacAdam wrote.[29] About a dozen American bankers and businessmen who lived in Kobe gathered around the bar to discuss race strategy. None of the group had firsthand experience, but most of the foreign residents said they didn't know if it was possible to make the trip in a car. The Zust and de Dion had taken a more northerly route. "I've heard that there are a number of precipitous mountain ranges between here and Tsuruga and I'm uncertain if anything leads over them but trails," one bystander said.

Charles Mancini, a Kobe shipbroker who had lived in Japan for eleven years and owned two of the city's six automobiles, volunteered to guide the Thomas crew to Kyoto. Having driven from Yokohama to Kobe and from Moji to Kobe, he knew the local conditions. Mancini and the local representative of the Hong Kong and Shanghai Bank joined the four others in the crowded car the next morning at 6:00 a.m. Leaving Kobe, they passed a golf course and a race course. Soon they reached Sannomiya, where Schuster squeezed the car down a typical village street. The path was about eight feet wide cluttered with children, merchandise, animals, and carts. "When the automobile suddenly appeared at the entrance of this lane, stopping it up almost as tight as a cork stops a bottle, there was a great scurrying," MacAdam said.

"Those who were in the street ran indoors, the women stopping just long enough to seize their children, the shopkeepers to gather up their merchandise; those who were indoors rushed to the house front to see what manner of strange thing was causing such a commotion; cartmen frantically backed their horse and bullock carts into side alleys; and then as the machine slowly passed, women, children, shopkeepers, cartmen, all flocked from their havens of safety and trailed along behind, their wooden sandals making a clatter that could be heard above the unmuffled chug-chugging of the motor."[30]

Driving through the villages gave the motorists a closeup glimpse at Japanese life. The car moved slowly down the narrow streets, sometimes just inches away from the screens of oiled paper in front of the houses on each side. "In the daytime these are slid back so that everything stands open to view—exactly like the front of a doll's house. To the traveler through one of these streets, the entire life and industry of the village passes in panoramic review on either side," MacAdam said.

He saw shopkeepers seated on yellow mats of rice straw, drinking tea with customers. He also inspected miniature gardens filled with bright flowers. When the car came to a sharp corner, Schuster had to back up and make several attempts to complete the turn, "as close-fitting an operation as that of putting on a pair of tight gloves," MacAdam said.

The route across central Japan took them through Osaka, which MacAdam labeled the Pittsburgh of Japan for its growing industrial activity. "The old hand labor of Japan has here been superseded by the machine labor of the Western World. High brick chimneys belching thick clouds of smoke dominate the horizon. Osaka is one of the scenic blots, now rapidly growing in number, on the face of old Japan," MacAdam said.

The Thomas Flyer is loaded on a flatboat at a Japanese harbor before being hauled aboard a ship bound for Vladivostok. (*OUTING*)

Beyond Osaka the racers found a taste of old Japan on a highway that cut a narrow line through one-acre farms. Some fields sprouted green barley plants, while others bloomed with the pale yellow flowers of mustard. Flowering azaleas along the roadside, houses with white walls and red-tiled roofs, and the bright kimonos worn by the Japanese girls left a lasting impression on MacAdam. "I have traveled in but one other country that is so gayly colored," he joked, "the land of primary colors."

The farm roads were only a few inches wider than the car, which meant that whenever an ox-cart approached from the opposite direction, the cart's driver had to drop a wheel into one of the deep drainage ditches on either side of the path. Pedestrians and cartmen usually refused to move out of the way, and sometimes even blasts on the horn and shouts failed to get the message across. Like the people in the car, the cartmen assumed they had the right of way. The village bridges had as much spring to them as any mattress advertised in the

back of a magazine, MacAdam said. Whenever the Thomas came to one of these, only the driver would remain in the car. Upon reaching the other side, someone would always shout: "All aboard for Paris."[31]

On the road outside of Kyoto, merchants spread their wares on the ground in front of their shops. Because rain threatened, awnings had been hung over the merchandise. This didn't leave enough room for the car, so Hansen and MacAdam jumped out and brusquely swept aside the goods, so that the car's wheels didn't destroy them. "To try to help the shopkeepers straighten out their tumbled wares would have been useless," MacAdam said, "So not without a twinge of conscience, we continued our disturbing course. And in the entire length of that street, not an angry word, not even a frown."

MacAdam may have been right that the shopkeepers didn't mind their goods being tossed in a heap, but it's more likely that the tradesmen kept their emotions under wraps, as is the Japanese custom.

At a crossroads beyond the village of Yasu, the racers encountered a priest dressed in a gaudy costume, followed by twenty young people wearing white tunics and carrying a large wooden shrine. The Thomas passed that procession without incident and Hansen even asked if he could take a picture of the priest in the car, which he did. Around the next corner, Schuster slowed down as a crowd filled the street from one side to the other. Several men shook their fists at the car and screamed. One man came within striking distance before being pulled back by others. The Japanese guide said the men had drank too much sake and did not want to see a car on the same road as their religious procession. MacAdam wrote later of a night spent at a Japanese inn in the village of Maibara. Villagers crowded around to watch the men remove each other's wet, muddy boots. "These little tugs-of-war, resulting in muddied hands and exposure of holey socks, made the

George Miller fills the radiator of the Thomas Flyer, as a crowd of Japanese villagers watch the operation closely. (*OUTING*)

crowd shake with laughter," MacAdam said. After taking their boots off, they walked on a floor as slippery as glare ice and "cut some strange antics" before sitting down to eat.

After consulting with local experts, who measured the car and decided the regular trail would be too narrow, the Thomas crew took a seventy-mile detour in central Japan. The recommended route was treacherous enough. Schuster couldn't see the edges of the trail beneath the running boards, and pedestrians had no problem keeping up with the car. As many as two hundred people from several villages walked behind it at one point, but by evening all but about forty of them had gone home. As the trail climbed into mountainous territory, about thirty people pulled on a rope and ten others lifted the driving wheels on the increasingly steep and sharp corners.

The men spent the night in a house on the mountaintop and asked that the villagers return the next morning to help them descend by reversing the process. The rope was tied to the rear axle and the

Japanese lifted first the front axle and then the rear axle over the corners. When the car returned to flat ground, Schuster gave fifty yen to the men, the equivalent of twenty-five dollars, and bid them goodbye.

Shortly before arriving at Tsuruga, where the S.S. *Mongolia* waited to take the car and crew to Siberia, Schuster pulled into the village of Takefu to buy more gasoline. The mayor met them and spoke to the translator, S. R. Ito. The mayor said that this was the first, and probably the last chance, that anyone in his remote village would ever have to see an automobile. "He asks if the honorable gentlemen will be so courteous as to travel through the main street of the town, so that all may see," Ito said.

Schuster complied with the request and took a quick tour through the town, which was bedecked with banners, streamers, and lanterns for a religious festival. The men sat back in their seats, smoked cigars, and enjoyed the scenery until they reached the ship.

They had driven 350 miles to cross the ninety-mile-wide island. Mindful of the Thomas company's instructions about playing up the obstacles overcome by the car, MacAdam wired the *New York Times*: "We do not know yet what awaits us at Vladivostok, but have lost none of the confidence which we had when we arrived back in Seattle and found our opponents had gained a week's start on us by sailing to Japan while we were still en route back from Alaska. We believe, however, that the car is fully equal to its task, no matter what we may find."[32]

The S.S. *Mongolia* sailed at 4 p.m. on May 16. MacAdam wrote that there was great interest in the race among the cosmopolitan crowd on board the ship. The correspondent filled his pocket-sized notebooks with his observations, writing in a neat, precise script. At first, he

wrote with a fountain pen in black ink. At times, he had to forego that luxury and write in pencil. MacAdam usually referred to himself as *Times* in his notebooks, in which he gathered the raw material for his reports to New York. Some stories never got into print except in his notebooks, such as the difficulty he faced in getting a drink on the ship to Vladivostok. MacAdam had gone to a room that looked like the proper lounge, but when he ordered a cognac the waiter paid no attention. He repeated himself three times. Finally, an officer motioned that MacAdam should go down a deck to see the bushy-haired chief steward. The correspondent was led into a room with plain tables and chairs with no backs.

"Times realized flannel shirt had caused him be taken for steerage passenger. Motioned to sit down. Did so. After 15 minutes wait concluded too long for even steerage passenger. Went on deck, discovered smoking room," MacAdam said.[33]

There he found Captain Hansen, enjoying a drink. "Cap, you're right," MacAdam said. "A man must have a uniform here in Russia. I think I'll get one myself." The captain brushed a speck off his gold lace on his shoulders and replied, "You want to be sure you have a right to wear one."

"I'll send for a volunteer fireman's uniform," MacAdam answered. "I once held the bottom of a ladder at a Tarrytown fire."[34]

NINE

THE SIBERIAN EXPRESS

ON MONDAY, MAY 18, the Thomas Flyer and its crew arrived in Vladivostok aboard the S.S. *Mongolia*, setting the stage for the final stretch in the race around the world. After a long wait, customs officials cleared the car for landing. Hansen, Schuster, Miller, and MacAdam lowered their bags over the ship's side to waiting sampans, then slid down ropes and went ashore.

The Germans, Italians, and French had arrived several days earlier. The visitors said the city had muddy roads, white houses, and legions of military men. It looked like an armed camp. As might have been expected, Scarfoglio did not like what he saw. "Vladivostok is ugly, tremendously ugly, dirty, inelegant and useless. What is the good of it today and why does it exist? We are told that it is the focus of the trans-Siberian Railway. But had that famous line, which has served and serves no purpose except to frighten the Mongolian horses in the deserts of Transbaikalia, any need of a focus?"[1]

In the Italian's mind at least, the answer was obvious. Vladivostok's main street had cobblestones, but every side street was a muddy morass. There were new buildings in the city of nearly ninety thousand, but so many were decaying rapidly, MacAdam said, that Vladivostok

presented an incongruous sight, like a "youngster, bald and toothless."

Others who visited the city in that era believed Vladivostok was best viewed from the water. Norwegian polar explorer Fridtjof Nansen said he could scarcely conceive of a more beautiful setting than the terraced slopes that stretched down to the sea. "It reminds one a good deal of Naples; of course, there is here no Vesuvius in the background, but to make up for it there is this beautiful harbor and all the islands outside," Nansen said.[2]

The geography of the region helped explain much of its recent history. Vladivostok is on a narrow strip of Russian territory that extends like a finger along Manchuria's eastern border. Although nearly blocked off from the rest of the country, Vladivostok was Russia's principal port on the Pacific. The harbor froze over in winter, but icebreakers managed to keep a channel open for larger ships even in the coldest months.

Vladivostok's shortcomings had helped spur a Russian drive for a greater presence in the Far East. The Russians had occupied Manchuria during the 1900 Boxer Rebellion, ostensibly to protect the nine-hundred-mile railroad they had built across Chinese territory; the railroad connected Vladivostok with the rest of the empire. The tsar's government had also secured leases from China for two ice-free ports on the Yellow Sea and threatened to move into Korea.

These expansionist dreams gave the Japanese nightmares, for the island nation had hopes of adding the same territory to its domain. Early on a Sunday morning in 1904, while most of the Russian military slept, the Japanese attacked, laying siege to Port Arthur, an ice-free port leased by the Russians from the Chinese. In the battles that followed, Russia fell victim to inefficiency, corruption, and its

dependence on the single-track supply line of the Trans-Siberian Railroad. What remained of Russian naval power on the Pacific was centered in Vladivostok after the 1905 peace treaty.

The Russian defeat was one of many signs foretelling trouble for the imperial government, an inflexible regime still in control, but headed for collapse. Tsar Nicholas II, who assumed power in 1894 after his father's death, has been described by historian Barbara Tuchman as a "narrow, dull-witted young man of no vision and only one idea: to govern with no diminution of the autocratic power bequeathed by his ancestors."[3]

In the twilight years of the old order, however, a transportation revolution had been forged in steel across the largest country on earth. Praised by the Russian press as "the fairest jewel in the crown of the tsars," the Trans-Siberian Railroad marked the start of a new era. Before the building of the world's longest railroad, visitors crossed Siberia in horse-drawn vehicles along a system of post roads, a journey that could take months under normal conditions. The most common conveyance was a tarantass, an uncomfortable contraption that looked like a large basket and could carry two adults. George Kennan, an American journalist who investigated Siberia and the exile system in the 1880s, said that during one especially bad night of travel by tarantass, he was thrown against the roof of the vehicle at least three hundred times. "I felt as if I had been beaten from head to foot with a club and left for dead," he said.[4]

Kennan went to Siberia to write of another class of people—those who had been forced to walk to Siberia. The exile system had started in the seventeenth century as a way of getting criminals out of sight after they had been flogged, mutilated, or branded. Long after the government stopped the mutilation, exiles were herded to Siberia on

foot as a means of populating the region, Kennan wrote. The list of crimes that could earn a ticket to Siberia ranged from assault to cutting trees without a permit. Others found themselves in Siberia because of their religious or political beliefs. From 1800 to 1914 nearly one million people were sent into exile east of the Ural Mountains.

After decades of inaction, work began in 1891 on the Trans-Siberian Railroad, a project that would make Siberia more than a dumping ground for unwanted citizens. It would help Russia conquer the land barrier that had stymied growth to the east for generations. By 1908, the railroad had cut the travel time across Russia to under two weeks; it was now possible to buy a ticket for London in Vladivostok.

As the Paris racers made their rounds at this outpost on the eastern edge of the Russian empire, they were warned repeatedly that the cars would never make five hundred miles. The Russians advised them to give up and take the train.

Scarfoglio said the "great men of the Russian government, all covered with gold lace" offered many reasons why the venture would fail: "We shall be met on the road by Chunchuse brigands, Manchurian tigers, fever, plague, pestilence, famine—to say nothing of the mud after three months of rain, mosquitos as big as locusts and other similar delights."[5] Officially, however, the tsar's government had given its blessing to the race. Premier Peter Stolypin, the head of the honorary Russian race committee, had ordered his subordinates to assist wherever possible.

In Vladivostok, the crew on the Thomas settled in at the Grand Hotel. MacAdam was somewhat put out with the service: for three days the four men had to share one towel. He had to wait an hour after Schuster took a bath before there was enough hot water for a second bath. St. Chaffray asked that they drop by his hotel room. The

Commissionaire General was in no mood to chat about towels and bath water as he revealed his predicament: the Marquis de Dion had ordered him to drop out of the race. To seal the decision, de Dion had sold the car and made arrangements to ship it to a buyer in China.

St. Chaffray no longer had any wheels, but the man dubbed by *Le Matin* as the "Napoleon of the automobile," was not ready to abandon the race. "He declared that he would prevent the departure of the American car unless Schuster agreed to carry him to Paris," MacAdam reported. The story ran on the front page of the *New York Times* under the headline "ST. CHAFFRAY HALTS AMERICAN AUTOISTS." St. Chaffray asked that Schuster send Hansen and MacAdam ahead by train to make a place for him on the American car.

The Frenchman claimed that he had purchased all the gasoline available in the city from the German firm of Kunst & Albers. "There is no petrol: there are no means of getting any. What there was is in my possession and I offer it to the car which will agree to take me on board," St. Chaffray said, a proposal he also made to the Italians. The Commissionaire General said he could take an empty seat on the German Protos, but he wanted to reach Paris on the American or Italian car. "He further said that it would not look well for a Frenchman to ride on a German machine," MacAdam said.[6]

St. Chaffray's blackmail attempt provoked a predictable response from Schuster, who waited until the next day to reply. "He declared he would rather remain in Vladivostok than accept any such terms," MacAdam said. Scarfoglio said the Frenchman's proposal made him "furious" and the Italian set out to "find other means of procuring the combustible."

Gasoline had been stockpiled in Siberia along the more northerly original Siberian route by a representative of *Le Matin*. But with the

route change the racers would have to secure their own supplies on the nearly two thousand miles from the coast through Manchuria to Irkutsk. Although Schuster worried that he'd have to wait until more gas arrived from Yokohama, he told the Commissionaire General either to take the train or to start walking.

Schuster and his crew scoured the city in search of gasoline supplies overlooked by St. Chaffray. They began collecting fuel from some of the boats in the harbor. Schuster, who spoke German, visited Kunst & Albers, an aggressive department store chain that had outlets throughout eastern Siberia. Schuster placed a deposit with a low-level official for sixty gallons of gas and received a written receipt. Then, he talked to the manager and asked to buy some of the one thousand gallons of gas that had been carried aboard the ship that had transported the Protos to Vladivostok.

The manager refused and said he had no gas to sell, but Schuster produced the receipt and threatened to have MacAdam send a cable to the *New York Times* alleging that the company was part of a plot to delay the American car. The next morning the store sold Schuster three hundred more gallons at $1.25 a gallon. Schuster also bought fifty gallons from an apothecary shop.[7]

That was enough to break St. Chaffray's corner on the gasoline market: he accepted defeat and prepared to go back to France, signing over his gasoline stockpile to the Italians.[8] As the Americans prepared to leave Vladivostok, St. Chaffray went around and effusively shook hands with the crew. Upon his return to Paris by train, the Commissionaire General came in for severe criticism. "There are not many kind words in Paris and at the De Dion factory for St. Chaffray, who at the start was so much in the public eye and figured as the

mainspring of the trip," said a report in the *Automobile*, a New York magazine.

Autran, who had usually driven St. Chaffray's car, claimed that "it was the inexperience and ignorance" of the Commissionaire General that prevented the de Dion from making a better showing. Autran said he shuddered whenever his companion wanted the wheel. "St. Chaffray was only capable of driving an automobile under the most favorable conditions," Autran said. "Every time he took the wheel on the bad roads of America he ditched the car. By driving over a steep embankment he broke the frame of the car, and on two occasions unskillful handling was responsible for the breakage of the driving shaft."[9]

The German magazine, *Der Motorwagen*, wrote off St. Chaffray as an "imaginative Frenchman" who should have been an actor. It said that St. Chaffray wanted public attention and didn't care how he got it. Journalists who monitored the race from afar and considered St. Chaffray's final stunt a symptom of the problems with the whole affair now had only three teams to insult and ridicule.

The Americans and the Germans rolled out of Vladivostok on May 22, beginning a game of leapfrog that continued for more than two months. The Zust waited two more weeks, delayed by confusion over whether the car would continue in the race at all. Sirtori was recalled to Italy by the Zust Company for some silly reason, Scarfoglio said, and some of the Zust's financial backers had withdrawn their support. Scarfoglio and his German companion Haaga fell far behind while new backers were getting organized.

After the fiasco in Alaska, the tour through Japan, and the battle for gasoline in Vladivostok, the contestants still had more than eight

thousand miles to go before reaching Paris—almost three times the distance covered in the United States.

Hansen took charge of loading the extra tires, spare parts, and cans of gas and oil aboard a railroad car. Schuster, who had spent nearly all of the forty-eight hundred dollars he had received in Seattle from Eddie Thomas, hired a Russian to stockpile gas at five points along the Trans-Siberian between Vladivostok and Harbin, Manchuria.

At 11:30 a.m. Schuster said, "All aboard for Paris" and Miller turned the crank. The governor general in Vladivostok sent his adjutant to be the Thomas's guide for the first one hundred miles. For diplomatic reasons, the car now carried a Russian flag as well as the American flag. As the Thomas churned through the sloppy streets of Vladivostok, the men could imagine the muck and mud that awaited them.

However, to the newsmen in New York who consulted guidebooks and accounts by travelers to describe Siberia, the course seemed cut and dried. "For the greater part of the 5,400-mile journey from Vladivostok to Moscow, the great Russian post road will be followed, and close communication will be had at all times with the Trans-Siberian Railroad," the *New York Times* said.[10] The newspaper optimistically described the collection of muddy paths as "the longest modern highway in the world." The *Times* also included a more accurate description of conditions from a traveler who had visited Siberia: "In parts the road is accidentally good due to the firmness of the binding materials which happened to be there and rarely to the efforts of the road builder. It is not in a Russian to build a good road."

The press said the most difficult stretch was likely to be the first fifteen hundred miles through Manchuria to Chita, a section that had never been traveled by automobile before. A French engineer had put up a new one-thousand-dollar prize for the first car to reach Chita.

Loicq de Lobel, a member of the race committee, made the offer on behalf of the Trans-Alaska-Siberian Railway, a proposed round-the-world railroad he was trying to keep alive. The railroad would cross the Bering Strait and link up with the Trans-Siberian.

Lobel told the newspapers that his firm had wanted to honor the first car to make its way across Alaska to the Bering Strait and through Siberia to Irkutsk. Despite the change in the race route, Lobel said, the railway still wanted to recognize the bravery of the first auto crew to conquer the hardest part of the journey through Asia.[11]

Siberia's roads had been all but abandoned after the railroad went into service in 1904. The train was much faster and more convenient. Nature had started to reclaim the trails, leaving fallen trees, rocks, and deep puddles as the most consistent landmarks. In May 1908, rain had fallen for nearly three straight weeks, sending streams over their banks and creating a thick glue on the roads.

The drivers fought for every mile through mud that was worse than the Iowa gumbo. About sixteen miles outside of Vladivostok, the Thomas came upon the German car, stuck nearly to the top of its rear wheels. Koeppen and the two factory representatives who had joined him in Vladivostok, Robert Fuchs and Casper Neuberger, were trying with the help of their guide to move the car, but it was no use. Schuster wanted to drive on, but Hansen suggested that he stop and assist the Protos. The Thomas crew strung a towrope to the Protos and pulled the car out of the mire. Koeppen opened a bottle of champagne and toasted the men on the Thomas.

The mud showed no signs of drying up as the motorists slogged along. "Road endless streak of mud, except where pools too liquid to be called mud," MacAdam wrote in his notes. "Logs and stones been thrown in to give horses footing. Automobiles, to keep from sinking,

The Thomas Flyer pulls the German Protos out of the mud in eastern Siberia. Heavy rain had made the roads impassable in many spots and the cars soon took to the tracks of the Trans-Siberian Railroad. (COURTESY OF GEORGE T. MACADAM)

must be sent through full speed. Fearful wracking of machine when hits stones or logs. Over a dozen times Thomas shot into air all four wheels clear these bumps. Bridges rotten or gone entirely. To lighten load and find firmest and shallowest parts of road, crew except chauffeur wade through mud and streams. Frequently over boot tops."[12]

On the fourth day out of Vladivostok, Koeppen gave up on the flooded trails and took to the tracks of the Trans-Siberian Railroad. The Americans did the same a day later after getting stuck so solidly in a swollen stream that they had to be towed out by forty Russian soldiers. A man driving a cart told MacAdam that on the road ahead horses were getting stuck up to their bellies.

Rest stop along the Trans-Siberian Railroad between Vladivostok and Harbin, Manchuria. (COURTESY OF HENRY AUSTIN CLARK JR.)

The Americans bumped aboard the railroad tracks at 6:00 a.m., knowing they had to reach the next station twenty-one miles ahead by 9:30 a.m. to stay clear of scheduled trains. With watches in hand, the motorists pulled into the station on time, greeted by a railroad man who stood like a statue with a rolled green flag in his hand. All flagmen had orders to salute approaching traffic, even automotive traffic, MacAdam figured.

As the tracks climbed through the forested foothills toward Manchuria, the car encountered several tunnels and the men stayed alert for train traffic. "Listening for the toot of a locomotive became an absorbing occupation," MacAdam said.[13]

They traveled along many places with steep embankments on each side of the tracks. After one tunnel they saw a track walker frantically waving a flag and yelling "Express is coming." There was no place to pull off the tracks, so Schuster backed up quickly to the end of the tunnel to avoid a collision. "Nervous work," MacAdam wrote in his notes. "Puffing crew just get off as train appears. Has been flagged and is running slowly. Faces at all windows and doors. Cheers. Hansen jumps train. Returns through tunnel. Two bottles of beer for thirsty crew."[14]

Three times a week from each direction, the Moscow-Vladivostok "fast" trains rolled by. On some trains, the first-class passengers could listen to a piano, take a bath, or read in the library as they toured Siberia and Manchuria. The trains always ran on St. Petersburg time and passengers rarely knew the correct local time—it was not unusual for passengers to drink beer at 8:00 a.m. or eat supper at lunchtime. Travelers took a good long look at the scenery because the railroad never hurried. As English travel writer Harry de Windt put it, "I know of only one slower railway in the world, that from Jaffa to Jerusalem, where I have seen children leap on and off the car-steps of the train while in motion, and the driver alight, without actually stopping his engine, to gather wild flowers!"[15] The express trains on the Trans-Siberian rarely exceeded twenty miles per hour because of the flimsy track and the relatively low power of the steam locomotives.

Another traveler of the era, explorer Fridtjof Nansen, said he enjoyed his trip in a private railroad car, watching closely as "the wide country glided past our windows, spread out like a map."[16] He said that since the tracks on the Trans-Siberian were a few inches wider than those in the United States and Europe, the coaches provided a little extra room for the passengers to move about and a smooth ride.

The words *smooth ride* did not describe the experience of piloting a car on the rough-cut railroad ties. It was more like riding a bicycle on a set of stairs. In the best spots, where the ties were close together, the car swayed slightly and the occupants had the sensation of riding a galloping horse.

On the right side of the Thomas car, the tires occasionally rubbed the rails. Schuster wrapped sash cord around the tires to get more miles between blowouts. "There were places where traveling on the railroad was good," Schuster said later. "There were other spots where it was so shaky that I thought my teeth would drop out of my head."[17] Sometimes the ties were so far apart that the car tires would lodge between them unless the driver traveled at considerable speed.

Schuster cabled *Le Matin* and asked if he could use a set of flanged wheels to travel on the rails, which would have made for a smoother and faster ride. Motorists such as Charles Glidden used this technique to cover thousands of miles on the iron road early in the century. The Thomas car had an extra set of wheels that could have been adapted for railroad travel, but the race committee warned Schuster that any car using special wheels faced disqualification.

The Thomas took a break from the tracks on May 29 at Pogranichny, a settlement on the Manchurian border, 144 miles from Vladivostok. Felix Neuville, a gray-haired man who wore a derby and carried a cane, introduced himself. Neuville had set up the gasoline supply stations in Siberia for *Le Matin* along the original northern route of the race.

Impressed with the Frenchman's knowledge of the region, Schuster employed Neuville to help as a guide and make arrangements for the car's passage. On the trip through Manchuria and Siberia, Schuster often turned to Neuville for help and ignored Hansen, the official

navigator and interpreter. Hansen complained that Neuville was getting too much money and attention.

On a couple of occasions in the weeks ahead, Schuster threatened to fire Hansen if he didn't follow an order. "I said to Hansen, 'Do as you are told or you are through on the Thomas.' Hansen replied, 'I have a contract with E. R. Thomas. You have no authority to discharge me.'" Schuster said he cut short that debate by showing Hansen a letter from E. R. Thomas that gave Schuster total authority over the car.[18]

Some days later, when Hansen's refusal to ask for directions resulted in the Thomas going several miles off course, Schuster said, "Hansen, we can get along without your help. Get ready to leave us when we reach a railway station."

"You do that and I will put a bullet through you," Hansen said. Schuster shouted: "The only way you would shoot me is in the back. Not while I am facing you."

Miller broke in and said to Hansen, "If there is any shooting, you will not be the only one doing it, Cap."[19]

Schuster's version of that incident is the only one that survives. He said the pressures of the race caused the hard feelings. "We all felt pretty ragged at times, so it was not entirely the fault of any one person."

Part of the problem can be traced to Schuster's personality. He approached the race with an intensity unmatched by any other contestant. MacAdam told of one occasion when they stopped at a village at 2:00 p.m. and Schuster pulled out his watch and said, "Seven minutes for lunch." The natives laughed at the men's haste in devouring crackers, sausage, and a bottle of wine. MacAdam was still chewing when the car pulled away seven minutes later.

The Thomas Flyer rides a handcar on the Trans-Siberian Railroad to cross three miles of temporary track. The main line was washed out by a severe thunderstorm. (COURTESY OF HENRY AUSTIN CLARK JR.)

Schuster said his troubles with Hansen stemmed from the Norwegian's lack of cooperation and his failure to head off potential problems. While Hansen excelled at drinking protocol with the Russian officers—the proper procedure was to toast in turn the host, each corner of a room, and every ranked official—he failed more important assignments, according to Schuster. Hansen spoke Russian, but he neglected to secure gun permits in Siberia. There was also tension over money. Schuster didn't want to waste any and he played the role of a conservative banker, rejecting more requests than he approved. In Moscow, Captain Hansen pawned a Browning rifle for some temporary cash, but Schuster refused to give him funds to redeem the weapon.

The rough ride through Manchuria put tremendous stress on both men and machines. The machines cracked first. Fifteen miles outside of Pogranichny the Thomas Flyer jolted to a stop: six teeth on a pinion drive broke and the transmission case cracked open, stranding the car

on an uninhabited plain. Schuster and MacAdam made a return trip to Pogranichny on foot.

Schuster caught a train for Harbin to retrieve some spare parts, while MacAdam bought supplies for the unexpected Manchurian camping trip. Russian soldiers told him about bands of robbers who lived in the region. The Manchurian outlaws known as red beards operated so blatantly that until recently most people who shipped goods had submitted to the bandits, buying documents that allowed safe passage. A week before the Thomas arrived, three of the outlaws had been captured. They told authorities that they knew about the "projected trip of the rich automobilists through the country and believed a good ransom could be secured by their capture," the Russians told the Americans. "Added to the other difficulties we are experiencing, this indeed makes a pleasing prospect," MacAdam wrote.[20]

The correspondent worried about other dangers too. Before returning to the Thomas Flyer on a handcar with some Chinese workmen, MacAdam saw a tiger skin. It came from an animal killed one week earlier about fifty miles away. Hansen and Miller, meanwhile, created a patchwork tent of canvas and old rubber coats piled on heavy railroad timbers. They called it Camp Hard Luck. The tent provided some protection from the hot afternoon sun, but it did not keep the rain out during the frequent thunderstorms.

Remembering the warnings about bandits, the men decided to post a twenty-four-hour guard. MacAdam took the first night watch. "The night was melancholy and the only noise was the frog chorus. Songs failed to relieve the loneliness," he said. Then, MacAdam heard men approaching and wondered if the red beards planned to do him in.

George MacAdam and Captain Hansen relax at Camp Hard Luck, the spot in Manchuria where the car broke down and they waited while George Schuster went to Harbin to get spare parts. (COURTESY OF GEORGE T. MACADAM)

A pair of Russian soldiers appeared in the darkness and quickly stamped out MacAdam's campfire. Sent by the commander of the garrison at Pogranichny, the soldiers warned that the fire would provide an easy target for the outlaws. The soldiers, who carried rifles with bayonets, brought along three watchdogs and stayed the night. The bandits never struck, but other visitors stopped at Camp Hard Luck in the days ahead, including a man who had driven thirty-six cattle from Harbin. The cattle driver said in the last thirteen miles he had to cross four waist-deep rivers.

When MacAdam's tale about bandits and the Manchurian break-down appeared in the *New York Times*, the correspondent's brother went to the Times Square offices of the paper to ask if a relief expedition was in order. At first, editors at the *Times* had complained that MacAdam was not sending enough material, but with this article

"Chesty George" redeemed himself, wrote Harry Horgan, a friend of MacAdam's at the newspaper.[21]

During the race, Horgan wrote occasional letters to MacAdam, providing a fresh supply of office gossip. In one letter he enclosed a copy of a letter to the editor of the *Times* from a woman who said that through the detailed dispatches in the *Times* she had become thoroughly familiar with Schuster and Miller, but she had "looked in vain for some inkling to suggest who the man is who refers to himself so modestly as 'your correspondent.'"

"Will you not turn the limelight on him and satisfy a woman's curiosity?"

Her plea did not convince Managing Editor Carr Van Anda to drop his ironclad policy of keeping reporters out of the limelight. Except in a couple of rare instances—one of them an article he wrote on the twentieth anniversary of the race—MacAdam's stories on the contest carried no byline.

Horgan advised MacAdam to brag about the woman's letter in Captain Hansen's presence and tell him it was not the only query the newspaper had received about the correspondent. "I suppose it's another vindication of the old doctrine that it takes indifference to pique the ladies," Horgan said.[22]

Five days following the breakdown, the crew pulled up stakes at Camp Hard Luck. Schuster returned with the spare parts and fixed the transmission. He had no idea how long the emergency repairs would hold up, however, so back in Harbin, he had cabled the Thomas factory and asked that a new transmission be shipped immediately from Buffalo.

By this time, the Germans had built a 150-mile lead. The Thomas set out on the railroad tracks again, followed by a handcar occupied

by a telegrapher and Chinese workers. The workers used wooden planks to ease the car over spots where the tracks were under construction and where there was no rock ballast between the railroad ties.

Back in New York, the Thomas company grew increasingly concerned about the mechanical problems and delays in Siberia. The Germans had built a six-day lead; E. R. Thomas reacted like a baseball manager watching his team blow a big game. On June 4, he filed an official protest over the decision to allow the Germans to continue in the contest. He again claimed the cup offered by *Le Matin* for the winner and said all the other cars had withdrawn from the race. Spokesmen for the Zust denied reports that the Italian car had pulled out.

Thomas said he admired Lieutenant Koeppen, but "the New York to Paris automobile race is a most serious undertaking, involving reputation, money, endurance of car and men to the extreme and sentiment or errors should have no place in the decision."[23] Thomas said it wasn't fair to allow the Germans to continue because the Protos had been shipped by train to Seattle. The German knew this was not allowed, but did so anyway, according to Thomas. "We wish to be magnanimous, but the trip through Siberia at this season of the year is one full of danger to men and machines and accidents are liable to happen and hence it can hardly be called just to compel the Thomas car to run more than 1,870 miles further than the Protos, subjecting the car to just that much more strain," Thomas said.

The race committee in Paris rejected the protest and said the fifteen-day penalty against the Germans and the fifteen-day allowance for the Americans compensated for the trip to Alaska.[24] Technically, the Americans still held a big lead, but the German advantage in the race across Russia could turn into a public relations defeat for the

backers of the Thomas. Whichever car reached Paris first would at least drive off with a psychological victory, despite the thirty-day difference in the official record.

The Zust ran a distant third. Scarfoglio and Haaga left Vladivostok only after a prominent Italian sportsman agreed to help pay for the balance of the trip.[25] That ended Scarfoglio's money troubles, but the Italian journalist continued to have problems communicating with the home office. He tried to send a 1,921-word dispatch to Italy from Pogranichny, but the telegrapher refused, saying that it was illegal to send coded messages. Scarfoglio screamed and said the Italian language was not a secret code. Scarfoglio bribed the town druggist with five rubles to swear that it was not a coded message. Thus assured, the telegrapher agreed to send a sixty-word condensation.[26]

By now the Russian authorities had developed a plan for handling the cars on the railroad tracks. The railroad treated the Italian car as a special train and supplied red and green lamps and flags for the rough-riding Zust Special. "The continual bumping, the incessant dance of St. Vitus, which has seized both us and the machine, is most exhausting and exasperating," Scarfoglio said.

Scarfoglio said that Manchuria may have been Chinese territory, but the railroad was entirely Russian. The names of the stations and the "dragons embroidered in silver on the caps of the employees" were the only signs they were in China. "For the rest, China is far off, undiscoverable, fled before the invasion. Everybody speaks in Russian, curses in Russian, gets drunk on Russian poisons and eats a la Russe."[27]

The major Manchurian city on the railroad was Harbin, the Russian base for the exploitation of the region. Harbin was on the nine-hundred-mile Manchurian line known as the Chinese Eastern Railway. Russia had been forced to give up a southern branch of the

George MacAdam writes a dispatch for the *New York Times* while George Miller looks on. They stayed several days in a makeshift canvas tent when the Thomas Flyer was broken down. The car tires were wrapped in sash cord to prevent the rails from rubbing. (COURTESY OF GEORGE T. MACADAM)

Chinese Eastern Railway after the war with Japan, but the tsarist regime held on to the main east-west line. Work was just starting on an all-Russian railroad extension to the north along the Amur River, but in 1908 the Manchurian shortcut remained the only way to travel.

The wide-open town attracted adventurers from throughout Asia. MacAdam arrived there by train, temporarily leaving the Thomas Flyer to bump along the Manchurian railroad tracks without him. He checked into the Grand Hotel, where he waited three days for the car to arrive.

Although the Chinese officially controlled Harbin, the Russian authorities in the city did not hesitate to inspect the passports of foreign visitors. Built by the Russians on land leased for the railroad,

the city was only twelve years old, but its twenty-acre graveyard was already overcrowded with wooden crosses and decaying brick monuments, MacAdam said. Pigs ran in the main square, and ornate commercial buildings were losing their plaster-stucco and showing other signs of wear. A Harbin distillery produced three million gallons of vodka a year, and MacAdam reported "fearful squandering of money, particularly on women and wine." A hotel porter told him to take his revolver when he went out at night. The man told him that a few months earlier, robbers dressed as policemen had attacked and killed bank messengers at noon on a main street. Carrying his pistol, MacAdam took a walk on the wild side of Harbin, but had no dramatic encounters to report. Later, he went to the railroad station. "Soldiers and women promenading on railway platform at night in uniforms and spurs. Much clicking of spurs," MacAdam wrote. "Departure of St. Petersburg Express. Woman throwing violets. Soldier with baby's photograph."[28]

MacAdam kept meticulous notes of his trip across Manchuria and Russia, writing in pocket-size notebooks. He often wrote late at night, keeping a cross between a personal diary of what happened to Times and a chronological account of the people and places encountered along the way. He wrote of Russians who were always ready to toast Teddy Roosevelt and the tsar, of the raft that had to be built to float the Thomas across a Siberian river, and of the old man who had kissed Schuster's and Miller's heads after they allowed him to take a short ride in the car. The old man had to be evicted from the car after Schuster realized the Siberian passenger wanted to go to Paris. MacAdam said on Sundays in Russia, the racers were bothered by people drunk on vodka who stood in the middle of the road, with a quizzical expression when they saw a car for the first time.

MacAdam had various Russian phrases written in his notebook, such as "Someone who speaks English?" He produced the book and showed it to people when he needed help. He also said there was an all-purpose Russian word that depending on the circumstances, apparently could mean, "right away, tomorrow, next week or never." He tried sign language at times and imitated sounds to communicate, saying "choo-choo, choo-choo" when he wanted to go to the train station.

The Thomas reached Harbin on June 9, three days after the Germans had left the city. Determined to overcome that lead, Schuster had the car back on the road within five hours. Miller and Hansen each carried a five-gallon can of gasoline to extend the car's range. MacAdam and Neuville remained behind in Harbin a few days and arranged to meet with the Thomas farther west along the railroad. In place of MacAdam, a Manchurian guide took a seat on the car, pointing out the route through the windswept Khingan Mountains.

The Protos and the Thomas both took leave of the railroad tracks after Harbin. "The railroad is now extremely strict, and insists on holding the car at various stations until the stretch ahead to the next station is entirely clear," MacAdam said. "There are many delays in consequence, and faster progress is impossible. The new regulation came into effect after many narrow escapes from accidents, and while dictated by caution is galling to impatient tourists eager to end the hardships of travel on the ties."[29] Beyond Harbin, the trail crossed a great plain, occasionally passing a village or a railroad encampment. "There was not a road of any description," Scarfoglio said of this area. "The plain around us was the road, and near and far, amidst the tall grasses there passed Manchurian caravans, lines of low carts with solid wheels studded with nails. Dotted over the verdant plain like reefs in

the sea were little Manchurian villages, nestling around red or blue pagodas. They were populated by frightened crowds who stopped their ears and covered their eyes as we passed."[30]

The trail grew worse as the motorists approached the Greater Khingan Range, where thick broadleaf forests and muddy roads made for difficult travel. The passage of the Thomas caused such a commotion that leaders of one village postponed a circus performance. Beyond the mountains, the car crossed the northern reaches of the Gobi Desert and veered toward Chita, the capital of the Transbaikalia.

MacAdam, who had arrived a few days earlier by train, said Chita was the "best looking town so far." The correspondent found a woman who spoke English, giving him a break from sign language. At 11:00 p.m. he went to a cafe for a bottle of mineral water. MacAdam was the only paying customer, but the proprietor asked his twelve musicians to start playing. "Times ... feels ought to buy something more expensive than mineral water. Wants to go to bed but when only one in audience seems like insult to leave. Some other people come in and Times escapes to bed."[31]

He was just falling asleep when he heard the sound of a car in the street at 12:30 a.m. "Schuster, Hansen and Miller stagger in, gray with dust and fatigue, gaunt, hollow-eyed, been traveling since 6 a.m." MacAdam said. The first question they asked: "Where are the Germans?" The Thomas crew had been slowly cutting into the German lead, but Koeppen maintained a two-day advantage and had already claimed the one thousand dollar prize for reaching Chita first. Both cars stayed on the road nearly twenty hours each day, taking advantage of the long summer twilight. The Italian car was not a factor, having dropped nearly one thousand miles behind the Thomas Flyer.

In the hotel at Chita, Schuster took off his boots and went to bed. Hansen and Miller had something to eat, then they collapsed for the night. MacAdam stayed awake by candlelight, writing cables for *Le Matin* and the *New York Times*. MacAdam said that the Thomas men would ship home the extra rifles they had carried for protection and that they felt relieved to be beyond Manchuria.

"Americans can have no conception of the lawlessness of the Manchurian towns along the railroad. An idea of what it is like, however, is given by the fact that this spring, in the village of Manchesuria, the melting snow revealed 30 bodies of men lying a few hundred yards from the streets. All these men had been murdered," he said.[32]

At dawn, MacAdam took his report to the telegraph office before waking Hansen and Miller. In the confusion of the night before, none of them had noticed which hotel room Schuster was in. The reporter peeked through several keyholes, a "risky and unpleasant business," and took a few tentative taps on doors, but received no reply. "Times sees blue flannel shirt through keyhole, boosts Hansen on shoulders to transom. Schuster discovered."

The car needed lubrication, but the men had to improvise. The Americans bought forty pounds of Vaseline at a drug store to apply to the noisy transmission. Later, they had to use beef tallow, which made the car smell like a butcher shop.[33]

MacAdam said the rolling plains outside of Chita made for good traveling and Schuster tried to make up lost time. He drove three hundred miles in two days and two nights, stopping the car only when forced to. The route passed through valleys and grass bottomlands inhabited by Buryats, the Mongolian people of eastern Siberia. The Buryats lived in tents and wagons; they tended large herds of cattle, horses, sheep, and goats. "Auto causes great commotion among

animals," MacAdam wrote. "When hear or see auto, entire herd rushes toward it, even from distance, then bellowing or neighing, run ahead in panic, sometimes couple of miles."[34]

The racers not only had to compete with the Buryat herds for the right of way, they also had to deal with caravans of two-wheeled horse carts. MacAdam said the leading carts, which resembled "half-grown prairie schooners," contained a driver who was often sound asleep. This cart was usually followed by five or six driverless carts piled high with merchandise of all sorts. The approach of the noisy Thomas Flyer invariably panicked the horses, MacAdam said. "Driver clings to horse of leading cart. Others scatter in all directions. Occasionally runaway carts turn over. If horses wait until auto gets near enough, crew alight, hold rearing horses until auto passes."

Entering a village produced the same kind of bedlam on a larger scale. Frightened horses stopped grazing and ran along the muddy street, scattering people, chickens, and cattle. The dogs barked, the pigs squealed, and the children screamed. Outside of each village stood a gate on the trail that kept the livestock from wandering off. On one occasion, a gatekeeper refused to open up for the Thomas Flyer.

Hansen failed to persuade him with words, so Schuster got out of the car and wrestled the gatekeeper out of the way. During the fight, MacAdam slipped by and swung the gate open, while Miller took the wheel of the Thomas and sped through. The others hopped aboard the car, leaving the reluctant gatekeeper shouting in the dust.

TEN

THE DASH TO PARIS

THE ROADS OF Siberia weren't that much worse than those in his own country, George Schuster said later. He couldn't say the same about the sleeping and eating accommodations. At the end of a day fighting mud and miserable weather in the United States, the men could usually find a good meal and a nice place to sleep. In Siberia, a day of mud and misery was capped by a bug-ridden hovel worse than a barn. The unventilated rooms always smelled bad, and the food usually consisted of coarse black bread, eggs, and tea. Schuster said the crust was passable, but the inside of the bread was "absolutely indigestible."[1]

The crew of the Thomas had shipped their extra clothes ahead by train from Harbin because Schuster wanted to reduce the weight on the car. They slept in their clothes in post houses where the stench was awful. MacAdam made it a nightly ritual to open a window to get some ventilation, but the proprietor would always close it by morning. MacAdam would get outdoors as soon as he could to escape the smell.

Scarfoglio wrote at length about the evils of the hotels in Siberia's larger cities, where he said the motorists were received like "dogs in a church." There were extra charges assessed for water in the wash basin, soap, towels, blankets, sheets, candles, drinking water, and even electric

lights that didn't work. "You dare not take a single step across the room for fear of knocking against a piece of furniture or moving a chair, for which you would be asked to pay more and more kopecks," Scarfoglio said.[2]

He said the Siberian hotels appeared attractive only because anything was better than the dirty huts in the small villages. For days on end, the men consumed bread, eggs, and tea, while sleeping on dirty floors and facing attack by all manner of insects. The bugs enraged Scarfoglio. One night he jumped up, stripped off his clothes, and poured a bucket of cold water over himself, but it didn't stop the itching for long.

The rain, wind, mud, insects, twenty-hour days, and poor food combined to make the journey miserable for the men on all the cars. It seemed as if it would take forever to get through Siberia. "In Siberia nobody ever asks if or when the rain will finish," Scarfoglio said. "They inquire whether and when Siberia will end."[3]

The motorists realized that numbers alone do not do justice to the size of Siberia. Journalist George Kennan had discovered this two decades earlier when he compared the region to more well-known real estate: "If it were possible to move entire countries from one part of the world to another, you could take the whole United States of America from Maine to California and from Lake Superior to the Gulf of Mexico, and set it down in the middle of Siberia, without touching anywhere the boundaries of the latter territory. You could then take Alaska and all the states of Europe, with the single exception of Russia and fit them into the remaining margin like the pieces of a dissected map." After that exercise there would still be three hundred thousand square miles of Siberian territory to spare.[4]

After battling their way through more than one third of this vast territory, the Americans nearly pulled even with the Germans just east of Lake Baikal. The wooded country reminded some visitors of the hills of Scotland, but MacAdam thought of other things as Schuster pushed everyone to the limit on an all-night ride. "It was like motoring in a nightmare—the road was bad but the bridges were worse. Ice and mountain currents had carried away many of the undersupports, twisting the bridges out of shape, leaving them dangerous ventures even for a wagon," MacAdam said.[5]

It was near here the previous year that Prince Borghese's car fell through a decayed bridge. After that accident, Barzini said, they took all questionable bridges at top speed. "Each part of the bridge only supported for an almost incalculably small length of time the weight of the car, and so had actually no time to break under it," Barzini said.[6]

Employing similar tactics, the Thomas crew reached the village of Mysovsk four minutes before the Protos left aboard a freight train that connected with a ferry across Lake Baikal. The conductor said there wasn't time to hook another flatcar up, so the Americans waited twelve hours for the next train. The road ahead was washed out so Schuster had no choice.

Later that day, MacAdam tried to take a picture of the Thomas Flyer while railroad workers helped load it on a freight car for the trip to the steamer. A policeman stopped him, saying that no picture taking was allowed along the railway. MacAdam said it was a prime example of the "unreasoning bureaucracy" that plagued Russia and the "vast inertia of its immense body of guards and governors."[7] Luigi Barzini had run into the same prohibition the year before on the Peking-to-Paris expedition. "A strange country, this, where photography is a

forbidden thing and firearms are allowed! Since the war with Japan there has remained a kind of terror of espionage," Barzini said.[8]

With the Thomas aboard, the flat car that MacAdam was forbidden to photograph took on the appearance of a parade float, showing those who stood along the tracks the "simple life of the racing autoist," MacAdam said. Miller worked on the car as the train rolled along at something less than fifteen miles per hour. The other men ate and slept, using newspapers for mattresses. The Thomas crossed Lake Baikal on the S.S. *Baikal*, an ice-breaking train ferry designed to carry the coaches of an entire express train across the world's deepest lake. The ship's captain invited the motorists to take a steam bath. Miller, Hansen, and MacAdam gladly accepted. By 6:00 a.m. the car was back on the road and it pulled into Irkutsk within two hours.

The Paris of Siberia, as some of its boosters described Irkutsk, attracted gold miners, merchants, tea traders, political exiles, and ex-convicts. "What San Francisco was in '49 when it flourished as the gilded Gomorrah of the West, Irkutsk, the largest town of Siberia and metropolis of the Asiatic goldfields, is today—with additional trimmings," wrote journalists Richardson Wright and Bassett Digby after a Siberian tour a few years later.[9]

"Of the tens of thousands of convicts in Siberia, a large proportion make their way into Irkutsk at the expiration of these sentences, anxious to snatch a few weeks' enjoyment of the sights and sounds of this crude, overgrown mining camp before making plans for the future," they said.[10]

Irkutsk had wooden sidewalks, four breweries, a museum, a home for orphans, hospitals, a bicycle track, and the only department store in Siberia with a large electric sign. Two hours before the Thomas Flyer reached the Paris of Siberia, Koeppen had departed

The Thomas Flyer crosses a pontoon bridge in Siberia. (COURTESY OF HENRY AUSTIN CLARK JR.)

for the Paris of France. Schuster would have followed immediately, but he had to repair a broken motor support and find enough gas to fill the car. The drivers had to scrounge for fuel and fill their cars whenever they could, buying gas from a variety of businesses. By the time the Thomas Flyer's tanks had been filled, the Protos's lead had grown to ten hours.

The men sat in "grim silence," MacAdam said, as they rolled along through the endless larch, cedar, and pine forests of the Siberian taiga. Some years earlier Anton Chekhov, who traveled by horse-drawn vehicle, wrote of the tedious nature of an extended trip through the

taiga. "On the first day one does not take any notice of the taiga; on the second and third day one begins to wonder, but on the fourth and fifth day one experiences a mood as if one would never get out of this green monster."[11]

The men had to fight to stay awake, as Schuster roused his crew at 3:00 a.m. and kept going most days until 11:00 p.m. "Same weary grind," MacAdam wrote of this part of the trip. "Miller and Hansen falling asleep, swaying side to side. Times wishes he could follow suit, but just as reaches sleeping point, lurch of car awakens."[12] They had to make numerous ferry crossings. Schuster, who had refused to allow anyone else to drive since Vladivostok, often fell asleep while waiting for the ferries. MacAdam said they had many close calls and near misses on the road and this seemed "to have taken Schuster's nerve—afraid to let Thomas out." He drove at twenty miles per hour on sections of good road. When Schuster did allow Miller to take the wheel, the pace quickened right away, the correspondent said. "Thomas gets new life, immediately proving that after all its Asiatic troubles still has old vitality," MacAdam said. "Advantage taken every stretch good road. Hansen and Times feel really in auto race around world. But half-hour later fascination of driving proves too much for Schuster and he again takes wheel. Thomas again lags."[13]

The next day Hansen and MacAdam left the car to go to Tomsk, under orders from Schuster, who needed a break from his backseat drivers. Schuster said he wanted to lighten the load and give Hansen time to visit his family at Tomsk. Schuster and Miller drove for two days straight, taking turns at the wheel. The man who wasn't driving strapped himself into the passenger's seat to keep from getting bounced out of the car while dozing.[14]

The battered Thomas Flyer, with pick axe and tires strapped to the rear, during a stop in Siberia. The tires rubbed big grooves in the planks above the wheels. (COURTESY OF GEORGE T. MACADAM)

Meanwhile, Hansen and MacAdam took the Trans-Siberian to Taiga and rode on a branch line fifty miles north to Tomsk. A visitor to Tomsk seven years before the race described it as "half full of millionaires and ex-convicts."[15] Hansen went to see his wife and child, while MacAdam checked into the Hotel Russia, where an orchestra, complete with bass drum and trombone, kept him awake until 4:00 a.m.

The sound of a car in the hotel courtyard woke MacAdam at 10:00 a.m. It was the Protos and Koeppen. The German car was in a "sad condition of disrepair," MacAdam said, but Koeppen and his crew remained in good spirits. As with the Americans, the difficulty of finding gasoline and the bad roads put a great strain on the car and its occupants. MacAdam dined with the Germans that night and Koeppen said he would drop by the next morning to say goodbye before leaving.

The knock on MacAdam's door the next morning came not from Koeppen, however, but from Schuster. The driver was covered with dust, worn out from round-the-clock travel and worried about letting Koeppen slip away again. The Germans left at 1:00 p.m. Schuster and Miller spent the day repairing the Thomas, closely watched by a crowd of army officers, merchants, and laborers.

Schuster decided that he could take Hansen along in the car now, but he opted to carry an extra cask of gasoline instead of MacAdam. The next gas he knew of was 350 miles away across the green, swampy, flat lowlands of western Siberia. The men slept for 3½ hours that night, then got up at 3:00 a.m. for what MacAdam described as a "silent breakfast."[16]

Over the next two days, MacAdam traveled by himself on the railroad to Omsk, an agricultural center six hundred miles away at the confluence of the Om and Irtysh rivers. The cars sped along after the train, crossing the green, swampy steppes of Siberia. Outside of every settlement, windmills tilted in the breeze. For weeks, Schuster had fought to erase the gap between his car and the Protos. Finally, outside of Omsk, the Thomas regained the lead for the first time in three thousand miles. When the Thomas Flyer pulled ahead of the Protos at thirty miles per hour, the men shouted "Good morning gentlemen." The Germans waved back.

As soon as he learned that the Thomas Flyer had taken the lead again, E. R. Thomas released a statement saying his car had shown that "American cars are better for American roads and for Siberian roads" than cars from "France, Germany or other thoroughly settled continental countries."[17]

Ariving in Omsk, the Thomas crew received word that two weeks earlier William Howard Taft had won the Republican nomination for

president and that former President Grover Cleveland had died. Siberian communications were such that they learned nothing of a more mysterious event that had taken place the day before one thousand miles northeast of Omsk: an explosion in the far reaches of northern Siberia had devastated an area of nearly five hundred square miles and touched off a large forest fire.

The blast known as the Tunguska Marvel shook seismographs in Irkutsk and produced an atmospheric disturbance recorded in England and Washington, D.C. It took place in such a remote area that many years passed before the site was thoroughly analyzed. In the decades that followed, researchers offered many possible explanations for the explosion. Some said a meteorite or a comet collided with the earth, but no crater was formed, leading to speculation that the explosion took place several miles above ground. Modern analysis suggests that the explosion released the equivalent of twelve million tons of TNT. The atomic bomb dropped on Hiroshima had the force of twenty thousand tons of TNT.

To this day the cause of the blast remains in dispute. Some people won't accept the theory that it was an exploding comet. A 1969 bibliography cited 180 scientific papers, 940 articles, and 60 novels about the blast of 1908. One theory advanced by a prominent Russian engineer and science-fiction writer was that a spaceship went out of control and blew up. "Most of the Soviet scientific community reject this theory on the grounds that, as one of the investigators has said, 'There are no planets with a highly organized life from which such a ship could descend,'" historian Harmon Tupper wrote.[18]

The idea that a vehicle from outer space reached Siberia would have seemed about as farfetched to the average Siberian as the notion that self-propelled vehicles could travel from one end of the Russian

George Miller scratches his name on the monument marking the boundary between Europe and Asia outside of Ekaterinburg. (COURTESY OF GEORGE T. MACADAM)

empire to the other. Conclusive proof may never be obtained about the former, but the Thomas and Protos were well on the way to accomplishing the latter when the Tunguska Marvel shook the skies.

The Thomas left Omsk at 4:00 a.m. on July 1 and traveled thirty miles to the Irtysh River. Beyond the river, some gears on the transmission were stripped when Schuster drove through a swamp. About forty villagers took hold of a two-hundred-foot rope and pulled the Thomas into the next village, where Miller used screws to replace the broken teeth on the driving pinion. There was still no sign of the new transmission from Buffalo, and Schuster had serious doubts about the life expectancy of the old one.

On July 6 the Thomas arrived in Ekaterinburg, a city in the low hills of the Ural Mountains where the tsar, his wife, son, and four

daughters would be killed by local Bolsheviks ten years later. Two days after the Thomas reached the city, MacAdam stepped off a train at 1:20 a.m., having searched without luck for the transmission. He roused the hotel porter and learned that the Thomas was to leave at 3:00 a.m. MacAdam stayed awake and wrote a telegram for the *Times* about the car's progress. The Americans had a four-day lead on the Germans, who were stopped with mechanical problems and were waiting for a mechanic and a rear-axle assembly to arrive by rail.

The Thomas Flyer's new transmission was still lost in transit. Schuster sent Hansen and Neuville to look for it in railroad depots, while the three Georges drove through the Urals. Two hours out of Yekaterinburg, along a wide path that made for easy traveling, the Thomas stopped at the monument on the boundary between Europe and Asia. Miller and Schuster went inside the small wooden fence that encircled it and scratched their names on the pillar, which had Europe marked on one side and Asia on the other.

Weeks later, when Scarfoglio finally made it this far, he couldn't find the monument or the Ural Mountains. Scarfoglio had saved two bottles of champagne to drink when he passed into Europe from Asia. He and Haaga eventually asked a policeman where they could find the Urals and the obelisk. The man laughed and pointed back to a "brown line which broke the horizon at our backs." The Zust crew had crossed the Urals without knowing it.[19] As Luigi Barzini had said, the Urals "seem high and imposing only to the men of the steppes."[20]

MacAdam said this region reminded him of the plains of Indiana and Illinois. After passing the monument, he said, "even the air seemed to instantly change." The fields were fenced and better tilled, while the houses and horses were larger. MacAdam did not consider the bigger horses an improvement over the animals in Siberia. Nearly

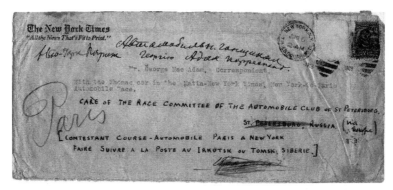

It was no easy matter to get mail forwarded to the contestants when they were in Siberia. (COURTESY OF GEORGE T. MACADAM)

every horse shied away at the sound of the motor, and MacAdam's job was to leap out of the car at the first sign of trouble and try to calm them.

That was no more difficult than calming down Schuster after he received a letter from E. R. Thomas asking if Montague Roberts should be sent to Europe to drive the Thomas Flyer on the final leg of the race. "This made me so mad I could have eaten nails," Schuster said.[21] He had a drink of cognac and responded with a telegram that said nothing about Roberts, but predicted that the car would probably reach Paris by July 26.

By now, the search for the lost transmission had finally produced results. Neuville found it more than two hundred miles ahead in Kazan. The only question was whether the Thomas would keep running long enough to get there. It was raining heavily, and Miller and MacAdam urged Schuster to stop until the clay roads dried out and hardened. They had a big lead on the Germans and there was no need to press their luck. Schuster didn't see it that way. He knew the transmission might fail, but he also knew that there was no guarantee that

road conditions would improve. He saw no choice, but to keep going. "As long as the wheels will turn, I'm going to drive this car," Schuster said.[22]

The end came as the car strained up a steep, muddy hill. The teeth on the drive gear snapped, making a loud cracking noise. The car sank along with the spirits of its occupants. They hired horses to tow the machine to the village of Zyatzy, where Schuster arranged to go 215 miles by horse-drawn cart to pick up new transmission. Hansen went ahead to Moscow. Miller and MacAdam, who stayed with the disabled car, communicated with the residents by sign language and became "village curiosities," MacAdam said.

"Indeed, so eager are the sightseers who gather every day to watch us that we have had to rope off the automobile to keep the crowd away," MacAdam said. Their host allowed his friends to come inside his house to watch the two Americans eat, wash, etc. The house was infested with vermin, and the air inside was terrible, so MacAdam and Miller slept outside in a cowshed. The delay made them restless and agitated.

MacAdam wrote a cable to the Thomas factory in New York that expressed his reservations about Schuster's driving: "Strongly urge appointment Miller driver. Only chance reaching Paris first."[23]

After four days, the repaired German car arrived at the village. Koeppen stopped long enough to greet Miller and MacAdam and commiserate with them before pushing on, "leaving us disconsolate with the peasants and the cows," MacAdam said. The next day Schuster returned, completing a 430-mile roundtrip in four days despite a fever and bad cold. He rode in one cart and the six-hundred-pound transmission in another. It took all day to install. By the time the car was ready to go, the Protos had a thirty-one hour advantage.

The Thomas stops at a statue in Nizhni Novgorod, Russia, a city now known as Gorki. (COURTESY OF GEORGE T. MACADAM)

As the cars entered European Russia, MacAdam's camera brought more smiles of recognition than in Siberia, where few people knew what it was. Not everyone knew what it took to make a good picture, however. At one spot, a man assumed a hostile pose with his fists clenched. "Where did they get the idea that this is what is desired in a photo?" MacAdam wrote in his notes.

A broken frame and leaky radiator slowed the car for ten hours on July 18. The Thomas caught up with Neuville at Nizhni-Novgorod, now known as Gorki, and Schuster took his shoes and clothes off for the first time in thirteen days. It was here that Dr. E. C. Lehwess had abandoned his plan to drive around the world six years earlier. This was the gateway to Europe; from here on the driving conditions allowed the cars to make better time. Schuster said the roads the rest of the way were so much better "that we imagined we were on feather beds."[24]

There were still problems, however. Over a forty-mile stretch outside of Vladimir, they were met by sullen and hostile people all along the road. Some threw sticks or stones at the car. Others put broken glass under straw in the road, shook their fists, and shouted curses as Schuster drove by. MacAdam dug his revolver out of his bag, not knowing what to expect. Schuster suffered a glancing blow on the head from a stick, while MacAdam had sand thrown in his eyes. MacAdam learned later that the previous year a pilot car for Prince Borghese had killed a child near here and no one had forgotten or forgiven the accident.

At Bogorodks, they met up with the first car they had seen since Vladivostok. It was driven by Alexis Shibaeff, the richest man in town. They ate supper on the veranda of his house and departed for Moscow. Schuster and Miller changed a flat tire at 3:00 a.m., and an hour later the car pulled up to the National Hotel in Moscow. Hansen stuck his head out of an upper window and yelled: "Well, you people make enough noise."

Schuster fell asleep in a chair in Hansen's room. MacAdam had the "luxury of five hours sleep," but it failed to revive his spirits. "Breakfast in room. Then to write dispatch and diary which had not been entered since Kazan. Head a stone, memory blank. Strong coffee and cigar little help. Past four days a confused and feverish mixture of detached events. Arouse memories mostly took form of unimportant roadside pictures, faces in crowd, etc. But Times sticks to the job and finally manages to do enough to have the matter off his conscience," MacAdam wrote.[25]

Schuster and Miller worked at the car all day in the hotel court-yard, surrounded by a large crowd. The mechanics repaired a broken motor support for the second time and fixed a problem with the clutch.

The Moscow Auto Club hosted a breakfast the next morning. Several cars accompanied the crew for some miles outside the city. It was farm country, rich with the smell of hay. Schuster took cat naps at the wheel, MacAdam said, and had close calls with a large stone in the road and a post. Miller took a turn driving and had just as much trouble keeping his eyes open.

On July 23, the Thomas reached the Russian capital of St. Petersburg. The crew stayed in the city four hours, attending a dinner given by Ludwig Nobel, president of the Russian oil trust. Members of the Imperial Automobile Club escorted the Thomas the last thirty-five miles into the city and made the crew honorary members. The organization had already bestowed its main prizes on the Protos two days earlier. By reaching St. Petersburg first, the German crew claimed a one thousand dollar prize and a silver cup. The tsar authorized the presentation of a gold medal, while Grand Duke Vladimir Michaelovitch said he would give a golden punch bowl to the first car to reach Paris.

By this time the Protos had crossed into German territory and was nearing Berlin. Koeppen wired the *New York Times* correspondent there: "Both the car and myself are in bully shape. . . . I expect to reach Berlin Friday morning and maintain our lead till we land in Paris definite winners."[26]

The Imperial Automobile Club of Berlin announced plans to celebrate Koeppen's "phenomenal victory," which it compared to the "glorious deeds accomplished by the German cars in the Grand Prix at Dieppe." The chairman of the Automobile Club of Koenigsberg said that Koeppen's showing proved that "German industry and German manhood were second to none." The car's triumph was an accomplishment of national importance, he said.[27]

Fifty cars escorted Koeppen the last thirty-two miles into Berlin on July 24. A squad of mounted police cleared a path for the final approach to the newspaper office. "Berlin has never known a more excited or a greater crowd than that which gathered in the streets today to honor the German crew in the around the world race," a dispatch to the *New York Times* said. "Hundreds of thousands of persons thronged the streets leading from the outskirts of the town to the headquarters of the *Zeitung am Mittag* on Kochstrasse, to which the Protos wended its way for a formal welcome."[28]

The Berlin newspaper's offices were draped with bunting of German, French, and American flags. Cheering spectators carried Koeppen inside. The officer said the German "Hochs" shouted by Berliners were "the first real music we had heard for half a year." The officer said the celebration equalled that given the victorious German Army when it returned from France in 1870, after the war that led to the consolidation of the German empire. He said more than one million people crowded the streets, making it almost impossible to move the car.

"We have done our best in this grinding, soul-wracking hurdle race across two hemispheres to live up to the famous command which was given to our troops by Admiral Seymour during the advance on Peking in 1900," Koeppen said, "Germans to the front.

"We have had the good luck to be in front tonight and victory smiles on us from across the Rhine, but who knows where we may be tomorrow night? While the cheers that seem to be voiced by all Berlin are ringing encouragingly in our ears as we chum our way through the crowded streets, the ominous tidings arrive that our gallant American competitor, by a magnificent spurt from St. Petersburg, has

Hans Koeppen at the wheel of an unidentified Protos car sometime after the race. (COURTESY OF THE SIEMENS MUSEUM, MUNICH)

crossed the German frontier and is making feverish haste to demolish what we had been thinking was a comfortable lead."[29]

He said he was in the lead, not because of anything he had done, but because of the skill of his drivers. Koeppen waited until the formal greeting was over before rushing into the arms of his white-haired father, a retired colonel in the army, who cried at his son's return. The German racers attended a lunch with military officers before setting off on the seven hundred dusty miles to Paris. The Germans held a five-hundred-mile lead on the Thomas.

Not once during the Berlin celebration did Koeppen or his sponsors take note of the thirty-day allowance accorded to the Thomas Flyer. The Germans acted as if there was no handicap and as if the first car to Paris would be the winner.

The Protos had traveled some of the world's worst roads in the preceding five months. On the final two-day dash to Paris, it traveled some of the best. Capable civil engineers and a French law that had required local road maintenance and taxes since 1836 had created an excellent road network where speeds of fifty miles per hour were often possible.

The Protos had no trouble on the trip through France. Koeppen, Fuchs, and Neuberger came to a stop in front of *Le Matin*'s offices at 6:15 p.m. on July 26. It had taken two months and four days to cover the 8,280 miles from Vladivostok.

Although they were hailed as heroes in Germany, the men on the Protos received little recognition from the French. *Le Matin* and the French auto establishment treated them as unwanted guests. After the de Dion's withdrawal two months earlier, coverage of the race had almost disappeared from the pages of most newspapers, restricted to an occasional short story on a back page. When the Protos arrived at *Le Matin*'s offices, the welcoming ceremony consisted of two members of the Automobile Club of France shaking hands with Koeppen and his men.

The *New York Times* found this reception puzzling. "For some reason, possibly not unconnected with national feelings which time has not quite assuaged, there was no official ceremony or reception to Koeppen on behalf of the French race committee." *Le Matin* tried to explain this by claiming that the German car had actually finished the race when it entered Berlin and there was no need for it to come to Paris. This took the *Times* and everyone else by surprise. The New York paper said that since "the finishing point was fixed at Paris and has not been changed, the basis of this view is not apparent."[30]

The Siemens Company acquired the Protos Company in 1908 and continued manufacturing cars until 1926. (COURTESY OF THE SIEMENS MUSEUM, MUNICH)

A small crowd followed the Germans into the Hotel Regina, where an impromptu reception lasted for several hours in the dining room. Koeppen planned to have lunch the next day with the German ambassador before returning to his homeland. He said his leave of absence ended August 1 and he had to get back to the army.

"We have had a splendid trip," Koeppen said in Paris, "and I'd like to take another such."[31] Taking note of the reception in France, he said that his real welcome had occurred in Germany. The brusque treatment of the racers did not go unnoticed in Germany, where the motoring magazine *Der Motorwagen* said the threat of competition from the German auto makers gave the French plenty of reason for worry. Had the Thomas reached Paris first, the magazine said, that

would have been acceptable because the American auto industry was not a serious international competitor. But the magazine said that following the German victory over the French in the Grand Prix, France could not stand another blow to its pride by recognizing the true victors in the race to Paris. "To hell with the sport if it ruins business, according to the *Matin*," *Der Moterwagen* said bitterly.[32]

American motoring journals interpreted the French reaction in much the same way. "The reception of the Protos at Paris was a most frigid affair compared to the great ebullition of joy which greeted the arrival of the German 'victor' at Berlin, this being the manner in which the Protos was generally hailed there," *Automobile* reported.[33]

The German car's arrival generated more enthusiasm in New York than it did in Paris. The news reached New York by cable within hours of the finish. The *Times* posted a bulletin in Times Square at 9:30 p.m. The managers of prominent German-American restaurants phoned the newspaper for details. At Pabst's Grand Circle restaurant at Fifty-eighth Street and Eighth Avenue, the manager stopped the music and spoke of Koeppen's success to an audience that included representatives of Lozier, White, and Cadillac automobiles. The men at the crowded tables jumped up and cheered, while the women waved handkerchiefs and clapped. The band then played "Wacht am Rhein" and "The Star Spangled Banner."

"The race could hardly have been more successful from the German-American point of view," said the manager of Luchow's Restaurant on East Fourteenth Street. "The German car has got in first, and the American car wins on time allowance."[34]

This latter point, although well-publicized in New York, received as little attention in Germany as the Protos had in Paris. The *Zeitung am Mittag* claimed an outright victory for its car. The newspaper said

the allowance given to the Thomas Flyer for going to Alaska was unfair and that Koeppen should never have been penalized for taking the train to Seattle. The newspaper decried the penalty as "wholly arbitrary and unsportsmanlike."

The Germans contended that the original race route across the United States had been abandoned and that all the cars were on an equal footing when they left Seattle. "If the course is radically altered, it is the rule in sport to arrange a fresh start, no matter where the contestants were when the old route was abandoned," the newspaper said in a complaint to the *New York Times*.[35] The *Zeitung am Mittag* filed a protest and reported that the Imperial German Automobile Club shared its view that the Protos was the winner. The newspaper urged the rest of the German press to take up the cause because the "matter has a certain national importance."

The *Times* said the German newspaper distorted the facts: the route had not been altered in the United States, and Koeppen knew he faced either disqualification or a penalty when he took the train. The *Times* said that while the German racers showed plenty of courage and determination, they did not win the race. "The Thomas car, which is now nearing Paris, is, of course, the winner of the race, and has won all the honors except the desirable one of reaching Paris first," the *Times* said.[36]

The Thomas Flyer entered Berlin at 8:00 a.m. July 27, and its occupants learned that the Germans had reached Paris the night before. The news did not discourage the men in the least, MacAdam reported, although Koeppen's father and others who greeted the Thomas crew seemed to think the Protos was the winner of the race. Schuster and his crew did not argue the point right then. For weeks they had known that the allowance accorded the Thomas car virtually guaranteed a first-place finish.

Slowed by fog and clutch trouble, it took the Thomas three days to reach Paris from Berlin. A large crowd of French drivers met the American car twenty-five miles outside of Paris and followed the Thomas into the city at 8:00 p.m. on July 30, four days after the Germans.

St. Chaffray and others responsible for the contest assembled at the offices of *Le Matin* and offered champagne to the men on the Thomas, but the reception was subdued. *Le Matin* had "apparently lost enthusiasm and made no pretense at drum beating," as one observer put it.

Twilight had changed to night as the car made its way to Fournier's garage, but not without a brush with authority that showed why the Paris police had a reputation for being tough on motorists. "You are under arrest," a policeman said to Schuster, stopping the car in front of the Cafe de la Paix. "You have no lights on your car."

St. Chaffray and a crowd of Americans from the cafe explained that the car had just finished a trip around the world and the headlights had been broken on the journey, but the policeman insisted. A man on a bicycle came by and offered his headlight. It could not be detached from the frame, so the bike was lifted into the car and placed between Schuster and Miller. The owner of the bike hopped aboard the rear of the car. With the bicycle lighting the way, the Thomas made it to the garage, while the men went to a dinner at the Grand Hotel.

The four men from the Thomas stood out in the crowd. Wearing dusty clothes, they looked like men who had spent the past 169 days in an open car. "There was as much hardship on this trip as any of us desired," Schuster said. "At times I doubted whether any car would get through. Now that we have finished, we are glad that we have got first place for America. We have been running on three hours' sleep

per night for so long and had had so little acquaintance with real beds for the last four months that I doubt if we shall be able to sleep tonight. I suppose there is a bath upstairs and we will try what hot water and clean sheets can do anyway."[37]

Schuster said if he lived to be one hundred, he would never have an experience to equal the trip to Paris. He also said he would not do it again under any circumstances and that he would always remember the "thousands of creepers that attacked us in some of the Siberian hotels, where cleanliness was an unknown quantity." When someone asked about driving through Alaska, Captain Hansen chimed in, "Time to think about that when airships are perfected."

The next day the racers bought new clothes and delivered the message to the French minister of war that they had carried from William Howard Taft. The race was analyzed and discussed at length. One enterprising Paris store acquired a pair of boots and placed them on display in its store window with a sign that said "Worn in the *Paris Matin-New York Times*, New York to Paris race."

An official welcoming ceremony took place in front of *Le Matin*. The car made its way along the Boulevard Poissonniere at 1:30 p.m. A crowd encircled the car and people fought to add their signatures to the hundreds that already covered it. Bystanders grabbed for a piece of the American flag on the rear, while Hansen fought to wrap up the flag and get it inside the offices of *Le Matin*. "When the four men had entered the offices, George Miller stepped out on the balcony," the *Times* reported. "His appearance was the signal for another great outburst. As the throng cheered him there were cries for a speech but Miller in expressive gesture indicated his inability to speak the language. The others then joined him on the balcony and were cheered again, as long as they remained in view."[38]

A crowd surrounds the Thomas Flyer in Paris, nearly six months after leaving Times Square. (COURTESY OF WILLIAM F. HARRAH FOUNDATION NATIONAL AUTOMOBILE MUSEUM)

Official representatives of the French auto industry skipped the ceremonies, "Those who make, sell and deal in cars shrugged their shoulders and remained sullenly at home," *Automobile* reported. *Le Matin* also paid little attention, wrapping up the arrival of the Thomas in one eighth of a column. Most other French newspapers devoted about eight lines to the finish.[39]

In New York, those responsible for the American entrant said they could hardly have been more pleased with the way things turned out. Just as the Germans had brushed off the thirty-day allowance given

to the Thomas Flyer, the Americans said it was of no consequence that the Protos reached Paris four days before the Thomas Flyer.

Privately, there was concern that the victory would be tainted. George MacAdam's father wrote to his son just before the end of the race: "We feel very much hurt because while your car seems to have done the best work, the German car seems about to acquire the glory."[40]

In the United States at least, that's not what happened. The thirty-day allowance had been heavily publicized for two months and that made all the difference. New York Thomas dealer Harry Houpt said the race had proven "that America produces the best car for service in the world" and that the Thomas was the best car made on American soil. E. R. Thomas said the Thomas could start from Paris and retrace its route to New York with no problem, except for the physical exhaustion of the crew.[41] The Thomas Flyer had traveled the equivalent of four trips across the United States.

Now that the race was over, Hansen said goodbye to the others on the Thomas Flyer, but not without one last squabble with Schuster over money. The captain asked Schuster for five hundred dollars before returning to his family in Siberia. Schuster cabled New York, and the Thomas company instructed him to pay two hundred dollars to Hansen, which infuriated the captain, who said he had been promised a larger bonus. Hansen apparently took what he was offered, but he wasn't on the best of terms with Schuster or a lot of people at the end.

Some Frenchmen blamed Hansen for the failure of the de Dion. While staying at the Grand Hotel, Hansen received an anonymous letter saying he had deserted the French car "for the filthy money of the Americans." The note, signed "Anti-Mercenary," accused Hansen of being a traitor. It's not known if the threat was connected, but after the race Hansen disappeared.

"The last we saw of Captain Hansen," MacAdam said three months later, "was when the racing party broke up in Paris. He had a considerable amount of money and was to start for his home in Tomsk, Siberia, where he has a wife and child. The first news of his disappearance came in a request from his mother, who is a Norwegian, that a search be made for him. Every one supposed him back in Tomsk with his family, but the latest advices from the other side are that he has not shown up there and none of his friends have heard from him since he told us goodbye in Paris."[42]

The Norwegian consul general in New York asked the Thomas company to aid in searching for Hansen. It's not clear why he disappeared, but Hansen's vanishing act may have been a simple matter of economics. A month before the race he said he had placed a bet of five thousand dollars that he would make it to Paris in less than one hundred days. He missed by sixty-nine days. If he actually made that bet, he didn't have the funds to cover his debt, warranting a temporary disappearance. Hansen took pride in his ability as a showman, and he tried to create an air of drama and suspense. In the end, he succeeded.

When the captain resurfaced, he was safe and sound, according to the files of the Royal Ministry of Foreign Affairs in Norway. Hansen moved from Tomsk to Biisk and later to St. Petersburg. The ministry says he was last heard from on June 26, 1911, when he was reported to be operating a roller-skating rink in St. Petersburg.[43]

ELEVEN

THE HOMECOMING

THE THOMAS FLYER and the three Georges sailed from Le Havre to New York on the S.S. *Lorraine*, the same ship that had carried most of the European cars to America six months earlier. The Lorraine docked at the French Line pier on a bright August morning, as more than fifty prominent automobile drivers waited to shake hands with Schuster, Miller, and MacAdam. Montague Roberts and the other two men who had taken turns at the wheel of the Thomas, Linn Mathewson and Harold Brinker, greeted the racers, as did E. R. Thomas, officials of the Automobile Club of America, and officials of the American Automobile Association.

MacAdam told newsmen of some of his experiences in Russia, including the time he grew excessively weary of the diet of black bread and tea and put his hands on his head to represent horns and made mooing sounds. The hotel proprietor eventually got the message, he said, and found some meat for dinner.[1]

The racers stopped by the offices of the *New York Times* and went to the Automobile Club of America clubhouse for lunch. Club official Robert Lee Morrell said this was the first international auto race won by an American car and a sign of things to come for the United States auto industry. "It shows the American car is on a par with the foreign

machine, and it marks the beginning of the end, in my opinion, of the European supremacy," he said.

E. R. Thomas said he would enter the car in the twenty-four-hour race at Brighton Beach in September, to show that it could stand any challenge. He said in good weather the trip to Paris could be made in half the time. A German engineer who had helped design the Protos and was working in New Jersey said that had his countrymen fully understood the reasons for the handicap awarded to the Thomas Flyer, they would never have filed a protest over the outcome.[2]

Newspapers compared the race results to the Olympic Games that summer in England, at which the United States won fifteen of twenty-eight gold medals. "America has gained another victory over the Old World," the *New York Evening Mail* said. The newspaper pointed out, however, that a relay race by runners might have beaten the Thomas to Paris by about a month.

The YMCA had just run a relay race from New York to Chicago in which the boys covered two hundred miles a day, nearly twice the daily average of the Thomas. "Thoreau used to hold that walking was more expeditious than travelling by train if you added to the time spent on the train, the time spent in earning the money to purchase your railroad ticket," the *Evening Mail* said. "A good walker could have circled the globe in less time than the Thomas machine, if you count in the time it would cost a man, on an average income, to earn the money needed to defray the expenses for maintenance and repair of the machine."[3]

The *Philadelphia Public Ledger*, which was owned by *New York Times* Publisher Adolph Ochs, said the completion of the race "belongs to the short list of the world's phenomenal, memorable, unsurpassable

deeds." Even the *New York World* said the *Times* deserved congratulations for the success of the event.[4]

The *New York Times* editorialized that the real significance of the race was that it showed the automobile was now to be taken seriously as an invention. Its durability had been proven as never before. "The self-moving car is to play a very prominent part in our future history. It is to be used for freight as well as passenger traffic, to supplant the trucks and vans drawn by horses, to be applied to farm machinery, to be of service in war," the newspaper said.[5]

Leading generals in Washington said the race had established that the motorized vehicle could be an asset in wartime, even in countries with primitive roads. "The automobile will never play an important part in the transportation of troops because automobiles large enough to carry any considerable number of men require roads of a high degree of excellence," predicted Brig. Gen. Clarence Edwards, chief of the Bureau of Insular Affairs. "But the movement of general officers is also an important factor in battles and it is here that the automobile will come in. In the transmission of dispatches, too, the automobile might prove valuable."[6]

A couple of days after the ship docked, the men returned to the wharf for a parade through Manhattan. A crane lifted the wooden container holding the car out of the ship's hold and lowered it to the wharf, as a crowd sang the national anthem. Workmen ripped open the crate, they filled the gas tank of the Thomas Flyer, and George Miller cranked the engine once more. Ships in the harbor and shorefront factories sounded their whistles, while the horns of thirty automobiles added to the chorus. The Thomas Flyer was dented and dusty; the boards that had been carried over its wheels to aid in crossing gullies were gone. The tread on the tires was worn and the

An eight-year-old boy awaits the arrival of the Thomas flyer in his soapbox car outside the Automobile Club of America in New York. When the Thomas and a procession of fifty cars arrived, the youngster was the center of attention, as the motorists signed his car and a pennant he was carrying. (COURTESY OF THE DETROIT PUBLIC LIBRARY)

body was covered with signatures, but the car was still running. People in the streets waved yellow flags that said "Thomas wins—New York to Paris.

Montague Roberts was back in the car with the others for the victory parade, but only because of Schuster. Roberts was persona non grata with the Thomas company because he had pointed out problems with the 1909 Model L cars being shipped to Thomas dealers across the country. The car was underpowered, it leaked oil, and Roberts said so. Company officials had said that Roberts wouldn't be allowed to ride in the car, but Schuster refused to participate without him. The company backed down.

The Thomas Flyer is uncrated in New York after its return from Paris, moments before a victory parade forms in the streets of Manhattan. (COURTESY OF GEORGE T. MACADAM.)

Schuster offered to let Roberts drive the car during the home-coming celebration, but the racer declined, saying that Schuster deserved the honor.[7] The men wore their dusty road clothes to help create an authentic atmosphere for the parade. A truck carrying a band led the way, followed by the Thomas Flyer and one hundred or more motorists. The procession went to City Hall, where Acting Mayor Patrick McGowan posed behind the wheel for the benefit of a dozen photographers. Six months earlier McGowan had presided at the send-off for Eugene Lelouvier and spoke of the trail to be blazed across a route that might one day carry intercontinental trains.

The failure to drive through Alaska and northern Siberia had not dimmed his enthusiasm. "This race around the world has been a

tremendous strain on both machine and men," McGowan said. "But now that I have seen the men I am not surprised that they withstood that test of muscle and endurance."

He added that E. R. Thomas deserved praise for "having the pluck and the patriotism to enter a car in this international event, and thus give these boys an opportunity to place our flag at the forefront of world sport—an event which, I should add, has happened with pleasing frequency this year."[8]

Later, the car returned to the Times Building, where it was placed on display under lock and key, so that no one could sneak in and make repairs to it. This was an advertising gimmick to prove that the car was still in good running order.

The next trip for the Thomas was a short one—out to Sagamore Hill on Long Island, so that President Roosevelt could pay his respects to the men and machine. At Oyster Bay, James Sloan, the chief of the Secret Service, joined the entourage. The car arrived while Roosevelt, dressed in a white flannel shirt and white knickerbockers, was playing tennis with his son Kermit and Postmaster General George Meyer. The president saw the Thomas and waved his racket in greeting.

Roosevelt shook hands with his guests, invited them inside, and ordered the butler to bring cigars and cigarettes. The president's view of the automobile had evolved considerably during his years in the White House. Three years earlier he had vowed not to travel by auto again because his driver had been stopped for speeding. By 1908 Roosevelt had softened his stance enough to allow himself to be photographed in the rear seat of a White Steamer. A car magazine greeted the turnabout with the headline: "PRESIDENT ROOSEVELT NOW VISITS IN AUTO."[9]

As they puffed away in the comfortable chairs of the presidential library, Schuster and the others told Roosevelt what it was like on the road. The *Times* reported later that Schuster mentioned tigers, wolves, and a savage band of outlaws that liked to roast the feet of victims over a slow fire. It's more likely that Schuster talked about transmission and clutch trouble and that the savages were created by a reporter for dramatic purposes.

"Were you well-armed Mr. Schuster?" the president asked. "Yes, Mr. President. We had express rifles, Colt revolvers, and shotguns."

"Sounds like my African trip, doesn't it?" Roosevelt said to the postmaster general.

Roosevelt was planning an expedition to Africa the next year to keep him occupied following his departure from the White House. He laughed when he was told that some of the worst roads on the entire trip were in the United States; he said he would have been surprised to hear differently. He said winning the race had been a great achievement for the racers and for the American car industry. Roosevelt said he was proud of people who did things, whether that meant going up in an airship, down in a submarine, or around the world in a car.

An impossible race from New York to Paris was a prime example of what Roosevelt called the "strenuous life." In his view, the only things worthy of achievement required a struggle to obtain them. Roosevelt once said it would be far better for people to "run the risk of wearing out than rusting out."

Roosevelt gave the men a guided tour of his favorite spots in the twenty-three-room house. He showed them a framed photograph sent to him by Pope Pius X and other prized possessions, such as regimental flags from his time with the Rough Riders. In the north room, they

saw wild boar tusks, bear heads, deer heads, and other hunting trophies, all shot by the president.[10]

Roosevelt examined the car closely before the men rode back to the city for more honors and recognition. In the weeks ahead, parades and celebrations followed in Albany, Utica, Syracuse, Rochester, and Buffalo. As the flag-waving and hoopla continued, everyone seemed to forget the race was not over for one of the cars.

When the Protos and the Thomas crossed the finish line, the Zust was still in Omsk, with five thousand miles to go. Mechanical problems, illnesses, and accidents had slowed Scarfoglio's progress. He had turned twenty-two in Siberia and must have thought he was in danger of growing old before getting to Paris. Numerous breakdowns stopped the car in out-of-the-way places. Haaga came down with a high fever in one primitive village and couldn't travel for days. Worst of all, the noise of the car spooked a team of horses: the animals ran over a small boy and killed him.

Scarfoglio and Haaga wrapped the tiny body and placed it in the back of the car. The dead child's sister rode with them to the next village, where Scarfoglio notified the authorities. It was a difficult ride, but not because of the terrain. The girl did not know that the bundle in the back was her brother, Scarfoglio said.[11]

The policeman Scarfoglio found at the frontier village of Tauroggen said he already knew about the boy's death. A telegram said that the car had killed the boy. Scarfoglio and Haaga protested that it wasn't their fault, but the policeman ordered them to jail. The two men found themselves in a cell with "fourteen delinquents who spoke all the languages of the world—except our own," Scarfoglio said. They spent the time "seated on a hard bench, eating a few spoonfuls of the daily

bean soup, scarcely daring to sip a drop of the infected water from a jug and not speaking a word."[12]

After three days, the police released the two men and apologized after learning the facts of the accident. Some days later, another accident temporarily took the zip out of the Zust. After traveling through Berlin, Scarfoglio and Haaga stopped for lunch, devouring sausages and a little too much wine. A representative from the Zust factory was also riding in the car when Haaga ran off the road. The impact knocked the three men out and a passerby found them, Scarfoglio and the factory man in the grass, and Haaga slumped behind the wheel.

After five days in the hospital, the bandaged and bruised motorists resumed the journey. They reached Paris on September 18, more than six weeks behind the leaders. "Our task was a rough one, but we persevered," Scarfoglio said. "America froze us; Asia flagellated us with its rain; Europe came to us with arms loaded with catastrophes. Today Paris appears, smiling in a brilliant sunset."[13]

The men on the Zust finished last, but they said they deserved to be first. According to Scarfoglio, both the Thomas and Protos should have been disqualified because of what had happened back in the United States.[14] The race concluded with all three finishers claiming victory. It seemed that the controversy over the run to Paris would prove as endless as the steppes of Siberia.

Before settling back in at his job at the Thomas factory, George Schuster made the first of many attempts to collect the one thousand dollar prize offered by Jefferson DeMont Thompson, the official of the Automobile Club of America and the American Automobile Association. The *Times* reported that Thompson had agreed to pay the prize, even though no cars had completed the original route.[15]

Schuster kept after Thompson, but more than two years passed without any action. Thompson had asked Schuster to help prepare a book on the race that would include a photograph of Thompson and an inscription. Schuster had refused, which may explain Thompson's failure to pay the prize.

In 1911, Schuster met with Thompson in New York City to renew his complaint. Thompson told him to bring the flag and leave it with a photograph in his office. Schuster followed instructions, but a few weeks later the flag and photo were returned to him without the money. Schuster kept the flag and it became one of his prized possessions, but the name J. DeMont Thompson was erased from it.

The *New York Times* had awarded a trophy to the Thomas for reaching San Francisco first. *Le Matin*, which had withdrawn its original prize after the arctic route proved to be impossible, eventually also paid tribute to the Thomas as well. A year-and-a-half after the contest the two newspapers jointly presented a trophy to E. R. Thomas, recognizing his entry as the overall winner.

The newspapers sponsored a banquet on January 8, 1910 in the main assembly hall of the Automobile Club of America. Photographs of the Thomas fighting snow in Indiana, mud in Iowa, and mosquitos in Siberia decorated the walls. The menu for the evening, on a brochure labeled "Proposed Route and Times Table," featured such delicacies as de Dion Olives, Zust Celery, Protos Nuts, Iowa Gumbo, Anti-Freezing Solution, Manchurian Weeds with French Dressing, and Alaskan Frost, with Vladivostok Cookies.

At a signal from the toastmaster, Schuster and Miller pulled wires that released the American flag draped over the trophy. A band struck up the national anthem and the flag fell, revealing a sixteen hundred

pound trophy. The longest race in history deserved the biggest car trophy in history.

It stood six feet, six inches high and featured a German bronze globe atop a base of pink French marble, mounted on a block of green Italian marble. An eagle topped the globe with its talons stretched across the American continent, "the very incarnation of victorious defiance," the *Times* said.[16] The race route was marked in American silver.

"Certainly no trophy ever presented had such a beautiful appearance, one so truly representative of the novelty of the affair which it commemorated," the *Times* said.

Victory in the New York–Paris race gave E. R. Thomas's car company an ideal opportunity to put its name before the public. The company advertised the Thomas Flyer as "The Car That Defends America Against the World" and "Ready for a Trip Around the World at any Minute." All correspondence from the company's Buffalo headquarters featured a letterhead showing the Thomas Flyer on the road and an American flag that took up one third of the page.

The company published a booklet on the race that described the Thomas as the "most reliable car in the world." The booklet failed to mention the major repairs made by Schuster and Miller, and it gave the impression that any mechanical problems on the way to Paris were of little consequence. Anyone who had followed the extensive news coverage of the race knew differently. The booklet also failed to mention that had the company acted faster in delivering a new transmission to Siberia, the Thomas would probably have been the first car to enter Paris. At least that's how Schuster saw it.

He said the exaggerated claims about the car's performance harmed the Thomas company's image, as did the mechanical problems that

afflicted newer models. The company produced some fine automobiles, Schuster said, but others were "poorly designed cars that caused endless grief to owners, dealers and the factory."[17] Schuster agreed with Montague Roberts that the Model L was "noisy, underpowered and literally leaked oil."

Production at the Buffalo factory peaked the year after the race, when the Thomas company built 1,036 vehicles. E. R. Thomas believed that car prices would never decline and that the future of the United States car market was in high-priced automobiles, not in "low-class autos." He was wrong. There was a growing demand for American cars, but not for the high-priced cars produced by the E. R. Thomas Motor Company.

Led by the success of Ford's Model T, overall United States automobile sales boomed in the years after the race to Paris, but the Thomas company showed a steady decline. Chronic problems with new models led many of the best dealers, including Harry Houpt in New York, to shift to other makes. Thomas sold the firm to Eugene Meyer, a New York banker, in 1911. Meyer brought in a group of executives from Packard, but they could not save the Thomas from a fatal crash.

The company sold only 350 cars in 1912. From there, it was a short step to bankruptcy. About six thousand of the seven thousand Thomas cars built remained on the road when the company went under.[18]

Shortly after the race, E. R. Thomas had given Schuster one thousand dollars and a promise of a job "as long as there is a Thomas company." Thomas said he had spent nearly one hundred thousand dollars on the race and couldn't afford to pay Schuster the ten thousand dollars that factory rumors said he was in line for. He asked Schuster if he wanted the Thomas Flyer he had driven to Paris. Schuster declined to take it, figuring it wasn't worth much because of its condition.

Despite advertisements such as this, the Thomas Company failed to translate its victory into increased auto sales. (*MOTOR*)

The car served as a pathfinder in 1909 for a race from New York to Seattle staged for the Alaska-Yukon-Pacific Exposition. The race was won by a Model T, generating free publicity for the car that became the world's workhorse. George Miller drove the Thomas Flyer, which broke down in Idaho and had to be shipped back to Buffalo.

E. R. Thomas talked of giving the Paris race car to the Smithsonian Institution, but the Thomas Flyer and the trophy were sold in a 1913 auction of the bankrupt company's assets. For many years, a former Buffalo newspaper publisher kept the car in his garage, where it continued to deteriorate. When Henry Austin Clark, Jr., bought the Thomas Flyer in 1948, it was a rusted wreck.

Despite its condition, Clark recognized the vehicle as an important piece of automotive history and displayed it at his Long Island auto museum outside New York City. Schuster, however, refused to believe it was the same car he had driven to Paris. He figured that the steering wheel, part of the seats, and maybe the axles were all that was original.

"Because I believed the essential parts were different, I refused many invitations to visit the museum and be photographed in the car there," Schuster said.[19]

The car changed hands again in the early 1960s, when gambling tycoon and automobile collector William F. Harrah added the Thomas Flyer to his collection. At the age of ninety-one, Schuster flew to Reno, Nevada, to inspect the car. "I am very glad to meet you," Schuster told Harrah, "But I am sorry to say that I do not think that the car you have is the one I drove into Paris."[20]

To find out for sure, Harrah's mechanics began taking the car apart piece by piece. While doing so, they discovered holes drilled in the frame as part of emergency repairs on the way to Paris. They also found the initials *M. B.* on the side of the left front seat. Schuster remembered that a Thomas employee had a girlfriend named Minnie Byers and that the factory worker had left her initials for posterity. Schuster dropped all his objections when the mechanics took apart the clutch. He saw the holes that had been drilled in the flywheel fifty-six years earlier when he fixed the car in Moscow.[21]

Harrah's crew rebuilt the car and Schuster returned to Reno to inspect the finished product in 1964. Schuster rode to his hotel in the old noisy Thomas Flyer, which, as in 1908, had no muffler. The restoration work was accurate, Schuster said, down to the seat belt on the passenger's side in the front and the red stripe on the gray body.[22] Harrah shipped the car to Tonopah, Nevada, where the arrival of the Thomas Flyer was re-enacted with Schuster at the wheel.

The restoration of the Thomas Flyer was part of a dream for William Harrah, who wanted to acquire at least one model of every important car ever made. He spent thirty years amassing fourteen hundred classic autos, one of the biggest collections in the world. After

his death in 1978, the Holiday Inn hotel chain purchased the cars along with Harrah's hotels and casinos. Holiday Corporation auctioned hundreds of the cars in sales that brought in at least $70 million.[23]

The company donated 175 of Harrah's cars and his library to the William F. Harrah Foundation National Automobile Museum. The museum in Reno, Nevada, offers one of the most comprehensive displays of cars in the United States. The Thomas Flyer is there, along with two hundred other relics such as the 1949 Mercury driven by James Dean in *Rebel Without a Cause*, a 1973 Cadillac owned by Elvis Presley, and a Philion steam carriage from 1890, one of the oldest automobiles built in America. A 1982 appraisal valued the Thomas Flyer at $1.5 million.[24]

Since its restoration, the Thomas Flyer has come out of retirement for exhibitions and a few cross-country tours. The car returned to Times Square in 1968 for the start of a transcontinental tour marking the sixtieth anniversary of the race to Paris. As part of that commemorative tour, a ninety-five-year-old man finally got what he deserved. Addressing what it said was "the slowest payoff in racing history," the *New York Times* delivered a one thousand dollar check to George Schuster, the money he had been promised so long before.[25]

The dollar had lost much to inflation, but the payoff at a banquet stop in Buffalo recognized one of Schuster's main accomplishments in a life spent largely in the automobile business. From 1920 until 1936 he had a Dodge dealership in a Buffalo suburb, but it folded during the Great Depression. Schuster retired in 1946, after spending ten years with Cutter Davis, a builder of gear reducers.

He corresponded regularly with Montague Roberts, who left the auto business in 1911 and was in charge of helium production for the United States government during World War I. Roberts worked for

The restored Thomas Flyer as it looks today in the William F. Harrah Foundation National Automobile Museum in Reno, Nevada. (COURTESY OF WILLIAM F. HARRAH FOUNDATION NATIONAL AUTOMOBILE MUSEUM)

The restored German Protos is now on display in the Deutsches Museum in Munich, Germany. (COURTESY OF DEUTSCHES MUSEUM)

a railroad supply company and a tool company until he retired. He died in 1957, when he was seventy-four. Mechanic George Miller died in 1937.

Schuster appeared on the television show "I've Got a Secret" in 1958, the year he took his first airplane flight. He wrote a first-person account of the race for *Reader's Digest* and then collaborated with Tom Mahoney on a book. In the final years of his life, Schuster grew tired of repeating his stories. He recorded them, so whenever anyone would ask him about it, he would let a tape recorder do the talking.

Schuster had predicted back in 1908 that if he lived to be one hundred, nothing would ever match his experience on the road to Paris. He died on the Fourth of July in 1972, seven months short of his hundredth birthday. His eyesight had failed, but he was hearty enough at ninety-eight to keep a long driveway shoveled. On his ninety-ninth birthday he said his only regret was that he had not accepted E. R. Thomas's offer to take the car that won the race.[26]

For all of the men who headed for Paris, the race was a highlight of their lives. Most disappeared from the public eye in the years after the contest. Scarfoglio wrote a book in 1909, *Round the World in a Motorcar*, that was translated into English and won praise from reviewers for its amusing detail. His writing owed something to his father, editor and author Edoardo Scarfoglio, who fought several duels and "considered himself a buccaneer floundering in nonheroic waters," one critic wrote.[27] In the mid-1960s, Schuster said that of those who took part in the race, apparently only he and Scarfoglio remained alive.[28] After the race, Scarfoglio helped manage his father's newspaper. With the rise of Mussolini, the paper was sold and he became a freelance writer because he objected to fascist rule. He died in 1969.

Hans Koeppen also wrote a book just after the race, *Im Auto um die Welt*. The book does not mention that the Thomas won the race. It says simply, and correctly, that the Protos was the first to reach Paris. After the race, Koeppen returned to active duty and fought in World War I, retiring after the war. Recalled to the army in the 1930s, Koeppen was made a general by the Nazis. According to his wife, he grew disillusioned with the regime and left the army in 1943 for health reasons. She said that later he was nearly beaten to death by Poles when they learned he had been a high-ranking officer. After the war, he was held virtually as a prisoner by the Russians until 1947, she said. He was released in ill health and died some months later.[29]

Today, the Deutsches Museum in Munich contains the restored Protos. The Siemens Corporation, now a major electronics firm, acquired the Protos Company in 1908 and continued building Protos cars until 1926 when it sold the auto subsidiary. The Protos was well-built, but too expensive for the average German. Production ended in 1934.

The two *New York Times* correspondents who covered the race went on to many journalistic achievements in later years. Skipper Williams, who was on the car from when it left New York until it reached Iowa, became the most prominent of the city's ship news reporters. He was a legend in the newsroom of the *New York Times*, where he worked until his death in 1942. In the days when everyone traveled the Atlantic by ship, Williams and the other ship news reporters would go out to meet the ships to interview newsworthy passengers and talk to the captains. "On the long waterfront of the great shipping port that was his 'beat' for many years, he was a familiar, almost Dickensian character—almost as familiar in fact, as the spars and stacks of the ships to which he was so devoted," the *Times* said in his obituary.[30]

He could conduct interviews in German, French, Italian, and Spanish and he probably knew more transatlantic visitors than any man in the city. For years, he also wrote wild tales about a set of imaginary characters he had created who traveled the world getting into trouble with "eight-foot head-hunters of the Wazza-bazza tribe" or "pink-faced zizza-zazzas." These tales appeared in the *Times* under ordinary one-column headlines that gave no hint that Marmaduke M. Mizzle and Ali the Egyptian were a figment of the Skipper's imagination.[31]

George MacAdam remained on the staff of the *Times* for about ten years. He later wrote for *World's Work*, one of the more influential magazines of the era. In 1925, he wrote a book called *The Little Church Around the Corner*, a history of one of New York's most famous churches. MacAdam especially admired the work of William Sydney Porter, the author known to the world as O. Henry, whose funeral was held in the Little Church. Porter shunned the life of a celebrity and gave only one interview in his life—to MacAdam. "I'll give you the whole secret of short-story writing," Porter said. "Rule No. 1. Write stories that please yourself. There is no Rule 2."[32]

As a freelance writer in later years, MacAdam sold dozens of stories to the *New York Times*. One of these was a 1928 retrospective on the twentieth anniversary of the race. Charles Lindbergh's thirty-three-hour flight to Paris in 1927 was much on MacAdam's mind when he thought of the race to Paris. "Can you find a more vivid illustration of the world's mechanical progress than Lindbergh's long, clean leap across space compared with the earth-bound grueling plug, plug of twenty years ago? The airman soaring over oceans, mountains, asking naught but that his propellers continue to whirr; the motorist stuck in a humble mudhole, his drivewheels spinning impotently in the slop?"

MacAdam recounted the days and nights of travail, relying on the notebooks and diaries he had kept about the event. "If ever again I participate in a New York to Paris race, it will be in an airplane," he said.[33] He never made that flight. After a long illness, MacAdam died in 1929 at the age of fifty-three.

In the decades after Lindbergh's leap across the Atlantic, a succession of more powerful and larger airplanes redefined attitudes about speed and world travel. In a few hours more than it took Lindbergh to go from New York to Paris, airplanes now circle the globe. But it seems that someone is always out to shave a few minutes off the record for world travel by air, land, or water. Phileas Fogg haunts us yet.

As part of the American bicentennial in 1976, an organization of auto enthusiasts planned a race from Paris to New York by way of Siberia. The owners of more than a dozen pre-1914 cars pledged to enter. They made one concession to modern technology: the cars would cross the Pacific Ocean on a Boeing 747 instead of in the hold of a cargo ship.

One proponent of the race said the venture "would give the same personal satisfaction as a trip to the moon or the Lewis and Clark expedition."[34] After a year-and-a-half of negotiations, however, the Soviets shot down the plan to drive across Siberia along the 1908 route. The racers had to settle for a tour of Europe and a trip across the United States. The Russian government concluded that the race "was just not practical," a spokesman for the race planners said.[35]

By any measure, the 1908 race was far more impractical. A 1916 history of the automobile said that of the thousands of publicity stunts designed to promote the automobile, none equalled the trip to Paris. "The single fact that three automobiles were able to run from New York to San Francisco in winter under their own power and at high

speed, everything considered, shed new light upon the sturdiness and power of the motor car and gave it a tremendous lot of publicity in the public prints," historian James Rood Doolittle wrote.[36]

Other automobile historians found little good in the race. In 1912, Frederick A. Talbot called the race a "dismal failure." Had the original route been followed, the cars would have been en route to Paris as he wrote, Talbot said.[37]

Poor organization, bad planning, accidents, and ignorance of world geography plagued the race from start to finish. The *New York Times*, which printed more than 280 articles on the race, performed a credible job in handling its share of the organizational work, but *Le Matin* created confusion by allowing the race rules to change more often than the weather. The Paris newspaper lost interest altogether when the race left American soil and the last of the French competitors fell by the wayside.

Le Matin had a circulation of nearly 1 million by 1910, but its reputation declined as the years passed. For forty-five years the newspaper was under the control of Maurice Bunau-Varilla, described by most historians as an unprincipled tyrant. Bunau-Varilla was a "flamboyant, mad-dictator type of press magnate," involved in many questionable practices, historian Theodore Zeldin wrote.

"My paper is, one may say, without limits," Bunau-Varilla said. "What it wants, it accomplishes; and it never wants anything but good things, useful to the greatest number."[38]

Bunau-Varilla thought it was a good thing to cooperate with the Nazis in World War II, which assured the newspaper's downfall. He died in 1944. Stephane Lauzanne, long-time editor of *Le Matin*, was convicted that year of collaborating with the Nazis. Lauzanne had praised the United States in 1908 when he visited New York for the

start of the race, but he turned against the Allies in World War II. He was seventy years old when a Paris court sentenced him to twenty years in jail and confiscated all of his possessions. Lauzanne was pardoned in 1951.[39]

While *Le Matin* went the way of the E. R. Thomas Motor Company, the other newspaper that sponsored the race to Paris became the preeminent newspaper in the United States, following Adolph Ochs's credo "To Give the News impartially, without fear or favor, regardless of any party, sect or interest involved."

The *Times* would never again go to such great lengths to promote the automobile. In a 1921 history of the newspaper, Elmer Davis devoted one sentence to the race to Paris. He said that since automobile news was such a prominent feature of so many publications, the *Times* "had no occasion to do in this field anything like its work in aviation and wireless. One event, however, it did promote—a New York-to-Paris automobile race, in collaboration with the *Paris Matin*, early in 1908."[40] By the time Meyer Berger wrote a company history in 1951, the race did not rate a single line.

After the race to Paris, the *Times* paid far more attention to the other machine that changed the twentieth century—the airplane. The newspaper offered a series of prizes for various achievements, such as the first roundtrip flight to Philadelphia and the first flight from Boston to Washington.

By the 1920s, the managers of the *Times* had decided to abandon the technique of promoting adventurers altogether, and "sternly held to the principle that they would not capitalize on another man's daring," Berger said. Ochs, Van Anda, and those who followed them at the *Times* committed themselves to covering news of exploration and adventure, instead of creating it. The *Times* achieved "a series of

impressive beats in pioneer aviation and exploration, but after the early prize ventures they never sent an explorer, a scientist or a flyer to risk his life for mere benefit of newspaper circulation," Berger said.[41]

The two men most responsible for the victory of the Thomas Flyer never stopped believing that the race to Paris did more than sell newspapers: if nothing else, it helped sell Americans on the practicality of the automobile for rough roads, according to Montague Roberts and George Schuster. In 1955, when Roberts was seventy-two and George Schuster eighty-two, the two men met together in New York City for the first time since 1910. They toasted each other and talked of the glory days. They spoke of the doctor in Tonopah who allowed Schuster to strip his car of everything he needed to keep the Thomas Flyer going.

"Now people raise the roof if they're held up five minutes at the toll gate," Schuster said. "Can you imagine the Union Pacific rearranging the timetable to give us time to get through the tunnel?"

The two men put their arms on each other's shoulders. "I'd do it again just to get off by myself. I never dreamed the roads would get so crowded," Schuster said.

Roberts nodded and said, "Amen."[42]

NOTES

Chapter 1: The Long Way around the World

1. *New York Times Film Reviews* (New York: New York Times, 1968), 568.
2. *Automobile*, February 13, 1908.
3. *New York Times*, February 17, 1908.
4. *Automobile*, February 13, 1908.
5. *New York Times*, January 5, 1908.
6. Ibid., February 11, 1908.
7. *Horseless Age*, April 22, 1908.
8. Edwin Emery, *The Press and America, An Interpretive History of the Mass Media* (Englewood Cliffs, N.J.: Prentice-Hall, 1982), 307–321.
9. Paul W. Harvey, *Tacoma Headlines, an Account of Tacoma News and Newspapers* (Tacoma, Wash.: Tribune Publishing Co., 1962), 22–28.
10. George Francis Train, *My Life in Many States and in Foreign Lands: Dictated in my Seventy-Fourth Year* (New York: Appleton, 1902), 339.
11. T.R. Nicholson, *The Trailblazers: Stories of the Heroic Age of Transcontinental Motoring* (London: Cassell, 1958), 1–9.
12. *Autocar*, September 14, 1907.
13. Luigi Barzini, *Peking to Paris in a Motor-Car* (1907; reprint, New York: The Library Press, 1973), 2.
14. Ibid., 15.
15. Ibid., 111.
16. T.R. Nicholson, *Adventurers Road: The Story of Pekin-Paris, 1907 and New York–Paris, 1908* (London: Cassell & Co., 1957), 130.
17. *New York Tribune*, February 23, 1902.
18. *Seattle Post-Intelligencer*, August 12, 1900.
19. Harry de Windt, *My Restless Life* (London: Grant Richards, 1909), 247–248.
20. Ibid., 301.

21. Harry de Windt, *My Notebook at Home and Abroad* (New York: E.P. Dutton & Co., 1923), 92.
22. *Autocar*, February 8, 1908.
23. *Automotor Journal*, February 29, 1908.
24. Jeannette Mirsky, *To The Arctic!* (1934; reprint, Chicago: University of Chicago Press, 1970), 273–278.
25. *New York Times*, December 1, 1907.
26. *Autocar*, December 14, 1907.
27. Pierre Berton, *The Klondike Fever* (1958; reprint, New York: Alfred A Knopf, 1977), 233–234.
28. *New York Times*, January 19, 1908.
29. Ibid., January 26, 1908.
30. Ibid., December 8, 1907.
31. Ibid., February 3, 1908.
32. Barnett Fine, *A Giant of the Press* (New York: Editor & Publisher Library, 1933), 41.
33. *New York Times*, February 11, 1908.
34. Ibid., December 1, 1907.
35. Ibid., December 2, 1907.
36. Ibid., February 17, 1908.
37. George Schuster and Tom Mahoney, *The Longest Auto Race* (New York: John Day Co., 1966), 140; *Scientific American*, January 16, 1909.

Chapter 2: The Road to Paris

1. *Automobile*, February 13, 1908.
2. *New York Times*, February 9, 1908.
3. Richard Kluger, *The Paper: The Life and Death of The New York Herald Tribune* (New York: Alfred A. Knopf, 1986), 186.
4. *New York World*, February 12, 1908; *New York Tribune*, February 12, 1908.
5. *New York Times*, February 12, 1908.
6. Ibid., January 2, 1908.
7. *Automobile*, February 13, 1908.
8. *New York Times*, July 27, 1908.
9. Ibid., February 8, 1908.
10. Ibid., February 22, 1908.
11. Antonio Scarfoglio, *Round the World in a Motor-Car* (London: Grant Richards, 1909), 24.
12. *New York Times*, August 16, 1908.
13. Ibid., February 11, 1908.

14. Ibid., February 10, 1908.
15. Allen Andrews, *The Mad Motorists: The Great Peking-Paris Race of '07* (New York: Lippincott, 1965), 249–250; *Autocar*, February 29, 1908.
16. *New York Times*, September 21, 1957; Schuster and Mahoney, *Longest Auto Race*, 27–28.
17. *New York Times*, February 12–13, 1908.
18. Ibid., February 11, 1908.
19. Ibid., February 13, 1908.
20. Ibid., February 13, 1908.
21. Scarfoglio, *Round the World*, 26.

Chapter 3: Snowbound

1. Joe McCarthy, "The Lincoln Highway," *American Heritage*, June 1974, 32–37.
2. *New York Times*, December 1, 1907.
3. *New York World*, February 13, 1908; *Philadelphia Inquirer*, February 13, 1908.
4. *Automobile*, February 20, 1908.
5. *Seattle Post-Intelligencer*, April 20, 1908; *Seattle Times*, April 21, 1908.
6. *New York World*, February 23, 1908.
7. Drake Hokanson, *The Lincoln Highway: Main Street Across America* (Iowa City, Iowa: University of Iowa Press, 1988), 45.
8. *New York Times*, January 19, 1908.
9. Ibid., February 9, 1908.
10. *Chicago Tribune*, February 9, 1908.
11. *New York Times*, February 13, 1908.
12. Scarfoglio, *Round the World*, 35.
13. *Buffalo Express*, February 15, 1908.
14. *New York Times*, February 15, 1908.
15. Ibid., February 16, 1908.
16. Ibid., February 16, 1908.
17. James E. Vance Jr., *Capturing the Horizon: The Historical Geography of Transportation since the Transportation Revolution of the Sixteenth Century* (New York: Harper & Row, 1986), 494.
18. Allan Nevins, *Ford: The Times, the Man, the Company* (New York: Charles Scribner's Sons, 1954), 387.
19. Ibid., 404–406.
20. *New York Times*, October 16, 1910.
21. *Buffalo Express*, February 17, 1908.
22. *New York Times*, February 17, 1908.

23. Maurice D. Hendry, "Thomas!," *Automobile Quarterly*, vol. 8, no. 4, 1970; *Automobile*, December 17, 1908.

24. *Buffalo Express*, March 2, 1908.

25. Ibid,, March 2, 1908.

26. *New York Times*, February 17, 1908.

27. Scarfoglio, *Round the World*, 30.

28. *Chicago Tribune*, March 2, 1908.

29. *Automobile*, May 28, 1908.

30. *New York Times*, February 17, 1908.

31. Ibid., March 16, 1908.

32. Ibid., February 19, 1908.

33. Ibid., October 10, 1942.

34. David Halberstam, *The Powers That Be* (New York: Alfred A. Knopf, 1979), 212.

35. *New York Times*, February 18, 1908.

36. Ibid., February 21, 1908.

37. Ibid., January 1, 1905.

38. Ibid., February 17, 1908.

39. Scarfoglio, *Round the World*, 41.

40. Ibid., 68–69.

41. Barzini, *Peking to Paris*, xv.

42. *Chicago Tribune*, February 20, 1908.

43. Ibid., February 20, 1908.

44. *New York Times*, February 21, 1908.

45. Scarfoglio, *Round the World*, 53.

46. *New York Times*, February 22, 1908.

47. Ibid., February 22, 1908.

48. Ibid., February 22, 1908.

49. Ibid., February 27, 1908.

50. Ibid., February 22, 1908.

51. Ibid., February 26, 1908.

52. *Rocky Mountain News*, March 22, 1908.

53. *New York Times*, March 1, 1908.

54. Ibid., March 1, 1908.

55. Ibid., February 21, 1908.

56. Ibid., February 22, 1908.

57. *Chicago Tribune*, February 25, 1908.

58. Ibid., February 26, 1908.

59. *New York Times*, February 25, 1908.

60. *Chicago Tribune*, February 27, 1908.

61. *New York Times*, February 29, 1908.

62. Scarfoglio, *Round the World*, 70–71.

63. *Chicago Tribune*, February 29, 1908.

64. *Chicago Tribune*, February 28, 1908; *Chicago Times-Herald*, February 28, 1908.

65. E.C. Morse, commercial manager of the E. R. Thomas Company, letter to George MacAdam, May 2, 1908.

66. *Omaha World-Herald*, March 9, 1908.

67. *Chicago Tribune*, March 2, 1908.

68. Nicholson, *Adventurers Road: The Story of Pekin-Paris, 1907 and New York–Paris, 1908*, 169.

69. *Autocar*, February 29, 1908.

70. Ibid., May 9, 1908.

71. Ibid., February 28, 1908.

72. Ibid., March 1, 1908.

73. *Automobile*, March 19, 1908.

74. *New York Times*, March 6, 1908.

75. Ibid., March 1, 1908.

76. Ibid., March 2, 1908.

Chapter 4: Of Mud and Motorists

1. Federal Writers' Project, *Iowa: A Guide to the Hawkeye State* (New York: Viking Press, 1938), 86.

2. Lincoln Highway Association, *The Complete Official Road Guide to the Lincoln Highway* (New York, 1921), 178.

3. *New York Times*, February 28, 1908.

4. Hokanson, *The Lincoln Highway*, 7.

5. Ibid., p. 106.

6. *New York Times*, March 1, 1908.

7. *Tonopah (Nevada) Daily Bonanza*, March 31, 1908.

8. *Chicago Times-Herald*, March 4–5, 1908.

9. *New York Times*, March 5, 1908.

10. *Chicago Tribune*, March 4, 1908.

11. *New York Times*, March 6, 1908.

12. Ibid., March 3, 1908.

13. Ibid., March 2, 1908.

14. Ibid., March 4, 1908.

15. Ibid., March 6, 1908.

16. Ibid., March 7, 1908.

17. Ibid., March 14, 1908.

18. Ibid., March 13, 1908.

19. Scarfoglio, *Round the World*, 82.

20. *Omaha World-Herald*, March 4, 1908.

21. Scarfoglio, *Round the World*, 86.
22. *Omaha World-Herald*, March 4, 1908.
23. *Denver Post*, March 8, 1908.
24. *Omaha World-Herald*, March 5, 1908.
25. Nellie Yost, *Buffalo Bill, his Family Friends, Fame, Failures, and Fortunes* (Chicago: Sage Books, 1979), 346–347.
26. *New York Times*, January 25, 1908.
27. Ibid., March 15, 1908.
28. Gene Fowler, *Timber Line* (1933; reprint, Comstock Edition, Sausalito, Calif., 1974), 191–206.
29. Frank Luther Mott, *American Journalism: A History, 1690–1960* (New York: Macmillan, 1962), 306–309.
30. *Rocky Mountain News*, March 3, 1908.
31. Ibid., March 7, 1908.
32. Ibid., March 8, 1908; *Denver Post*, March 10, 1908.
33. *Cheyenne Daily Leader*, March 24, 1908.
34. Ibid., March 10, 1908.
35. Ibid., March 10, 1908.
36. Ibid., March 22, 1908.
37. *New York Times*, March 21, 1908.
38. Scarfoglio, *Round the World*, 148.

Chapter 5: Riding the Rails
1. *Cheyenne Daily Leader*, March 10, 1908.
2. Floyd Clymer, *New York to Paris, 1908* (1908; reprint, Los Angeles: Floyd Clymer, 1951), 2–3.
3. *New York Times*, March 18, 1908.
4. Schuster and Mahoney, *Longest Auto Race*, 52.
5. The Home Insurance Co., *News from Home*, June–July 1952, 2–5.
6. Charles Edgar Ames, *Pioneering the Union Pacific: A Reappraisal of the Builders of the Railroad* (New York: Appleton-Century-Crofts, 1969), 537–541.
7. *Denver Post*, March 10, 1908.
8. *Horseless Age*, September 2, 1908.
9. *Denver Post*, March 11, 1908.
10. Ibid., March 11, 1908.
11. Scarfoglio, *Round the World*, 105.
12. *New York Times*, March 12, 1908.
13. *Denver Post*, March 13, 1908.
14. Ibid., March 13, 1908.
15. *Rocky Mountain News*, March 18, 1908.

16. *Denver Post*, March 20, 1908.

17. *New York Times*, March 16, 1908.

18. *Denver Post*, March 21, 1908.

19. *New York Times*, March 22, 1908.

20. Scarfoglio, *Round the World*, 113.

21. *New York Times*, March 29, 1908.

22. Ibid., March 29, 1908.

23. Dee Brown, *Hear That Lonesome Whistle Blow* (New York: Bantam Books, 1977), 30, 124.

24. *New York Times*, March 18, 1908.

25. Scarfoglio, *Round the World*, 124.

Chapter 6: Through the Gold Fields

1. Barton Currie, "The Gasoline Camel of the American Desert," *Harper's Weekly*, March 16, 1907.

2. Schuster and Mahoney, *Longest Auto Race*, 63.

3. Phillip I. Earl, "New York-to-Paris via Nevada: The Great Auto Race of '08," *Nevada Historical Society Quarterly*, Summer 1976, 105–127.

4. *New York Times*, April 1, 1908.

5. Scarfoglio, *Round the World*, 140.

6. *New York Times*, April 7, 1908.

7. Ibid., March 23, 1908.

8. *San Francisco Examiner*, March 23, 1908.

9. *New York Times*, March 19, 1908.

10. *San Francisco Chronicle*, March 25, 1908.

11. *San Francisco Examiner*, March 25, 1908.

12. *New York Times*, March 25, 1908.

13. *San Francisco Examiner*, April 18, 1908.

14. *New York Times*, April 7, 1908.

15. *San Francisco Examiner*, April 19, 1908.

16. Ibid., March 25, 1908.

17. Ibid., March 27, 1908.

18. *Omaha World-Herald*, March 18, 1908.

19. *Rocky Mountain News*, March 22, 1908; *Denver Post*, March 22, 1908.

20. *Denver Post*, March 25, 1908.

21. *San Francisco Chronicle*, April 15, 1908.

22. *San Francisco Examiner*, April 15, 1908.

23. *San Francisco Chronicle*, April 15, 1908.

24. *Automobile*, May 21, 1908.

25. *Motor*, May, 1908.

26. Schuster and Mahoney, *Longest Auto Race*, 56.

27. *Automobile*, April 2, 1908.
28. Schuster and Mahoney, *Longest Auto Race*, 71.
29. *San Francisco Examiner*, March 24, 1908; *New York Times*, March 25, 1908.
30. *New York Times,* March 28, 1908.
31. *Automotor Journal,* July 15, 1908.
32. *New York Times,* April 2, 1908.
33. Ibid., March 28, 1908.
34. Ibid., April 4, 1908.
35. Ibid., April 5, 1908.
36. Ibid., March 29, 1908.

Chapter 7: North to Alaska

1. Mirsky, *To the Arctic!*, 306–310.
2. *Seattle Times*, March 30, 1908; *Seattle Post-Intelligencer*, March 30, 1908.
3. George MacAdam, letter to his mother, March 31, 1908.
4. E.C. Morse, letter to George MacAdam, March 25, 1908.
5. Ibid., March 25, 1908.
6. E.C. Morse, letter to George Schuster, March 25, 1908.
7. George MacAdam, letter to his father, March 31, 1908.
8. Ibid.
9. *New York Times*, April 2, 1908.
10. George MacAdam, letter to his mother, March 31, 1908.
11. Terrence Cole, "Klondike Contraptions/Geniuses," (Fairbanks, Alaska, 1989).
12. Ibid., p. 7.
13. *New York Times*, April 2, 1908.
14. Schuster and Mahoney, *Longest Auto Race*, 75.
15. *New York Times*, March 28, 1908.
16. George MacAdam, "On Board the Santa Clara," April 8, 1908.
17. Ibid.
18. *New York Times*, March 28, 1908.
19. MacAdam, "On Board the Santa Clara," April 8, 1908.
20. *New York Times*, February 23, 1908.
21. Ibid., February 3, 1908.
22. *Anchorage Daily News*, April 9, 1967.
23. MacAdam, "On Board the Santa Clara," April 8, 1908.
24. MacAdam, "On Board the Santa Clara," April 16, 1908.
25. *Dawson Daily News*, November 29, 1907.
26. *New York Times*, December 22, 1907.

27. *Tanana Tribune*, February 29, 1908.
28. Claus Naske, *Paving Alaska's Trails: The Work of the Alaska Road Commission* (Lanham, Md.: University Press of America, 1986), 84.
29. *New York Times*, February 5, 1908.
30. *Nome Daily Nugget*, March 18, 1908.
31. Ibid., February 5, 1908; *Weekly Star*, February 14, 1908.
32. *New York Times*, February 5, 1908.
33. MacAdam, "On Board the Santa Clara," April 16, 1908.
34. *New York Times*, April 11, 1908.
35. Ibid., April 12, 1908.
36. *Nome Daily Nugget*, April 28, 1908.
37. *Alaska-Yukon Magazine*, April 1908.
38. *New York Times*, April 4, 1908.

Chapter 8: An Act of Splendid Folly

1. *Seattle Times*, April 14, 1908.
2. *New York Times*, April 15, 1908.
3. Scarfoglio, *Round the World*, 157.
4. *New York Times*, April 12, 1908.
5. *Seattle Times*, April 15, 1908; *New York Times*, April 16, 1908.
6. *New York Times*, April 20, 1908.
7. Ibid., April 18, 1908.
8. Ibid., April 17, 1908.
9. *Seattle Times*, April 19, 1908.
10. Commercial Department of the E. R. Thomas Motor Co., letter to George MacAdam, April 13, 1908.
11. E.C. Morse, letter to George MacAdam, May 2, 1908.
12. Ibid.
13. Commercial Department of E. R. Thomas Motor Co., letter to George MacAdam, April 14, 1908.
14. *New York Times*, April 19, 1908.
15. Ibid., April 22, 1908.
16. Scarfoglio, *Round the World*, 161.
17. Ibid., 168.
18. Ibid., 169–177.
19. Ibid., 178.
20. *New York Times*, May 18, 1908.
21. Ibid., May 4, 1908; May 20, 1908.
22. *Automobile*, April 8, 1908.
23. Scarfoglio, *Round the World*, 190.

24. Schuster, "The Thomas Flyer Automobile in the Race New York to Paris," handwritten account in the library of the William F. Harrah National Automobile Museum, 74.

25. T.R. Nicholson, *Adventurers Road: The Story of Pekin-Paris, 1907 and New York-Paris, 1908*, 189.

26. *New York Times*, July 19, 1908.

27. Theodore Roosevelt, *Letters of Theodore Roosevelt*, ed. Elting E. Morison (Cambridge, Mass.: Harvard University Press, 1952), 1012. Roosevelt to Kermh Roosevelt, April 19, 1908.

28. *Automobile*, August 13, 1908.

29. George MacAdam, "Across Japan in a Motor Car," *Outing Magazine*, August 1909, 575.

30. Ibid.

31. *New York Times*, July 19, 1908.

32. Ibid., May 17, 1908.

33. George MacAdam, notebook, May 16, 1908.

34. Ibid.

Chapter 9: The Siberian Express

1. Scarfoglio, *Round the World*, 215.

2. Fridtjof Nansen, *Through Siberia, The Land of the Future* (London: Heinemann, 1914), 341–342.

3. Barbara Tuchman, *The Proud Tower: A Portrait of the World Before the War, 1890–1914* (New York: Macmillan, 1966), 236.

4. George Kennan, *Siberia and the Exile System* (1891; reprint, New York: Russell & Russell, 1970), 356.

5. Scarfoglio, *Round the World*, 220.

6. *New York Times*, May 21, 1908.

7. Schuster, "The Thomas Flyer Automobile in the Race New York to Paris," 86–87.

8. Scarfoglio, *Round the World*, 216.

9. *Automobile*, July 9, 1908.

10. *New York Times*, May 17, 1908.

11. Ibid., May 20, 1908.

12. MacAdam, notebook, June 1908.

13. *New York Times*, July 29, 1928.

14. MacAdam, notebook, June 1908.

15. Harmon Tupper, *To the Great Ocean* (Boston: Little, Brown & Co., 1965), 251.

16. Nansen, *Through Siberia*, 281.

17. *Automobile*, August 13, 1908.

18. Schuster, "The Thomas Flyer Automobile in the Race New York to Paris," 117.
19. Ibid., 122–123
20. *New York Times*, May 29, 1908.
21. Harry Horgan, letter to George MacAdam in Siberia, June 4, 1908.
22. Harry Horgan, letter to George MacAdam in Siberia, July 21, 1908.
23. *New York Times*, June 5, 1908.
24. Ibid., June 7, 1908.
25. Ibid.
26. Scarfoglio, *Round the World*, 229–230.
27. Ibid., 239.
28. MacAdam, notebook, June 6, 1908.
29. *New York Times*, June 12, 1908.
30. Scarfoglio, *Round the World*, 251.
31. MacAdam, notebook, June 16, 1908.
32. *New York Times*, June 18, 1908.
33. Schuster and Mahoney, *Longest Auto Race*, 104.
34. MacAdam, notebook, June 17, 1908.

Chapter 10: The Dash to Paris

1. *Automobile*, August 13, 1908.
2. Scarfoglio, *Round the World*, 304.
3. Ibid., 293.
4. Kennan, *Siberia and the Exile System*, 56.
5. *New York Times*, July 29, 1928.
6. Barzini, *Peking to Paris*, 178.
7. MacAdam, notebook, June 20, 1908.
8. Barzini, *Peking to Paris*, 182.
9. Richardson L. Wright and Bassett Digby, *Through Siberia: An Empire in the Making* (New York: McBride, Nast & Co., 1913), 81.
10. Ibid., 83.
11. V. Kuranov, *The Trans-Siberian Express*, trans. Anatol Kagan (New York: Sphinx Press, 1980), 124.
12. MacAdam, notebook, June 22, 1908.
13. Ibid., June 23, 1908.
14. MacAdam, notebook, June 24, 1908; Schuster and Mahoney, *Longest Auto Race*, 109.
15. Tupper, *Great Ocean*, 296.
16. MacAdam, notebook, June 27, 1908.
17. *New York Times*, July 2, 1908.

18. Tupper, *Great Ocean*, 294.
19. Scarfoglio, *Round the World*, 329.
20. Barzini, *Peking to Paris*, 244.
21. Schuster and Mahoney, *Longest Auto Race*, 120.
22. Ibid., 120.
23. MacAdam, notes, undated.
24. *New York Times*, August 16, 1908.
25. MacAdam, notebook, July 22, 1908.
26. *New York Times*, July 23, 1908.
27. Ibid., July 24, 1908.
28. Ibid., July 25, 1908.
29. Ibid.
30. Ibid, July 27, 1908.
31. Ibid.
32. *Der Motorwagen*, August 31, 1908.
33. *Automobile*, July 30, 1908.
34. *New York Times*, July 27, 1908.
35. Ibid., July 29, 1908.
36. Ibid.
37. *Automobile*, August 13, 1908.
38. *New York Times*, August 1, 1908.
39. *Automobile*, August 13, 1908.
40. George MacAdam Sr., letter to George MacAdam, July 23, 1908.
41. *New York Times*, July 31, 1908.
42. Ibid., October 31, 1908.
43. E.W. Norman, Royal Ministry of Foreign Affairs, to author, July 24, 1990.

Chapter 11: The Homecoming

1. *New York Evening Mail*, August 15, 1908.
2. *New York Times*, August 16, 1908.
3. Ibid., August 2, 1908.
4. Ibid., July 29, 1908.
5. Ibid., August 1, 1908.
6. Ibid., July 28, 1908.
7. Schuster and Mahoney, *Longest Auto Race*, 135.
8. *New York Times*, August 18, 1908.
9. *Automobile*, August, 1908.
10. *New York Times*, August 21, 1908.
11. Scarfoglio, *Round the World*, 356.
12. Ibid., 355–359.

13. Ibid., 367.

14. *London Times*, September 25, 1908.

15. *New York Times*, August 16, 1908.

16. Ibid., January 9, 1910.

17. Schuster and Mahoney, *Round the World*, 143.

18. Maurice D. Hendry, "Thomas!," *Automobile Quarterly*, vol. 8, no. 4, 1970.

19. *Horseless Age*, September 4, 1912.

20. Schuster and Mahoney, *Longest Auto Race*, 149.

21. Ibid., 150.

22. Ibid., 152–153.

23. *Buffalo Courier Express*, December 6, 1964.

24. *Los Angeles Times*, January 3, 1987.

25. Leon Mandel, *American Cars* (New York: Stewart, Tabori & Chang, 1982), 41.

26. *New York Times*, June 12, 1968; June 17, 1968.

27. *Buffalo Evening News*, July 5, 1972.

28. Horatio Smith, *Columbia Dictionary of Modern European Literature* (New York: Columbia University Press, 1947), 724.

29. Schuster and Mahoney, *Longest Auto Race*, 146.

30. Alise Whiticar, *The Long Road* (Wake-Brook House, 1973), introductory note.

31. *New York Times*, October 10, 1942.

32. Ibid., May 12, 1929.

33. George MacAdam, "The Only Interview O. Henry Ever Gave," *Mentor*, February 1923, 42–43.

34. *New York Times*, July 29, 1928.

35. Ibid., September 11, 1975.

36. Ibid., July 15, 1976.

37. James Rood Doolittle, *The Romance of the Automobile Industry* (New York: Klebold Press, 1916), 401.

38. Frederick A. Talbot, *Motor-Cars and Their Story* (New York: Funk & Wagnalls, 1912), 94–95.

39. Theodore Zeldin, *France: 1848–1945* (Oxford: Clarendon Press, 1977), II, 531–532.

40. *New York Times*, October 30, 1944; October 31, 1944; March 15, 1951.

41. Elmer Davis, *History of The New York Times, 1851–1921* (1921; reprint, New York: Greenwood Press, 1969), 291.

42. Meyer Berger, *The Story of The New York Times*, 1851–1951 (New York: Simon & Schuster, 1951), 1970.

SOURCES

THE NEWS COVERAGE in the *New York Times* provided much of the basic information about the events described in this book. For more than eight months, the *Times* reported on all aspects of the story in hundreds of articles. These included first-person accounts by the drivers, reports from the Associated Press, and dispatches from the two correspondents the newspaper assigned to the contest, Skipper Williams and George MacAdam.

Newspapers in major cities along the race route also reported on the race in detail when the cars were close by. Other major sources include the journals of George MacAdam, letters from the E. R. Thomas Motor Company to MacAdam, numerous articles in major automotive magazines in the United States and Europe, and the writings of George Schuster and Antonio Scarfoglio.

MacAdam's journals, to which I was granted access by his son, George T. MacAdam of Newark, New Jersey, were especially valuable in providing a sense of the day-to-day hardships encountered on the trip across Siberia. A handwritten account by George Schuster in the files of the William F. Harrah Foundation National Automobile Museum in Reno, Nevada, revealed much about Schuster's character and his determination to win.

The Transportation Library at the University of Michigan at Ann Arbor and the Detroit Public Library contain a wealth of research material on the history of the automobile. The Ann Arbor library maintains a comprehensive collection of early automotive periodicals that was useful in documenting the industry's early development.

Archivists at the *New York Times* were helpful, but there is almost nothing in the company files about the contest. Publisher Adolph Ochs destroyed many of his personal papers.

The following is a partial list of the major sources used in the preparation of this book.

NEWSPAPERS AND PERIODICALS

Alaska Prospector
Antique Automobile
Autocar
Automobile
Automobile Quarterly
Automotor Journal
Bakersfield Californian
Buffalo Evening News
Buffalo Express
Buffalo Courier
Cheyenne Daily Leader
Chicago Record-Herald
Chicago Times-Herald
Chicago Tribune
Collier's
Dawson Daily News
Denver Post
Der Motorwagen
Ely Weekly Mining Expositor
Harper's Weekly
Horseless Age
Illustrated London News
La Vie Automobile
Life

Los Angeles Times
Motor
National Observer
New York Evening Mail
New York Journal
New York Times
New York Tribune
New York World
New York World-Telegram and Sun
Nome Daily Nugget
North China Herald
Omaha World-Herald
Outing Magazine
Overland Monthly
Philadelphia Inquirer
Rocky Mountain News
San Francisco Examiner
San Francisco Chronicle
Seattle Times
Seattle Post-Intelligencer
Tanana Tribune
Tonopah Daily Bonanza

BOOKS

Ames, Charles Edgar. *Pioneering the Union Pacific: A Reappraisal of the Builders of the Railroad*. New York: Appleton-Century-Crofts, 1969.

Andrews, Allen. *The Mad Motorists: The Great Peking-Paris Race of '07*. New York: Lippincott, 1965.

Barzini, Luigi. *Peking to Paris in a Motor-Car 1907*. Reprint. New York: Library Press, 1973.

Berger, Meyer. *The Story of The New York Times, 1851–1951*. New York: Simon and Schuster, 1951.

Berton, Pierre. *The Klondike Fever*. 1958. Reprint. New York: Alfred A. Knopf, 1977.

Brown, Dee. *Hear That Lonesome Whistle Blow*. New York: Bantam Books, 1977.

Clymer, Floyd. *New York to Paris, 1908*. 1908. Reprint. Los Angeles: Floyd Clymer, 1951.

Davis, Elmer. *History of The New York Times, 1851–1921*. 1921. Reprint. New York: Greenwood Press, 1969.

De Windt, Harry. *My Restless Life*. London: Grant Richards, 1909.

——. *My Notebook at Home and Abroad*. New York: E.P. Dutton, 1923.

Doolittle, James Rood. *The Romance of the Automobile Industry*. New York: Klebold Press, 1916.

Emery, Edwin. *The Press and America, An Interpretive History of the Mass Media*. Englewood Cliffs, N.J.: Prentice-Hall, 1982.

Federal Writers' Project. *Iowa: A Guide to the Hawkeye State*. New York: Viking Press, 1938.

——. *A Guide to Alaska: Last American Frontier*. New York: Macmillan, 1945.

Fine, Barnett. *A Giant of the Press*. New York: Editor & Publisher Library, 1933.

Flink, James J. *America Adopts the Automobile, 1895–1910*. Cambridge: MIT Press, 1970.

Fowler, Gene. *Timber Line 1933*. Reprint. Sausalito: Comstock Edition, 1974.

Halberstam, David. *The Powers That Be*. New York: Alfred A. Knopf, 1979.

Harvey, Paul W. *Tacoma Headlines, an Account of Tacoma News and Newspapers*. Tacoma: Tribune Publishing Co., 1962.

Hokanson, Drake. *The Lincoln Highway: Main Street Across America*. Iowa City: University of Iowa Press, 1988.

Hosokawa, Bill. *Thunder in the Rockies: The Incredible Denver Post*. New York: William Morrow, 1976.

Hunt, William R. *Alaska: A Bicentennial History*. New York: W.W. Norton, 1976.

Jackson, Robert B. *Road Race Round the World: New York to Paris, 1908*. New York: H.Z. Walck, 1977.

Kennan, George. *Siberia and the Exile System, 1891*. Reprint. New York: Russell & Russell, 1970.

——. *Tent Life in Siberia*, 1871. Reprint. Layton: Gibbs M. Smith, 1986.

Kluger, Richard. *The Paper: The Life and Death of The New York Herald Tribune*. New York: Alfred A. Knopf, 1986.

Kuranov, V. *The Trans-Siberian Express*. Translated by Anatol Kagan. New York: Sphinx Press, 1980.

The Lincoln Highway Association. *The Complete Official Road Guide to the Lincoln Highway*. New York, 1921.

Mandel, Leon. *American Cars*. New York: Stewart, Tabori & Chang, 1982.

Mirsky, Jeannette. *To The Arctic!* 1934. Reprint. Chicago: University of Chicago Press, 1970.

Morison, Samuel Eliot. *The Oxford History of the American People*. New York: Oxford University Press, 1965.

Mott, Frank Luther. *American Journalism: A History, 1690–1960*. New York: Macmillan, 1962.

Nansen, Fridtjof. *Through Siberia, The Land of the Future*. London: Heinemann, 1914.

Naske, Claus M. *Paving Alaska's Trails: The Work of the Alaska Road Commission*. Lanham: University Press of America, 1986.

Nevins, Allan, with the collaboration of Frank Ernest Hill. *Ford: The Times, the Man, the Company 1865–1915*. New York: Charles Scribner's Sons, 1954.

Nicholson, T.R. *The Trailblazers: Stories of the Heroic Age of Transcontinental Motoring, 1901–1914*. London: Cassell, 1958,

——. *Adventurers Road: The Story of Pekin-Paris, 1907 and New York-Paris, 1908*. London: Cassell, 1957.

Olson, Kenneth Eugene. *The History Makers: The Press of Europe from its Beginnings through 1965*. Baton Rouge: Louisiana State University Press, 1966.

Rae, John B. *The American Automobile: A Brief History*. Chicago: University of Chicago Press, 1965.

——. *American Automobile Manufacturers: A History of the First Forty Years*. New York: Chilton, 1959.

Roosevelt, Theodore. *Letters of Theodore Roosevelt*. Edited by Elting E. Morison. Cambridge: Harvard University Press, 1952.

Scarfoglio, Antonio. *Round the World in a Motor-Car*. London: Grant Richards, 1909.

Schuster, George and Tom Mahoney. *The Longest Auto Race*. New York: John Day, 1966.

Smith, Horatio, ed. *Columbia Dictionary of Modern European Literature*. New York: Columbia University Press, 1947.

Talbot, Frederick A. *Motor-Cars and Their Story*. New York: Funk & Wagnalls, 1912.

Talese, Gay. *The Kingdom and the Power*. New York: World Publishing Co., 1969.

Train, George Francis. *My Life in Many States and in Foreign Lands: Dictated in my Seventy-Fourth Year*. New York: Appleton, 1902.

Tuchman, Barbara. *The Proud Tower: A Portrait of the World Before the War, 1890–1914*. New York: Macmillan, 1966.

Tupper, Harmon. *To the Great Ocean*. Boston: Little, Brown & Co., 1965.

Vance, James E. Jr. *Capturing the Horizon: The Historical Geography of Transportation since the Transportation Revolution of the Sixteenth Century*. New York: Harper & Row, 1986.

Whiticar, Alise Barton. *The Long Road: The Story of the Race around the World by Automobile in 1908*. Fort Lauderdale: Wake-Brook House, 1971.

Willis, Thornton. *The Nine Lives of Citizen Train*. New York: Greenberg, 1948.

Wright, Richardson L. and Bassett Digby. *Through Siberia: An Empire in the making*. New York: McBride, Nast & Co., 1913.

Yost, Nellie. *Buffalo Bill, his family friends, fame, failures, and fortunes*. Chicago: Sage Books, 1979.

Zeldin, Theodore. *France: 1848–1945*. Oxford: Clarendon Press, 1977.

INDEX

ABOUT THE AUTHOR

DERMOT COLE, A former reporter for the Associated Press, is assistant managing editor of the *Fairbanks Daily News-Miner* in Fairbanks, Alaska. A journalist for fifteen years, he has received numerous state and regional journalism awards for his reporting on Alaska and was named a Michigan Journalism fellow in 1986.

Growing up in Quakertown, Pennsylvania, Cole completed high school in Tainan, Taiwan, subsequently studying Chinese at the Chinese University of Hong Kong and traveling throughout Asia. Later he attended Montana State University in Bozeman, Montana, before moving to Alaska in 1974, where he earned a bachelor's degree in journalism at the University of Alaska in Fairbanks. While living in Alaska, he has covered the oil industry, state politics, and written extensively about Alaska history. His first book, *Frank Barr: Bush Pilot in Alaska and the Yukon*, was published in 1986.

Dermot Cole is married to journalist Debbie Carter. They have a son, Connor, and a daughter, Aileen. Cross-country skiing, traveling, and reading E. B. White and Red Smith are some of his hobbies.